Anonymous

Bhagavadgita, translated into English blank verse
With notes and an introductory essay by Kashinath Trimbak Telang, etc.

ISBN/EAN: 9783337946135

Printed in Europe, USA, Canada, Australia, Japan

Cover: Foto ©Paul-Georg Meister /pixelio.de

More available books at **www.hansebooks.com**

Anonymous

Bhagavadgita, translated into English blank verse

With notes and an introductory essay by Kashinath Trimbak Telang, etc.

BHAGAVADGÎTÂ

TRANSLATED INTO ENGLISH BLANK VERSE

WITH NOTES

AND

AN INTRODUCTORY ESSAY

BY

KÂSHINÂTH TRIMBAK TELANG, M.A., LL.B.,

SOMETIME SENIOR DAKSHINA FELLOW, ELPHINSTONE COLLEGE,

ADVOCATE, HIGH COURT, BOMBAY.

———◆———

𝔅𝔬𝔪𝔟𝔞𝔶:

ATMARAM SAGOON & Co., KALBADEVI ROAD.

———

1875.

Price Rs. 2—8.

BOMBAY:

PRINTED AT THE " INDU-PRAKÂSH " PRESS.

PREFACE.

THE translation of the Bhagavadgîtâ which appears in this volume was originally undertaken merely as an exercise in versification, without any view to its ever being published. After considerable portions of it had been prepared in this way, it occurred to me, that it might be useful to print and publish it, as there had been no rendering of the Gîtâ into English verse. I thought that a metrical translation would be, in sundry respects, a better representative of the Sanskrit original than a translation into prose, even though the latter might in its own class be entitled to a higher rank than the former in its class. Under this view I finished the translation, and submitted it for revision to my very able friend Mr. Âbâjî Vishnu Kâthavaṭe. He did the work of revision with a fulness and patience for which I cannot sufficiently thank him. Most of his corrections and suggestions—indeed, I may say, all except, perhaps, four or five—have been after consideration adopted by me. And I would add, that although the responsibility for all the errors in this work must undoubtedly be mine, a great deal of such value as the translation may be found to possess, whether in respect of accuracy of rendering or otherwise, is due to Mr. Kâthavaṭe's labours.

One point there is as to which I have not acted upon my friend's suggestion, though I have felt, and still feel, considerable diffidence as to the propriety of the course which I have pursued. Mr. Kâthavaṭe thinks, that our native mode of pronouncing names ending in 'a' as if they ended in a consonant is quite incorrect and ought not to be stereotyped. I fully appreciate the force of this. Nevertheless I find it very difficult to reconcile myself to the outlandish pronunciation which results if the suggestion is adopted. In my difficulty as to how to proceed, I turned to the excellent metrical translation of the Râmâyan by Mr. R. T. H. Griffiths. But there I found on one and the same page two such lines as the following :—
        "The As'vamedh was finished quite"
And "And Das'aratha ore they went." (Vol. I. p. 97.)
Nay we have even such lines as these :—

" Râma and Lakshman next obtained" (I. 129)

And " Yea, Râma Bharat's self exceeds." (I. 378.)

Similarly in Mr. Muir's metrical translations at the close of the Second Volume of his Sanskrit Texts, we read :—

" I know thee Râvan who thou art."

and a few lines further on;

" And won great Râma for her lord."

Obviously, both Mr. Muir and Mr. Griffiths have scanned the names as the exigencies of the verse required in each particular case.

I have taken a somewhat different course. The following lines will exemplify the principles I have adopted :—

(I.) The prince Duryodhan to his teacher went.

(II.) And Dhrishṭadyumna, Saubhadra of large arms.

(III.) Who meditates on Brahma in the act.

It will be seen that where the consonant preceding the ' a ' is a simple consonant (I.), the 'a' is treated as having no value for purposes of scansion and is omitted in the spelling. Where it is preceded by a conjunct consonant (II. and III.), the 'a' is pronounced in all cases, except a few in which the following word begins with a vowel, and the 'a' coalesces with that vowel in scansion. As remarked already, this is not quite a satisfactory solution of the difficulty, but I think it is a convenient one, and is based, at all events, on a uniform principle.

It may be useful to add, that the whole poem is in the form of a dialogue between Sanjaya and Dhritarâshtra ; and the speeches of Krishna and Arjun are merely reported by the former to the latter. The prefixing of the names of Krishna and Arjun does to a certain extent disguise this fact, and to some of the speeches in the first two chapters the names have by mistake not been prefixed, though one might expect them there according to the rule followed in the subsequent chapters. But I do not think that there will be any misunderstanding in practice caused by these circumstances.

In my translation I have nearly always followed the interpretations of the commentators, S'ankar, S'ridhar, and Madhusûdan. Wherever the text seemed to me to require explanation, I have given it in footnotes. Additional explanation, where it seemed to me on further consideration to be necessary, has been added in the Notes and Illustrations, in preparing which I had the advantage of consulting a commentary by Râghavendra Yati—a writer of a different school from S'ankar and the rest. I have to thank my friend Mr. Vyankaṭrâv Râmchandra of Puna for his kindness in lending me his copy of that commentary. I can, of course, scarcely expect that there are no material deficiencies in the notes, but I have endeavoured to give as full explanations as I thought necessary. I am sorry that by an oversight some explanations which ought to have appeared in footnotes were not given there; but I have added them now in the Notes and Illustrations.

With regard to the Introduction I may state, that the nucleus of it was a paper read by me before the Students' Literary and Scientific Society in December 1873. But the expansions and additions have been so considerable that it may be said to be an altogether new essay. As to the questions discussed in it concerning the first introduction of Christianity into India, and the translations of the New Testament in the first centuries of the Christian Era, and kindred matters, I need scarcely say, that not having bestowed any special study on them except for the purposes of this essay, I should have been glad to avoid the discussion of them. But this I could not do, as they furnish a very important link in the chain of reasoning by which Dr. Lorinser supports his theory. "Supernatural Religion" and "Literature and Dogma" have evoked very considerable discussion of important points connected with the early history of Christianity and of the New Testament, and I have availed myself of some of the points made in that discussion. But my treatment of the subject is avowedly very far from full. It seems to me to be enough for my argument, if it can be shown—and this I think will not be denied—that there is a real and *bona fide* difference of opinion among persons qualified to judge in the matter, as to some of the points which Dr. Lorinser takes for granted. This fact, coupled with the circumstance noted at the top of p. xxiv. of the essay, appears to me to fortify the position I have taken up, nearly as much as a complete study of the whole discussion on the age and authenticity of the Gospels could have enabled me to fortify it.

As the sheets were passing through the press, some discussion was going on in the literary world concerning various points connected with the early history of Christianity, parts of which have a bearing upon the subject discussed by me. But I can only give a general reference to it, as I was not able to study it sufficiently to consider the points of contact between that discussion on the one hand and this essay on the other. There is also a paper by Dr. Muir in the *Indian Antiquary* Vol. IV. p. 77, the conclusion of which seems, at least in some measure, to coincide with ours, which we may express in the following words of Dr. Strauss:— "However high may be the place of Jesus among those who have shown to mankind most purely and most plainly what it ought to be, still he was not the first to do so nor will he be the last. But as he had predecessors in Israel and Hellas, on the Ganges and the Oxus, so also he has not been without followers," (Life of Jesus. Vol. II. 437).

CONTENTS.

——000——

ADDENDA ET CORRIGENDA.

P. IV. line 26. Add note 'But see p. xciv. *infra.*'

P. V. last line. For 'I' read ' we.'

P. XXI. l. 26. After 298 add 377.

P. XXIV. l. 30. Add 'also that cited at p. lxiv. *infra.*'

P. XXX. l. 14. Add note ' See Meghadût St. 15.'

P. XLV. l. 22. Delete the words ' are something which.'

P. LIV. l. 6. For ' not '*not* sweet to do" read *not* ' sweet to do' and in l.
11. after ' next' insert ' passage.'

P. LVII. l. 15. For ' believe' read ' maintain.'

P. LXXV. l. 32. Add ' also Thomson's Gîtâ, Introd. p. xxvi.

P. LXXVI. l. 24. Add after 236 'XII. *5 et seq.*' And in l. 26 ' Also
Lalit Vistar 159 and Müller's Anc. Sans. Lit. 517.'

P. LXXIX. l. 24. After ' Tyndall's' insert a comma.

P. LXXXII. l. 28. Add 'Vol. IV. 125 and Ind. Ant. Vol. IV. 81.'

P. LXXXVIII. l. 1. On ' veneration' add note ' See Kâdambari p. 127.
(Târân. Ed.) and other passages.'

P. LXXXIX. l. 16. On ' S'abar Svâmi ' add note ' See Colebrooke
Essays I. 297-8.'

P. CVII. l. 7. For ' allowable in the Classical Literature' read 'allowed by the strict rules of grammar.'

P. CXVI. l. 6. For 'Manu and the Gîtâ' read ' the Gîtâ and
Manu.'

P. CXVIII. l. 4. For ' set' read ' put'.

P.   4 l. 12. For ' my kin. Oh Krishna "! read ' my kinsmen. Krishna"!

P.   5 ,, 4. For ' treachery' read ' injury.'

P.   6 ,, 15. For ' wise' read ' good.'

P.   8 ,, 18. After 22 add ' (line 708.)'

P.   7 ,, 27. For ' distinguish' read ' interpret accurately.'

P.   12 ,, 22. After 53 add (line 300); in l. 29 after 21 add (lines 1055
and 1171).

P.   13 ,, 18. Add ' See Manu I. 26.'

P.   15 ,, 31. Add ' Comp. line 1639.'

P.   16 ,, 22. Add 'see Wilson's Essays Vol. III. p. 130 and note.'

P.   17 ,, 33. After 27 add (line 450).

P.   18 ,, 27. Add see line 2010.

P.   19 ,, 22. Add after 60 (line 2299).

P.   21 ,, 16. Add 'Compare Haug's Aitareya Brâhman Pref. p. 4 note.'

P. 22 l. 30. Add after 9 (line 661 *et seq.*)

P. 24 „ 23. After nature, add 'is'.

P. 28 „ 19. Add after 13 '(line 539)'; in l. 20 after 14 '(lines 540-42)'; in l. 28 after 62 '(line 329)'; and in l. 29 after 24 '(lines 749 and 820).'

P. 29 „ 27. After 9 add (line 396).

P. 31 „ 12. For 'thus' read 'this.'

P. 32 „ 27. Add ' See line 659,'; last line, for 13 read ' 45 (line 271)'.

P. 33 „ 28. For ' 2 *et seq.*' read ' 3 *et seq.* (line 2116).'

P. 34 „ 7. For 'touched' read 'stained.' On l. 17 add note 'S'vetâs'vatar III. 18' and in line 32 after 30 add (line 461).

P. 35 „ 20. For ' and Madhusûdan say' read ' says.' In l. 23 before प्रकृति add आविद्याङ्क्षणा.

P. 37 „ 23. For 1037 read 1035.

P. 38 „ 29. After 770 add ' and line 389.'

P. 41 „ 7. After ' which' insert ' too.'

P. 42. The notes * and † should interchange places.

P. 45 „ 11. For ' some alone' read ' only some.'

P. 48 „ 20. For 1860 read 1866.

P. 49 „ 33. For 1671 read 1675 and for 1823, in l. 34, 1827.

P. 53 „ 21. For 2075 read 2081.

P. 54 „ 27. Add ' and Manu I. 52'; in l. 31 for 1870 read 1876.

P. 58 „ 33. After ' deluding' add ' But see Kirât. XIV. 19.'

P. 61 „ 25. For 1978 read 1986.

P. 65 „ 24. For 2320 read 2307.

P. 68 „ 20. For ' St. 33 S'ankar' read 'St. 33 (line 1330) S'ridhar. '

P. 70 „ 28. Add ' comp. S'ankar's note at foot of page 118.'

P. 72 „ 3. For ' with the' read ' His.'

P. 74 „ 16. For ' first' read ' chief.'

P. 88 „ 4. For ' roach' read ' reached.'

P. 95 „ 31. For 2322 read 2305.

P. 96 „. 26. For 2324 read 2307.

P. 117 „ 20. For Chhândogyopanishad read S'votâs'vataropanishad.

Some minor errata, and some errors of punctuation &c., have been omitted from the above list.

———

INTRODUCTORY ESSAY.

It is proposed in the present essay to review the question of the originality and antiquity of the Bhagavadgîtâ. We have here considered that question mainly with reference to the theory advanced by Dr. F. Lorinser in the Appendix to his " Die Bhagavadgîtâ," which has been translated into English for the *Indian Antiquary*. It appears to us, however, that the investigation of the question, if confined within the limits marked out in Dr. Lorinser's Appendix, will be altogether imperfect. And accordingly we shall endeavour in the present essay not only to discuss the points taken by Dr. Lorinser, but also other points, which are very material in this investigation, but which have not recieved due, or indeed any, consideration at Dr. Lorinser's hands.

And first, it will be convenient to state in the form of distinct propositions those conclusions of Dr. Lorinser's inquiry, with which we are here primarily concerned. As far as practicable, I use Dr. Lorinser's own words, as they appear in an English dress in the *Indian Antiquary*. His propositions, then, are these :—

I. On the one hand it is certain that the Bhagavadgîtâ dates after Buddha.*

II. On the other hand its composition must be attributed to a period terminating several centuries after the commencement of the Christian Era.†

III. It can be sufficiently proved that the composer of the Bhagavadgîtâ knew and used the New Testament.‡

* *Indian Antiquary*, Vol. II. 283*a*.
† *Ibid.*
‡ *Ibid* 284*a*.

IV. The date after which the Gîtâ could not have been composed must be left an open question till, we are certain when S'ankarâchârya lived.＊

Such are the propositions to which Dr. Lorinser's theory about the Gîtâ may be reduced. We shall now address ourselves to the consideration of them in their order.

And first, as to the Bhagavadgîtâ dating after Buddha. On this point, Dr. Lorinser feels no hesitation in using so strong a word as "certain." But although I may once more expose myself to the charge of not being "sufficiently acquainted" with what is dignified with the appellation of "the present state of scientific research" on this point, I must humbly inquire—How has this been rendered "certain"? Where has it been proved? And by whom has it been proved? Dr. Lorinser himself has shown no grounds for his position. He has not thought fit even to follow the ordinary practice of giving in a note the references to the authorities on which he relies. Speaking for myself, I confess, I am quite unprepared to accept this proposition of Dr. Lorinser as "certain," and the mere *ipse dixit* of Dr. Lorinser, or for the matter of that, of any one else, will not be enough to convince me of it. The only *argument* upon the point, which I am aware of, is one to be derived from a statement contained in Professor H. H. Wilson's Review of Schlegel's edition of the Bhagavadgîtâ. Commenting on Gîtâ XVI. 7. the Professor observes as follows :—"It is clear from the subsequent passage that the Bauddhas are especially intended as the beings of the demoniacal order."† Now it need scarcely be said. that if this were correct, it would be conclusive. But it is not correct. For mark what follows.

＊ *Indian Antiquary*, Vol. II. 283a.

† Essays on Sanskrit Literature, Vol. III. 150.

' S'ankara,' Professor Wilson goes on to say, " states them to be the members of the Lokâyatika sect, which was a division of the Bauddhas." Now remarking parenthetically, that not only S'ankar, but also Madhusûdan Sarasvatî and S'rîdhar Svâmî, explain the passage as alluding to the Lokâyatiks, I must point out, that Professor Wilson has fallen into error in speaking of the Lokâyatiks as a division of the Bauddhas. And his learned Editor, Dr. Reinhold Rost, shows himself to be of this opinion by putting a Quære against the Professor's remark. The Lokâyatiks, as every reader of Mâdhav's Sarvadars'anasangraha is aware, are in truth identical with the Chârvâks or Materialists, a sect essentially different from the Buddhists. And the conclusion, therefore, seems to me to follow, that Professor Wilson, in speaking of the allusion to the Bauddhas as clear, was himself clearly committing a mistake. But further, while I concede, that the doctrines alluded to in the passage under discussion are very like those of the Lokâyatiks, still it seems to me that they do not appear there in that developed and definite form in which they appear even in the work of Brihaspati, as we know it from the extracts in the Sarvadars'anasangraha.* That work exhibits them, I think, in a more advanced and fully developed form, and probably therefore belongs to a considerably later age, than the Bhagavadgîtâ. Now Brihaspati appears to have been the first author of a systematic Lokâyatik work, and the Bhâgurî

---

* First section *passim*. Madhusûdan's and S'rîdhar's commentaries on Gîtâ XVI. 11. contain quotations from Brihaspati not in verse but in sûtras. And this was probably the oldest form of Brihaspati's work. What is the relation to it of the work cited from by Mâdhav? I have no access to either the sûtras or the verses in original, and cannot answer the question. The argument in the text must, therefore, be taken subject to considerable allowances.

Ṭikâ alluded to in Patanjali's Mahâbhâshya[*] was very probably a commentary on Bṛihaspati's work. See then how
the matter stands. The Gîtâ may be taken as standing
chronologically prior to Bṛihaspati ; Bṛihaspati as prior to the
Bhâgurî Ṭikâ ; the Bhâgurî Ṭikâ as prior to Patanjali ; and
Patanjali as prior to the beginning of the first century
before Christ.[†] How old, then, must the Gîtâ be ? True,
the argument here is based, in very great measure, not on
ascertained facts, but on mere presumptions. But on the
other hand, it must be remembered, that these presumptions
are such as the facts before us render very likely. And if
they are correct, they lead logically to the conclusion, that the
Gîtâ is much older than Dr. Lorinser's school would fain allow
it to be.

But apart from this last branch of the argument, which, as
just remarked, is mainly based on presumptions ; if it is true,
as I contend it is, that the Gîtâ does not contain that allusion
to the Buddhists which Professor Wilson thought it contained ;
and if it therefore follows, as it must be admitted to follow,
that the conclusion which might be drawn from the supposed allusion must fall to the ground ; then it seems to me
a very pertinent inquiry to ask—what ground Dr. Lorinser
has for the very unqualified and unhesitating assertion, which
he has ventured to make about the relative dates of the composition of the Gîtâ and the rise of Buddhism. Of any other
ground than that above disposed of I cannot see the slightest trace. And I do not think it at all unlikely, that
the statement of Professor Wilson above referred to has

---

[*] Under Pânini VII. 3. 44 (Banâras Ed. p. 115) and see Kaiyaṭ
on the same.

[†] See the introduction to our Edition of Bhartṛihari (Bombay Series
of Sanskrit Classics) where the authorities on this point are collected.

been taken by some later writers as laying down a finally established proposition, to be treated in all discussions on the subject as embodying, in Dr. Lorinser's language, one of the 'results already won,' or as Professor Weber phrases it, as forming part of 'the present state of scientific research.' I know, and have elsewhere pointed out, at least one instance of an assertion, made by one scholar with words of limitation and qualification, which has been afterwards repeated by another scholar without any such diluting expression, as if it were a proved and well recognized truth.[*] And the scholar who copies in this fashion is a critical German, 'whose authority in the sphere of Indian Philology', as we are for the first time told by Dr. Lorinser, 'is recognized even in India.'[†]

That being so, the question still remains—Is or is not the Gîtâ older than Buddhism? I own that in forming an opinion on this point, the materials at my command are unfortunately very scanty. But in the absence of anything else, I think that they furnish quite sufficient ground for holding, at least as a sort of provisional hypothesis, that the Gîtâ is older, and not later, than the rise of Buddhism. For in the first place, as is, and indeed must be, admitted on all hands, there is no express mention of the name or doctrines of Buddha in the Bhagavadgîtâ. In the second place, there is not even any implied allusion to either Buddha or his doctrines, the only passage which has been relied on as containing such an allusion having been shown above to refer to a totally different sect. Now I admit at once, what, indeed, I have elsewhere contended for, that a merely negative argument of this nature is not in ordinary cases of much value.[‡] Nor do I adduce it

[*] See *Indian Antiquary*, Vol II. 73.
[†] *Ibid* 284.
[‡] See 'Was the Râmâyana copied from Homer'? p. 41. I may,

here as entitled to much force. Nevertheless, in view of the fact that the Gîtâ, in some parts, is concerned with topics identical with those to which Buddhism addresses itself, and in view of this other fact, that various opinions held by other thinkers° are alluded to in the course of the work, this negative argument does appear to me to be worth some consideration. Further, I think, that the way in which the Veds are spoken of in more than one passage of the Gîtâ, shows that the composition of the work must be referred to a time when no attack had as yet been made on their authority.† For being, as is conceded even by Dr. Lorinser, the work of one who was himself thoroughly orthodox,‡ it is not likely, that the Gîtâ would add strength to the hands of the heterodox Buddhists, by showing a split in the phalanx of orthodox Hinduism at the main point of contest between the two parties. It seems to me more likely, that the Gîtâ was a work of the age immediately preceding the Buddhistic revolution—one outcome, probably, of that general upheaval of religious feeling, which culminated at last in the heresy of Gautam Buddha.

Now in this state of the case, I repeat, I am entirely un-prepared to accept Dr. Lorinser's statement, that it is "certain" that the Bhagavadgîtâ "dates after Buddha." Dr. Lorinser adduces no argument, does not even refer to any authority for his position. And this leads to a remark,

perhaps, be permitted to point out that Prof. Lightfoot in his review of 'Supernatural Religion' has expressed a view agreeing with ours, as to this 'negative agreement.' See Contemporary Review (January).

* See XIII. 4 or XVIII. 2,13 among other passages.

† See II. 42, 45 or VI. 44 or IX 21. Of course there is no direct defiance of the authority of the Veds but the reverse. Nevertheless the way they are spoken of is worthy of note, and seems to mark a sort of compromise.

‡ *Ind. Ant.*, VI. II. 284a and see Thomson's Gîtâ *passim.*

which I may have to make in several places in the course of this discussion, that Dr. Lorinser very rarely refers his readers to the authorities for his assertions. I own, I find it quite impossible to satisfy myself, that there are more than a very few facts in the history of Sanskrit Literature, which we are entitled to speak of as historically "certain." That being so, I think, every reader has a right to expect, that the authorities for all important statements involved in any discussion should be always very carefully referred to. And I may say, that this is the general, if not the universal, practice. Dr. Lorinser, however, has laid down several propositions in the course of his essay, like the one which we have just been discussing, without giving his readers the slightest clue to the arguments or the authorities by which those propositions are supported. And the consequence is, that it is exceedingly difficult to deal with them except by the method of giving a bare denial to a bare assertion.

We now proceed to the second point, and I think it need not detain us long; for I at once confess, that I cannot understand the meaning of Dr. Lorinser's words. "A period terminating several centuries after the commencement of the Christian Era,"* may mean all the time from the beginning of the world to the year of Grace one thousand eight hundred and seventy-five! It is, of course, clear, that Dr. Lorinser means something less vague than this, but what that something is, I have hitherto failed to perceive clearly. It is possible, that Dr. Lorinser means by it a period marked by certain noteworthy characteristics, which closed several centuries after Christ. But if so, I submit, that Dr. Lorinser ought to have told us what those characteristics are, and also, for the purposes of the present argument, when the

* *Ind. And.*, Vol. II. 283a.

period in his opinion commenced. For a work may belong
to a period "terminating several centuries after the commencement of the Christian Era," and yet may itself have
been composed even before the birth of Christ. However, as
already stated, no information on these matters is furnished
by Dr. Lorinser; and his proposition without such information is so very vague, that it is impossible to grapple with it.
We shall, therefore, proceed without further ado to the third
of Dr. Lorinser's points as stated above.

This third point is really the most important point of
all; it is, as I may say, borrowing the language of Prof. Max
Müller, the sheet-anchor of Dr. Lorinser's theory. The
point is, that it is possible to prove that the author of the
Gîtâ knew and used the New Testament. Let us endeavour
to see how Dr. Lorinser satisfies himself that he has proved
this. His argument seems to be as follows:—S'ankarâchârya
lived in the eighth century A. C.; from that it is to be
inferred that the Gîtâ was composed *at the earliest* some five
centuries earlier; at that time there were Christian communities in India; and there was also an Indian Translation
of the Bible belonging probably to the first or second century
A. C. "In this way," Dr. Lorinser then goes on to observe,
"the possibility that the composer of the Bhagavadgîtâ may
have been acquainted not merely with the general teaching
of Christianity, but also with the very writings of the *New
Testament*, might be shown in a very natural way, without
the necessity of having recourse to rash hypothesis."[*] And
next, coupling with this possibility "the fact that we can
find in the Bhagavadgîtâ passages, and these not single and
obscure, but numerous and clear, which present a surprising
similarity to passages in the New Testament," Dr. Lorinser

---

* *Ind. Ant*, Vol II. 284a.

sees "conclusive proof that the composer (of the Bhagavad-gîtâ) was acquainted with the writings of the New Testament, and used them as he thought fit."* Q. E. D.

Now it appears to me, that every single step in this reasoning is open to objections of a more or less grave character. Let us take the several steps in their order. It is by no means certain that S'ankar flourished in the eighth century A. C. Dr. Lorinser himself thinks that the "reasons" on which this hypothesis rests, though "weighty," "can make no claim to irrefragable certainty."† I quite concur. But when Dr. Lorinser indulges the hope, that S'ankar's date may prove to be later than the eighth century,‡ I entirely differ from him. My expectation, on the contrary, is that the correct date will turn out to be at least a century or two earlier. I cannot go into the question at length on this occasion. I shall only refer in brief to some considerations which appear to me to support my position. In his paper on the antiquity of the Mahâbhârat, Professor Bhâṇḍârkar, arguing from the data furnished by certain inscriptions which he refers to, suggests two alternative dates for S'ankar, the later of which is earlier by two centuries than the date fixed by the "usual hypothesis."§ Again Mâdhavâchârya in his S'ankarvijaya —a work which dates from about 1350 A C.‖— speaks of S'ankar as स्तुनः सम्यक्विभिः पुराणैः, (anglice, "well extolled by ancient poets,") and of his own work as one in which प्राचीनशंकरजये सारंसंगृह्यते स्फुटम्.¶ (" the substance of the old work on the victories of S'ankar is clearly stated.") Now it seems to me, that before a person

---

* Ibid 286.

† Ibid 283b.

‡ Ibid 296a.

§ Journal B. B. R. A. S. Vol. X. p. 89.

‖ See Cowell's Kusumânjali, Preface p. x.

¶ S'ankarvijaya I, 1 and 4 &c. Prof. Wilson's essays &c, III, 192-3.

like Mâdhav could speak of a writer as पुराणकवि or ancient poet, this latter must have preceded him by a considerably long period of time, say five or six centuries at the very least; while the hero of the predecessor's laudatory work must also have probably gone before his biographer by about a century or two. Furthermore, I find that the records of the Math of S'ringerî, which owes its first establishment to S'ankarâchârya, exhibit a list of the several occupants of the Gâdî, which according to the ordinary computation would send S'ankar into a much higher antiquity than the "usual hypothesis" gives him.* Once more, the Editor of Ânandagiri's S'ankarvijaya states that according to the traditions which have descended to him in a line of literary succession, S'ankar must have lived about 1200 years ago.†

But let that pass. Let us for the moment concede to Dr. Lorinser that S'ankar did flourish in the eighth century. Still I fail to see, by what possible process of ratiocination that alone could enable either Prof. Lassen, or Dr. Lorinser, or any one else, to say that the Gîtâ could not have been composed *earlier* than the third century after Christ. The reasoning is simply beyond me. Unfortunately, Dr. Lorinser, here as elsewhere, gives no references, even though he does not set out the arguments for his propositions. But if the opinion of Lassen which he refers to is that expressed in the Preface to his edition of Schlegel's Bhagavadgîtâ, I must say, that I think Dr. Lorinser has not correctly stated Prof. Lassen's view. That view is, in Lassen's own words, as follows :—"Si conjecturam facere par est, quinque fere saeculis ante S'ankaram editam fuisse Bhagavadgîtâm facile credider-

---

* In fact the records give his date also, but I cannot yet make up mind to place reliance on them. See Journal B. B. R. A. S. Vol. X. 373.

† See preface.

im."＊ Thus far Lassen. Contrast Lorinser. "It must not be forgotten, that it (*scil.* Lassen's inference) only professes to give the *earliest* date at which the Bhagavadgîtâ could have been composed."† Is this a correct interpretation? Surely what Prof. Lassen can "easily believe" is not the utmost that he will believe. On the contrary, the inference which I think may legitimately be drawn from Prof. Lassen's words as above quoted, especially when taken in connection with the preceding argument which is summed up in them, is that the interval he mentions is in his view much nearer the minimum than the maximum interval. But however that may be, it is perfectly clear, that the fixing of a *terminus ad quem* can never by itself lead to the *terminus a quo;* and even if I have misunderstood Lassen, I still contend, that the argument which I am now combating is essentially illogical, and such as no amount of mere authority can support.

The next step in Dr. Lorinser's argument brings us to the question of the earliest existence of Christian communities in India. Now on this point again, Dr. Lorinser's deliverance is remarkably positive. "We know," he says in one part of his Dissertation, "we know that there were already at that time Christian communities in India."‡ And in another part, he says in even more powerful language, "we know for certain that there were numerous Christian communities in India in the first century of the Christian era, which continued under the name of Thomas Christians and were found by the Portuguese."§ This is decidedly a rather strong

---

＊ P. XXXVI.

† *Ind. Ant.*, Vol. II. 283a.

‡ *Ind. Ant.*, volume II. 283b.

§ *Ibid* 285a. In the seventh volume of the Asiatic Researches, there

thing to say, but of course Dr. Lorinser cites no authority
for his assertion, shows no means of "certain knowledge." Dean
Milman, indeed, says, that "even of Andrew in Achaia and
in Scythia, of Thaddeus in Edessa, Matthew or Matthias in
Æthiopia, of Thomas in Parthia and Southern India, of
Bartholomew in Judæa, there remain but vague, late, contradic-
tory rumours which hardly aspire to legends."* But then
Dean Milman is only a prosaic historian after all. And
Gibbon is no better, seeing that he talks of " the *legend* of
antiquity which tells of St. Thomas's preaching the Gospel in
India."† I will not quote Wheeler‡ or Kaye§ in order further to confirm this view about the reality of St. Thomas's
mission. But it does seem to me, that this instance of
Dr. Lorinser's dogmatism in the teeth of such a mass of
authority—and powerful authority too—is not calculated to
impress one favourably about the value to be attached to

is a paper on the history of this Malabar community of Christians,
and we learn there, that "the affiliation of that community on the
Apostle St. Thomas was an invention of the bigoted Portuguese
missionaries," opposed to all the traditions of the community itself.
And the writer expresses his surprise, that the story "unsupported
as it is by historical proof is asserted and repeated by even Protes-
tant writers as Baldæus and Valentyn" (see p. 366).

* History of Christianity I. 387. Another orthodox historian
of Christianity, Dr. J. C. L. Gieseler, seems in effect to concur in
this view, for he thinks it probable that the tradition is of Manichœan
origin (see Vol. I. of Gieseler's Ecclesiastical History p. 79), and the
Manichœan sect rose about the close of the third century A. C. Dr.
Gieseler says generally (p. 76). " The history of the other apostles"
(*scil.* except St. Paul) " and their early pupils is involved in great
obscurity and has frequently been much disfigured by mistakes and
fabrications"—a passage which furnishes an instructive commentary
on Dr. Lorinser's words above quoted.

† Decline and Fall of the Roman Empire (Bohn's Ed.) Vol. V. 261.

‡ History of India, Vol. III. p. 390.

§ Christianity in India p. 3 *et seq.*

his strong asseverations. And when Dr. Lorinser goes on to refer to Eusebius as an important witness, he seems to forget, that out of his own mouth, Eusebius has been all but convicted of being rather a romancer than a sober historian. For we read in Gibbon:—"The gravest of the ecclesiastical historians, Eusebius himself, indirectly confesses that he has related whatever might redound to the glory, and that he has suppressed all that could tend to the disgrace, of his religion." "Such an acknowledgment" Gibbon very justly goes on to say, "will naturally excite suspicion that a writer who has so openly violated one of the fundamental laws of history has not paid a very strict regard to the observance of the other."* And it is not entirely unworthy of note, that whereas the Gospel which, upon the authority of Eusebius, is supposed to have been found in India in the second century after Christ, was the Hebrew Gospel of St. Matthew,† Dean Milman declares, that "where that Gospel was written, in what language originally, are questions to which no authoritative answer can be given."‡ Upon the whole, I think,

---

* See Decline and Fall, Vol. II. 68. Compare Milman's Hist. of Christ. Vol. III. p. 360. The notes there and also at p. 17 of Gieseler's History above referred to show how even Eusebius has found his advocates. "Probably" says Dean Milman "Eusebius erred more often from credulity than from dishonesty." Be it so. Nevertheless the value of Eusebius's statements, even on this view, must be very small indeed. As to Eusebius's intellectual aptitude as a historian, see Strauss Life of Jesus (1865) Vol. I. 35; and also that wellknown work, Supernatural Religion, Vol. I. p. 124. We may add here, that it is on Eusebius's authority, that Dr. Gieseler seems to accept the reality of St. Bartholomew's mission to India (p. 79).

† *Ind. Ant.* Vol. II. p. 283. Even Eusebius puts it no higher than 'it is said that he found' &c. See Westcott on the Canon p. 70.

‡ Hist. of Christ Vol. I. p. 386; and see too Greg's Creed of Christendom I. p. 111 *et seq.*; and Supernatural Religion Vol. I. p. 473 *et seq.*

it must necessarily be admitted by every unbiassed inquirer into this subject, that the evidence for this early existence of Christian communities in India, looked at from any point of view whatever, is of the weakest possible description. If we judged simply by the weight of authority, it would be far more safe to abide by the conclusions of two such eminent historians as Gieseler and Milman, than by the biassed statements of any other writer, even of Eusebius or Lorinser. If we applied to these various stories the historical tests laid down by Grote and Cornewall Lewis, and insisted on contemporary evidence, refusing to believe any statements that were not substantiated by such evidence, we should, I think, *ex concessis,* have at once to reject these stories. But even examining them by less exacting rules of historical criticism, they do not appear to me to be sufficiently vouched for. For there is not, I believe, any older writer than Eusebius to whom the stories can be traced ; yet St. Thomas and St. Bartholomew lived in the first century after Christ, and Pantænus[*] in the second, while Eusebius himself belongs to the middle of the fourth century. The truth seems to be, as remarked by Dr. Gieseler, that " the real but later founders of churches

---

[*] Sir John Kaye says (p. 6 n). "There is no reason, indeed, to doubt that Pantænus visited India, in all probability the island of Ceylon and the Malabar Coast." I cannot find, that this rests on any older authority than the statements of Eusebius and Ambrose (1 Gieseler 230, where the remark on Pantænus in the text ought to be noted, as also the diverging accounts referred to in the note about the succession of teachers in the school to which he belonged). It is also to be remarked concerning Pantænus that, as admitted even by Sir John Kaye, "it is not easy to say what he left behind him or who succeeded him in the great work. The history of the Christian Church in the east here sinks into a clould of obscurity." Col. Wilford (Asiatic Researches Vol. X. p. 69 *et seq.*) has some observations as to St. Thomas and Pantænus, but it is impossible to attach any weight to them.

have been frequently transferred to the times of the apostles by tradition"—a circumstance very natural and easy to understand, and one which, according to the writer in the Asiatic Researches above referred to, is known to have actually come to pass with regard to the Christian Church at Malabar.

Dean Milman has said :—"The other scattered communities of Christians disseminated through various parts of Asia, on the coast of Malabar, perhaps in China, have no satisfactory evidence of Apostolic or even of very early date ; they are so deeply impregnated with the Nestorian system of Christianity, which during the interval between the decline of the reformed Zoroastrianism and the first outburst of Islamism spread to a great extent throughout every part of the Eastern continent, that there is every reason to suppose them Nestorian in their origin."[*] To a somewhat similar effect is the following passage from Dr. Gieseler: " The Persian church had now broken off all connexion with the church of the Roman empire, and the Kings of Persia from *Pherozes* onward (461-488) favoured this separation for political reasons. These Christians, who had the bishop of Seleucia and Ctesiphon, were called by their opponents *Nestorians*, though they called themselves Chaldæan Christians, and in India Thomas-Christians."[†] But it is unnecessary to further labour this point. Dr. Lorinser brings forward no evidence in support of his position ; and on such a point, it might even be enough to pit against his assertion the above passages from the writings of two such historians as Milman and Gieseler, who, if they had a bias at all, would have a bias in favour of Dr. Lorinser's position.

---

[*] Hist. of Christ. II. 31.
[†] Eccles. Hist. I. 404.

We next come to a point, which, as stated by Dr. Lorinser himself, "is of peculiar importance in the present discussion ;" and I would, therefore, first set forth in Dr. Lorinser's own words what he says upon it. "Further" he says "there already existed an Indian Translation of the New Testament, of which we have positive proof* in the writings of St. Chrysostom, which seems to have been till now overlooked by Indian Antiquarians. The place in question is Evang. Joan. Homil. I. cap. 1 and runs as follows :—

"The Syrians too, and Egyptians, and Indians, and Persians, and Ethiopians, and innumerable other nations, translating into their own tongues the doctrines derived from this man, barbarians though they were, learnt to philosophise."† Now a variety of observations arises on this passage. And first I must say, that on a point of such "peculiar importance," I wish Dr. Lorinser's words had been perfectly precise, even beyond the reach of cavil. It may be my fault, or Dr. Lorinser's, or of Dr. Lorinser's translator; but what is precisely meant by the word "already" in the above sentence, and what precise fact it is of which we have "positive proof," seems to me very far from clear. I, however, take "already" to mean before the third century, and the "positive proof" to apply only to the fact of the existence of the translation, apart from the date to which that translation is to be referred. This being premised, let us now examine the real value of this new evidence. Who, in the first place, are the Indians ? Is it "positively proved" that the word Indians here means the people of this country? The

* It may be useful, considering the strength of this expression, to refer to the observations of Strauss at pp. 48 *et seq.* of the first Volume of his Life of Jesus. And see our remarks further on upon this point.

† *Ind. Ant.* Vol. II. 283b.

question is put for a variety of reasons. Writing of the reign of Constantine—and Chrysostom flourished in the same century with him—Dean Milman says:—"The Romans called this country (namely that about the Red Sea with that of the Homerites on the other side of the Arabian Gulf) by the vague name of "the nearer India;" while our country seems to have passed under the name of Further India.[*] This alone would throw considerable suspicion on the theory identifying Chrysostom's "Indians" with the people of this country. But secondly, the maxim of *noscitur a sociis* also points in the same direction ; for the other peoples enumerated by Chrysostom belong exactly to that part of Asia which might be regarded as connected with the "nearer India" of the Romans. And lastly, when St. Chrysostom is pleased to speak of all the nations named by him as " barbarians" whom the study of the doctrines of Jesus, for the first time in their national life, taught how to philosophise, those expressions also, even taken *cum grano* as we shall show further on they must be taken, apply more properly to the people about the Red Sea than to the countrymen of Patanjali, of Kâlidâs, of Varâhamihir. These considerations, it is submitted, throw at the very least an extremely strong suspicion upon the identification of the "Indians" and the Hindus.[†]

---

[*] And see too Gieseler Vol. I. p. 79 where India is stated to be probably identical with Yemen, and several authorities are cited for this view. See also Mr. Burnell's elaborate paper in 3 Indian Antiquary 309*a*. note and 1 Supernatural Religion p. 476 *et seq.*

[†] Sir John Kaye, speaking of Pantænus's visit to India, says (p. 6 note) that "the balance of evidence collected by Mr. Hough in his ' History of Christianity in India' is against the latter hypothesis," namely, " that the scene of Pantænus's labours was the coast of Arabia." I confess, I cannot bring myself to this conclusion. The contrary, I must say, appears to me more correct. Besides the evidence collected by Mr. Hough is not in my opinion of very much historical value, and the arguments adduced are extremely weak. Mr.

But further. It appears to me clear upon the very face of the passage, that the author is a rhetorician indulging in hyperbolical language. And what we are able to infer from this passage is amply confirmed by the information about St. Chrysostom which we receive from Gibbon. This, indeed, seems to have occurred to Dr. Lorinser also. But he says, that the consideration " loses its force, when we remember that all the translations mentioned by name in this passage, with the single exception of the Indian, are known to us from other sources and are still extant."✲ Upon this one or two observations arise, and again by reason of Dr. Lorinser's reticence as to his authorities. Are the dates of these translations perfectly well settled ? And if they are, are they settled upon authority independent of this statement of St.

Hough says in one place :—" Baronius the Martyrologist concluded that there were two Bishops named Frumentinus, one presiding over the church of Ethiopia, and the other over that of India proper ; the reader will judge whether this is a more reasonable way of solving the difficulty than by drawing a summary conclusion which would deprive the History of the Indian Church of this interesting narrative." Not having any wish as to the preservation or otherwise of this " interesting narrative," I own, that I consider the suggestion of Baronius the less reasonable of the two hypotheses. Clemens Alexandrinus's description of India need not necessarily have been learnt from Pantænus. And there seems to be some doubt as to Pantænus's exact relation with Clement. See Gieseler I. 230 and II. Supernatural Religion 191. The opinions of Fabricius and Niecamp are not anything like conclusive evidence, even if they are of any force at all, as to the reality of Pantænus's mission to India. Bunsen (Hippolytus and his age I. 235) speaks of Pantænus's Mission to India— " which means or includes, South Arabia." Dr. Westcott by putting India between inverted commas, seems to indicate at least a doubt as to the precise scene of Pantænus's labours. (Westcott on the Canon p. 297.)

✲ *Ind. Ant.* Vol. II. 184. If this statement be correct, it certainly becomes all the more remarkable that the ' Indian Translation' alone should not be forthcoming. Does it not lend some support to the view put forward in the text ?

Chrysostom ?* These questions are of very great moment, for
unless they can be answered in the affirmative, we cannot
obtain that corroboration for St. Chrysostom which Dr. Lorinser endeavours to find for him. And further it must be
remembered, that taking this statement of St. Chrysostom
at the best, we have to weigh against it the unquestionable
circumstances that no such Indian Translation is now forthcoming; that such a translation is never alluded to any where
else; that if there had been any such translation, the Christians would have taken very good care that it should
not be lost; and that in those early years of Christianity, it is not very likely, that Christian Missionaries
should have come over to India, and been able to master
even one of the languages of the country sufficiently to trans-

---

* These questions were suggested, only because Dr. Lorinser expresses himself in various places as thoroughly satisfied about things as
to which the evidence is of a very meagre and weak description. Since
this was written, however, I have found, that there is some
foundation for Dr. Lorinser's assertion. At the same time it
is remarkable, and of very great importance in this argument, that the dates of these translations are not themselves
well settled at all. As to the Syriac see Davidson Biblical Criticism
p. 597; as to the Egyptian p. 653; as to the Ethiopic p. 648-9: as to
the Persian p. 667 though this, by the way, does not seem to be mentioned in Smith's Dictionary of the Bible, which may be consulted as
to all the version, under the article Versions (ancient.) I may also
quote here the following words of Dr. Davidson as affording very
strong confirmation to the view I have ventured to express in the
text as to the value of Chrysostom's testimony. After mentioning
Chrysostom's "boast" about numerous translations, Dr. Davidson
says, "But we are scarcely justified in attaching much significance to
this language. The eloquent father speaks in the hyperbolical, exag-
gerated strain of the orator, rather than in the sober tone of truth
and reality. The Greek passage need not be quoted, as it may be
found in Marsh's Michaelis, where the learned translator observes,
that Chrysostom has weakened his own evidence by the addition of
the words 'innumerable other nations.' "

late the Bible into it. Dr. Lorinser thinks, " we may be
certain that Chrysostom would not have expressly mentioned
the Indian if he had not had positive knowledge of a translation in their tongue."○ There is some force in this remark.
On the other hand, it is certainly not necessary to suppose
any personal or positive knowledge. A mere rumour is quite
sufficient for the purposes of a rhetorical flourish, though it
is quite insufficient for the purposes of sober trustworthy
history. And St. Chrysostom's words above cited appear
to me, I confess, to have too much of the rhetorical ring
about them. It is well known, too, that he was a man of a particularly fervid imagination, one who had gone through a
regular training in rhetoric, and one, therefore, not likely to
weigh his words with much accuracy.† Upon the whole, then,
I do not think that any weight is due to the statement of
St. Chrysostom which Dr. Lorinser values so highly.
It is probably of as much, or rather as little, value as the
rumour mentioned by his namesake Dio Chrysostom about
an Indian Translation of Homer, which also has recently
been raised to the dignity of a historical truth.‡

One word more on this important point. "The Indian
Translation" says Dr. Lorinser "of which he (*i. e.* Chrysostom) knew must have existed for at least a hundred years
before information about it could in those times have reached
him."§ Very likely. But this remark, it seems to me, has
also a value on the opposite side. If the mere information
would take a hundred years to reach Chrysostom, surely a
considerably longer period than a hundred years would be

---

* *Ind. Ant.* Vol. II. 284*a.*

† See Gibbon (Bohn's ed.) Vol. III. p. 501.

‡ See *Ind. Ant.* Vol. I. 176; and see "was the Râmâyana
copied from Homer?" p. 11.

§ *Ind. Ant.* Vol. II. 284*a.*

required for the Missionaries of Christianity to come as far as India, to learn even one of the Indian languages, and to prepare a translation of the Bible into that language. And if we remember further, that the real propagation of Christianity among the " Heathen" did not commence till the time of St. Paul, and was not commenced even then without something like opposition from the older Apostles,[o] surely we must come to the conclusion, that when Dr. Lorinser asks us to believe, that the date of this translation may possibly reach to the *first* or second century A. C.[†] he makes a somewhat strong demand upon our credulity. And this quite apart from the question which will be referred to further on as to the dates of the composition of the original Gospels themselves.

But at this part of the argument, a suspicion seems to have crossed Dr. Lorinser's own mind, that this story of an Indian Translation of the New Testament is so indifferently vouched for, that it may probably not be of much historical value. And so he proceeds to discuss another alternative. " But even" says he "if we shut our eyes to the existence of an Indian Translation of the New Testament, it would still be possible that a Brâhman acquainted with the Greek language may have known and used the original text."[‡] According to the maxim that nothing is impossible except what involves a contradiction, this possibility may be accepted. But it seems to me that all the

---

* Strauss Life of Jesus I. 298. Milman also, (Vol. I. 380-1) seems to admit this.

† Dr. Davidson's highly reasonable observation may be quoted upon this. He says : " No man could think, as Marsh rightly affirms, of translating the Greek Testament before its several parts were connected and united in a volume, that is before the canon was formed. But the canon was not formed before the middle of the second century." See Biblical Criticism p. 597.

‡ *Ind. Ant.* II. 284a.

probabilities point exactly the other way. It must be remembered, that in the days to which these matters are
to be referred, the Christian came not as a ruler as he comes
now, but as one going to interfere with the religion of the
people, without the power of physical force to back him,
and without being able to dangle before their eyes any
temporal reward to be secured by conversion to Christianity.
And when we remember this ; when we remember also that
there has always been a prejudice against foreign tongues
among our people which is preserved in the line न वदेद्यावनीं
भाषां प्राणै: कण्ठगतैरपि ; when we remember further, that
even in our own days it is because of the ulterior advantages
which the study of the English language affords that that
language is learnt by many of our people ; once more when
we remember that, even in spite of these advantages, those
strata of our society which have not directly or indirectly
much connexion with the foreigner in other ways still
continue impervious to the influences of the English language ;
when we remember all this, and couple with it the just
assertion of Professor Wilson that Alexander's invasion had
but little influence on India ;* we cannot but come to the
conclusion, I think, that it is an exceedingly "rash hypothesis," which, without a scintilla of evidence, imagines a
Bráhman of the first or second century after Christ to have
been acquainted with the Greek language. The rashness of the
hypothesis appears to me, I confess, to be increased immensely, when we are asked to believe, that the Greek work
which the Bráhman studied and used was the New Testament,
the Holy Book of a religion which sent out its Missionaries
with the avowed object of destroying all the other religions

* See Mill's British India by Wilson Vol. I. p. 118. And compare
Wheeler's India Vol. III. 240.

f the world, and among others the religion of this same
Brâhmanical student of the language of Greece. Dr. Lorinser
eems to think, that his supposition may perhaps find con-
irmation in the circumstance, that "besides the New Testament,
here are traces of the use of the Book of Wisdom which
vas originally written in Greek."* But the existence of
hese traces descried by Dr. Lorinser has itself never been
roved. Parallels between the Gîtâ and the Book of Wisdom
here may be. These, too, however, may be only apparent
nd unreal. But even if they were very substantial and
eal, I should still strongly demur to the inference that
he Gîtâ must have borrowed from the Book of Wisdom.
Iuch more strongly should I demur to the use of this illo-
;ical deduction as a premiss upon which to base any further
:eduction. What if I said, that the supposition that the
Vew Testament borrowed from the Gîtâ may perhaps find
onfirmation in the circumstance that the Book of Wisdom
lso shows traces of its use?

And here a question of the last importance in this inquiry
resents itself. While Dr. Lorinser is talking of the existence
f translations of the *New Testament* in the first and
econd centuries after Christ, is it not a matter of at least
;rave doubt whether the original itself existed at that
arly period? Dr. Lorinser writes as if the conclusion which
e draws was not at all in conflict with conclusions arrived
t by other writers on independent reasoning. He does not
ven passingly notice any such conclusions. I shall therefore
otice them. For although Dr. Lorinser may conveniently
gnore the work of his countryman, Dr. Strauss, and others,
am of opinion that a complete investigation of the point be-
ore us requires that it should be discussed. And all the more

* *Ind. Ant.* Vol. II. 184a.

will one insist upon this, when one observes, that the methods
of criticism adopted with regard to the Gospels by Dr. Strauss
and the other writers on their age and authenticity, are
similar to the methods which have been applied to our own
literature, as well sacred as profane, in the discussions upon our
ancient history. Now in the first place, taking the four Gospels alone into our consideration, "we do not find certain
traces of the existence of our first three Gospels in their present form until towards the middle of the second century;"*
while as to the Fourth Gospel that is chronologically posterior to the other three. If so, no translation of these gospels
into any language whatever could possibly have existed in
the first century, nor it may be safely added, I think, even
in the second century, except, *perhaps*, at its very close. It
need scarcely be added, that the case as to the existence of a
translation into Sanskṛit or any other language of this country is even stronger against Dr. Lorinser's view. Furthermore, the facts adduced by Dr. Strauss† very clearly show

* See Strauss Life of Jesus Vol. I. 76—100, and see too Greg's
Creed of Christendom Vol. I. Chap. VI. and VII. In the Contemporary Review for March 1875, Mr. Matthew Arnold referring to the
wellknown work called " Supernatural Religion" writes on this subject as follows:—" But this which it is the main object of his book to
show—that there is no evidence of the establishment of our four gospels as a Gospel Canon, or even of their existence as they now finally
stand at all before the last quarter of the second century, nay tha
the great weight of evidence is against it—he has shown, and in the
most minute and exhaustive detail" (p. 525.) And with this should be
coupled the remark of Marsh endorsed by Dr. Davidson which we have
quoted above.

† See *inter alia* pp. 60, 75 of his life of Jesus Vol. I. Compare also
Greg's Creed of Christendom II. 37, and other places. Mr. Matthew
Arnold, also, though he seems to refer more particularly to th
heretics of the early days of Christianity, says:—"The practice
of forgery and interpolation was notorious, and the temptation to i
was great." Contemporary Review for March 1875 pp. 516-7. So
too Supernatural Religion I. 464 also p. 472.

that there have been numerous alterations made in the reports of Christ's works and speeches, which, among other considerations, render it at least quite as likely that the Gospels in the course of their formation received accretions from foreign sources, as that after their formation the followers of other religious systems borrowed from them. And this, indeed, suggests one point of very great moment in the present discussion. The point is, that while Dr. Lorinser endeavours to interpret facts in unnatural ways in order to suit his hypothesis as to the mode of explaining the coincidences he observes, he does not even hint at the possible existence of an opposite mode of explaining those coincidences. While he strains every nerve to make out that the coincidences between the two works show the Gîtâ to have borrowed from the Bible, he propounds not a single argument to show that the reverse of his hypothesis is incorrect. There is nothing in this part of his essay which can furnish an answer to the query.—Might not the Bible have borrowed from the Gîtâ? My own belief is, that such a borrowing, whether directly or indirectly, is very likely. But as we shall have something to say on this point at a later stage of this discussion, we need not here dwell on it any longer.

So much for the arguments by which Dr. Lorinser thinks he has made out the possibility that the author may have made use of the New Testament. Here however, a very natural difficulty occurs to Dr. Lorinser himself. " But is it conceivable," he asks, "that a Brâhman, who holds fast to the traditional wisdom of his caste and puts it above everything, as the author of the Bhagavadgîtâ does, should have condescended to take such special knowledge of Christianity, and even to use some of its doctrines, and maxims from its holy

writings, in order to suit them to, and incorporate them with,
his own system ?"* Having raised this important question,
Dr. Lorinser proceeds to adduce passages from various
writers, which appear to him to bear upon it. These passages,
which are set out at length, show that in the opinion of certain Christian scholars, the character of Kṛishṇa in the Mahâbhârat has had attributed to it many of the acts and qualities attributed to Jesus in the Christian Scriptures;† and
that the worship of the Deity Kṛishṇa is a comparatively recent innovation not earlier than about the fifth or sixth century A. C., as it cannot be traced in Varâhamihir. Dr. Lorinser thence infers, that in the same way that the deeds of
Christ are ascribed to Kṛishṇa, the words of Christ and the
doctrines taught by him may have been fathered upon Christ's
Hindu analogue.

Now if we remember, that the frame of mind which led
the Greeks to "discover everywhere their Heracles and
Dionysos"‡ was by no means the peculiar property of that
people, we shall not for one moment regard it is unnatural,
that Christian writers should have "recognised the influence
of Christian doctrines and legends on the development of later
Brahminical wisdom."§ In one of the extracts from his writings
given by Dr. Lorinser, Prof. Weber attributes the mental pre-
possession here spoken of to the Hindus. I do not deny that
this is in some measure correct. But seeing that the Hindus
have long held the doctrine which Christendom has yet to
learn, but is now likely to learn under the teaching of men like
Herbert Spencer and others—the doctrine of what may be called

* *Ind. Ant.* Vol. II. 284a.
† Compare Mr. Growse's letter on the Kṛishṇa Janmâshṭamî in
Ind. Ant. Vol. III. 300a.
‡ *Ind. Ant.* Vol. II. 285a.
§ *Ibid.* 285b.

the relative truth of religious systems, it seems to me that the mental characteristic in question would be more potent in the Christian than in the Hindu. Bred up under a system of religion which holds its own dogmas only to be true, and the dogmas of all other religions to be wholly and entirely untrue, Christians would naturally be only too glad to believe and to teach that whatever was good and true in other systems was borrowed from their own.* But in a scientific inquiry, when we have to calculate the value of results which are offered for consideration by persons in this peculiar position, it behoves us to make allowance, so to speak, for the 'personal equation.'

What then is the true state of the case on this point? We shall go *seriatim* through Dr. Lorinser's citations. And first Professor Weber, in the first passage extracted from his *Indische Studien*, makes a supposition, which occurs to him involuntarily, that Bráhmans may have gone to Alexandria, or even to Asia Minor, at the beginning of the Christian Era, and learnt there the monotheistic doctrine and some of its legends, which in due course they may have afterwards transferred—whatever that may mean—to Krishna, to whom, nevertheless, divine honours may already have been granted.† This "supposition" of Bráhmans travelling in search of Christian doctrine to foreign lands, has, of course, no evidence at all to support it, and may be taken, accordingly, for what it is worth.‡ And in considering the worth of the supposition, the reader of these sentences will doubtless

* Strauss mentions "a legend of a connexion between Senecca and the Apostle Paul." Life of Jesus Vol. I. 251.

† *Indian Antiquary* Vol. II. 284b.

‡ Mr. Hough (Christianity in India Vol. I. 43) speaking of "strangers" from India and sundry other countries being drawn to Alexandria by the attractions of its mart, says:—"they came for the sake of

take due note of the auxiliary verb 'may' which is to be
observed in such profusion in them. We seem here to be dealing with that "German license of conjecture,"* which was
reprobated, and justly reprobated, by the late eminent Historian of Greece. And if Professor Weber really means to say,
what in the words above referred to he does seem to say, that
monotheism was introduced into India from Christianity, not
only is there no evidence to bolster up this supposition, there
is, I think, positive evidence to show that the supposition is
entirely incorrect.† However, Prof. Weber, continues :—"the
legends of the birth of Krishna and his persecution by

this world's traffic indeed ; but they found in the knowledge of the
Gospel infinitely more than they sought, and returned home freighted
with the merchandise of Heaven." I own this strikes me as utterly
illogical and unlikely. Men engaged in the "world's traffic" are
not, according to the ordinary modes of human action, the most eli-
gible persons for conversion to a foreign religion. And though the
knowledge of the Gospel may, in the eyes of a devout Christian like
Mr. Hough, be infinitely more than what the Hindu trader sought,
the Hindu trader is not very likely to have taken the same view of
the matter. At any rate his taking such a view is certainly not a matter of course. Mr. Hough next goes on to state, how some
Christian Missionaries preached at Socotora, and how some may have
gone on to India, and then winds up in this wise :—" who those heralds
of mercy were, or to what extent the great Head of the Church vouchsafed to prosper their endeavours, the pen of history has not recorded.
But this is of little moment. It is enough to know that their names
are written in Heaven." This again is a remarkable mode of writing
history. Mr. Hough has failed to show that the ' pen of history' has
' recorded' the fact of any ' herald of mercy' going to India. That
statement rests merely on a conjecture of his own. Yet in these last
sentences, he speaks as if that were quite settled, and the only doubt
was as to the precise persons who took part in the transaction, and as
to the precise extent of the success which they achieved.

* See Personal life of Grote by Mrs. Grote p. 264.

† Not to mention a legion of other passages, I may simply refer
to the verse एकं सद्विप्रा बहुधा वदन्ति quoted in Yâska's Nirukta,
and see Wilson. Essays on Sanskrit Literature Vol. III. 345,

Kansa remind us too strikingly of the corresponding Christian narratives to leave room for the supposition that the similarity is quite accidental." I am not quite so sure of that. But we shall suppose that Prof. Weber is perfectly right. What then? This does not prove that the Hindus borrowed from the Christians,＊ and certainly not that they borrowed in the particular mode which Prof. Weber's clairvoyance has descried. Prof. Weber goes on:—"According to Lassen (I. 623), the passages in the Mahâbhârata in which Krishṇa has divine honours attributed to him are of later origin (belong in fact, as I think, to the Purâṇa epoch) and the Krishṇa-cultus proper is not found before the fifth or sixth century." The question hinges really a good deal on this point. Is this view of Prof. Weber, correct? Prof. Lassen's opinion—into the grounds of which we shall not stay to inquire—is not by any means enough for the exigencies of Prof. Weber's conclusion. For, admitting the "later origin," the question still remains, later

＊ See the passage from Sir W. Jones cited in Mr. Greg's Creed of Christendom Vol. I. 140; see too 3 Wheeler's India 378 n.; and Moor's Hindu Pantheon p. 200 cited, apparently with approval, in Hardwicke's Christ and other masters p. 177. And see also Weber's Krishnajanmâshṭamî. *Indian Antiquary* III. pp. 21 *et seq.* It is worth remarking here, that this story of Kansa, on which Prof. Weber relies so much, is already mentioned in the Mahâbhâshya—a work which, even according to Weber, was composed before the death of Christ. On Prof. Weber's principle, the inference from this is irresistible, that the Christian story is borrowed from the Indian, as Mr. Greg suggests. A learned scholar, criticising in the *Bombay Gazette* a paper of Prof. Bhândârkar's referred to in the sequel, suggested that the passage might have been interpolated—upon what ground except its clashing with a foregone conclusion, it is difficult to say. Besides the writer is probably not aware, that the interpolation must have been made not only in the Bhâshya but also in the Vâkyapadîya and in Kaiyaṭ's gloss, for both those works refer to the story. See under Pâṇini III. 1-2. (Banâras Ed. p. 27).

than what period? Professor Weber's assertion, therefore, that the passages of the Bhârat in which Krishṇa is deified belong to the " Purâṇa* epoch," must be fortified with other reasons than the vague deliverance of Prof. Lassen. But the only other reason I can trace throughout the lengthy extract from the *Indische Studien* which is given by Dr. Lorinser, is that "there is no trace in Varâhamihira" of the worship of Krishṇa. And it must, I apprehend, be at once admitted, that at the best this is an extremely weak reason indeed. But the matter does not rest there. Bhartṛihari in his Nîtis'atak speaks of the Ten Incarnations of Vishṇu. Of course, therefore, he must have regarded Krishṇa as an incarnation of Vishṇu. And Kâlidâs expressly speaks of "Vishṇu in the guise of a cowherd." Now Dr. Bhâu Dâjî makes Bhartṛihari a contemporary of Kâlidâs, and both contemporaries of Varâhmihir.† What then becomes of the argument based on Varâhamihir's silence, when two of his contemporaries speak out in this wise? Still more, what becomes of it, if, as I contend, both Kâlidâs and Bhartṛihari must be placed a good deal, in fact two or three centuries, before the 6th century A. C?‡ Even yet, however, we have not

* What is the " Purâṇa epoch" of which Prof. Weber speaks? This is one of those vague expressions, highly objectionable and misleading as I submit, which occur with unfortunate frequency in the discussions on our ancient Literature. The Purâṇa epoch means, I suppose, the epoch in which the Purâṇas were composed. Who knows when that occurred? I have already lodged my protest against Prof. Wilson's opinion in this matter in the preface to my edition of Bhartṛihari (see pp. VII.—VIII.) So have Professor Bhândârkar and Bâbû Râjendralâl Mitra (see *Indian Antiquary* Vol. III. 16 and Chhândogyopanishad, Engl. Translation p. 53 note.

† J. B. B R. A. S. Vol. VI. 225, and J. R. A. S. (N. S). Vol. I.

‡ See "Was the Râmâyana copied from Homer?" p. 58. and Bhartṛihari (Bomb. Series of Sansk. Classics) Introduction pp. XII.—XIII.

traced the deification of Krishṇa up to the earliest testimony to its existence which we possess. There is in the Mahâbhâshya of Patanjali—an author who flourished before Bhartṛihari and before Kâlidâs—a body of evidence which is of the highest importance on this point. The strongest argument is that afforded by a passage to which attention was drawn by me in my essay on the Râmâyaṇ in reply to Professor Weber,[a] and by Professor Bhâṇḍârkar in his essay on the Antiquity of the Mahâbhârat.[†] Since then Professor Bhâṇḍârkar has collected several other passages from the Mahâbhâshya in which references are made to Krishṇa or his exploits.[‡] The conclusion is, therefore, irresistible, that apart from the weakness of the argument ab silentio, there is positive evidence on the other side to show that the divinity of Krishṇa is not a post-Christian innovation, but is as old at least as the time of Patanjali, if not as old as the time of Pâṇini.

I cannot leave this topic without entering an emphatic protest against the perfectly arbitrary method of fixing dates in the history of Sanskṛit Literature and Philosophy which this example well illustrates. I feel convinced, that the argument ab silentio has been in numerous cases impressed to do work to which it is not equal in any case, least of all in the case of a literature of which large portions can almost be demonstrated to have perished. While the chronology of our ancient literature and philosophy is yet entirely unsettled, there are not a few scholars who think themselves entitled to make dogmatic assertions about the dates of various works, and of the rise of various doctrines. But the evils of

---

* P. 27.

† J. B. B. R. A. S. Vol. X. 84

‡ Ind. Ant. Vol. III. 14-16.

this vicious method, of course, do not stop there. Not only
are hypotheses formed on the weakest possible foundations,
with the smallest possible collection of facts, but upon such
hypotheses further superstructures of speculation are raised.
And when that is done, the essential weakness of the base
is often effectually kept out of view. By such methods the
whole of Sanskrit Literature, or nearly the whole of it, is being shown to be much more recent than it has hitherto been
thought. It may be that we Hindus have in some measure
to thank ourselves for this result. It may be that our claims
to an exceedingly high antiquity have in the natural course
provoked this reaction. This may be. But if this is so,
then those who put themselves forward as workers in the
field of "oriental research," and connect with their labours
the venerable and dignified name of science, are bound to
be on their guard against this reaction.

But to return. After the evidence we have set out above
to show the antiquity of the belief in Krishna as a God, it
is not very necessary to go into the other surrounding
matters referred to by Professor Weber. Nevertheless as it
is not quite useless to do so, we shall take a rapid review of
them. I pass over the assumptions, which I contend are quite
unwarranted, contained in such expressions as "Individual
Christian teachers......would not be without influence in
the early time," or "Natives of India who filled up in their
own way what they had learned in foreign countries," or
"prepared by the current tendency of Indian Philosophy
towards a concrete unity."* I pass this over, and come to the
points on which, according to Professor Weber, "the whole
question turns." Now the statement of the first point by
Professor Weber himself shows how little any person is

* *Ind. And.* II. 285a.

varranted in talking about the borrowing of Christian dogmas
>y oriental people. It is difficult, as Professor Weber him-
elf admits, to say what has been borrowed by the Gnostics
rom the "Indians" and *vice versâ.* And the only remark
vhich I need make with reference to this is, that I am not
.ware that there is much more material for deciding on the
[uestion as applied to the period preceding the rise of the
Gnostic sects.* And when Professor Weber speaks of the
eciprocal action and mutual influence of Gnostic and Indian
conceptions in the first centuries of the Christian Era as being
'evident," I think, he might with advantage have shown the
grounds for this opinion; especially as it comes immediately
.fter the admission made by himself about the difficulty of say.
ng how much in each is original and how much borrowed.
The second point of Professor Weber refers to Varâhamihir's
ilence to which reference has been already made. The third
oint is a good specimen of the vagueness in which great
names can afford to indulge with impunity. "This worship
f Krishṇa," says Professor Weber, " has no intelligible connexion with his earlier position in the Brahmanical legends.
There is a gap between the two which apparently nothing '
>ut the supposition of an external influence can account for."
Now what is the "gap" which requires explanation? What
s the "external influence" which affords that explanation?
The gap, admittedly, is not wider than that between a great
numan hero, and a hero regarded as an incarnation of the Deity.
Is the transition from the one to the other such an immensely
sudden, unusual, and inexplicable transition, that you must
imagine some "external influence" to explain it? I have my

* About these sects there has been quite a legion of conflicting
opinions. See the sources of them collected in Gieseler's Compendium
of Ecclesiastical History Vol. I 135. One writer there mentioned
lerives the Gnostic doctrine from Buddhism.

own doubts as to the existence of this alleged "gap." But even assuming its existence, it appears to me that a fact of most frequent occurrence in the religious history of the Hindus—and also I may add of other peoples—is enough to account for it—the fact, namely, that a man who is thought to be remarkably superior to his contemporaries in any qualities of great worth is easily believed, in a certain condition of society, to have been more than human. And it must not be forgotten, that even in the case of Christianity itself, eminent critics have maintained, that "the New Testament alone represents several stages of dogmatic evolution," and that "no one can have attentively studied the subject without being struck by the absence of any such (scil. supernatural) dogmas from the earlier records of the teaching of Jesus."[*] Are we not here also to look about for some "external influence?" I own, it seems to me a thoroughly mistaken view, which always seeks for the causes of such 'gaps,' where they exist, in 'external influence.' In most cases, the natural evolution of the religious idea in certain conditions of society, is quite sufficient to explain them. What "external influence" was at work in the apotheosis of S'ankarâchârya in modern times, or of the Ribhus in the times of the Veds?

The legend of the S'vetadvîp, to which Professor Weber goes on next to refer, does not appear to me to be entitled to the weight which the Professor attaches to it. I confess, I cannot see the flimsiest possible ground for identifying the S'vetadvîp of the legend with Alexandria, or Asia Minor, or the British Isles,[†] or any other country or region

---

[*] Supernatural Religion II. ad finem.

[†] This has been done by Col. Wilford, Asiatic Researches Vol. XI.

in this world. The Dvíp is in the first place stated to lie to the North of the Kshírasamudra; and to the North West of Mount Meru, and above it by thirty-two thousand yojans. I should like to know, what geography has any notion of the quarter of this earth where we are to look for that sea of milk and that mount of gold. Consider next the description of the wonderful people inhabiting this wonderful Dvíp.

ते सहस्रांनिपं देवं प्रविशन्ति सनातनम् ।
आनेन्द्रिया निराहारा अनिष्यन्दा: सुगन्धिन: ॥ २५ ॥

It will be news to the world, that there were in Alexandria or elsewhere a whole people without any organs of sense, who ate nothing, and who entered the sun—whatever that may mean! Remember, too, that the instruction which Nârad receives in this wonderful land is not received from its inhabitants, but from Bhagaván, from God himself. Nor let it be forgotten, that the doctrines which the Deity there announces to Nârad cannot be shown to have any connexion whatever with Christianity. On the contrary, I think, it must be at once admitted, that the whole of the prelection addressed to Nârad bears on its face its essentially Indian character, in the references to the three qualities, to the twenty-five primal principles, to the description of final emancipation as absorption or entrance into the Divinity, and various other matters of the like character. Against all this what have we to consider? Why, nothing more than the description of the inhabitants as white, and as एकान्तिन: which, Prof. Weber thinks, means monotheists (Sed quœre). It appears to me, that the story is a mere work of the imagination, and that if anybody else had made any use of it as even in its nucleus historical, Prof. Weber himself and other European scholars would have objected to its use in any such way. And independently of this, I say, that historical or unhistorical, the story shows no tangible reference to Christianity or any Christian country.

We now proceed to Prof. Weber's fifth and last point, and here again we have an instance of that vagueness, which we have already complained of, and which it is so difficult to fairly grapple with. What explanation has Christianity to give of the legends corresponding to those referred to here by Prof. Weber ? What ground has Prof. Weber for saying that " individual Christian teachers" did not receive those legends in Hindu hands ? What has Christ got to do with ' life as a herdsman' ? The whole question appears to me to be looked at under such conditions, that the result presented is inevitably onesided.

Dr. Lorinser goes on next to refer to Mr. Wheeler, and to Mr. Wheeler's anonymous Reviewer in the *Athenæum*, who both assert this " borrowing from Christianity." It is perfectly useless, however, to multiply authorities in this fashion. The point which Dr. Lorinser is here endeavouring to make out is the probability of the author of the Gîtâ having made use of the New Testament. Dr. Lorinser admits, both expressly and by implication, the intrinsic improbability of such a thing. And that being so, the production of a whole Olympus of mere authority cannot outweigh that improbability. The question is not one to be decided by authority at all, and most assuredly not by the authority of a Weber or a Wheeler. Upon the question whether the Hindus have borrowed from Christians, the *mere authority* of Christian scholars, I must take leave to say, is in my opinion worth nothing at all. There is but one other remark which I need make upon this point, and that is, that the broad assertions of Wheeler and his Reviewer are all founded upon the very narrow and frail basis afforded by the assumption, that from the coincidence between Hindu and Christian legends the inference of the former being the copy and the latter the original is irresistible. I once more lodge my humble but firm protest against this unwarranted assumption.

To proceed. Having summed up the result of this part of the inquiry, Dr. Lorinser now goes on to couple with it an other argument, which according to him sublimates the " possibility" thus far proved into " conclusive proof." That other argument is based on the coincidences between passages in the Gîtâ and in the New Testament. These passages Dr. Lorinser marshals into three classes. Now although it is not to be denied, that his first and third classes of passages must be of some value in this discussion, I cannot admit that the second class of passages is worth anything at all. To draw conclusions from a comparison of the words of two works in original when divorced from their contexts is very dangerous; to draw such conclusions with one work in original and the other in a translation is more dangerous still; to draw such conclusions with both works in translations is most dangerous of all. But how much is even this superlative degree of danger heightened, when the translator is one who comes to his work with the spectacles of a theory? How much more is it heightened, when that theory is one propounded by the translator himself, and one, therefore, for which he would naturally feel that paternal love, which, as Plato tells us, every poet and every author feels for the work of his intellect ?

With this preliminary caution, let us now proceed to examine the first class of passages adduced by Dr. Lorinser. And on the very first passage (Gîtâ III. 6) it must be remarked, that the coincidence, if any, is a very slight one indeed. The passage in the Gîtâ deals with a case of difference between the inner and the outer man. The passage in Matthew has no reference at all to such a difference, but with regard to the inner man, it says, that a sinful feeling should not even be harboured in the heart, for to harbour such a feeling is itself to commit a sin. There is here, therefore, not merely a difference in expression, but also a difference in meaning. As to the note on this passage, it affords one out of the many instances of dogmatism in this essay of Dr. Lorinser's, and simply begs the question. "The peculiar stress," says Dr. Lorinser, "laid on the inner purity of the mind in the Bhagavadgîtâ would itself alone suggest the influence of Christian ideas, even if other vestiges of it could not be pointed out." It is scarcely necessary to pit against this wonderfully dogmatic asseveration anything better than a mere "Certainly not." But perhaps it may not be out of place to add that, having regard to the fact that Jesus's own doctrine as enunciated above comes by way of improvement on the previous teaching of the Old Testament, it is more likely, upon the principles of Dr. Lorinser and of his great authority Professor Weber, that Jesus only learnt it elsewhere and did not work it out himself. And we may also refer to the strong and clear statement of this very valuable idea in the Buddhistic Dhammapad.* On the second passage (III. 32) there is a note similar to the above as to S'raddhâ and Bhakti. The fact, however, is that while we have allusions to faith and its efficacy in Indian Literature of a date unquestionably prior to Christianity,

---

* See the passage cited at 5 Journal Royal Asiatic Society (N. S.) 229. About the antiquity of the Dhammapad which was commented on by Buddhaghosh about 400 A. C. (See "Was the Râmâyana copied from Homer?" p. 12) I do not think even Dr. Lorinser or Professor Weber will venture to raise any doubt. And see also 12 J. R. A. S. 179-80.

the Christian doctrine of faith is by Dr. Strauss pronounced a new-fangled one.* What is the conclusion hence derivable? With regard to the third passage (III. 34), 'desire and inclination' is evidently a mistake; it ought to be 'desire and aversion'; and it seems to me, that on this shoal some at least of Dr. Lorinser's argument is stranded. As to the coincidence, it is clear, that the passage of the Gîtâ has no reference to sin, which appears from the context to be the main idea in the passage in the Epistle; while 'lusts' also only represents one half of the idea in the Gîtâ, and indeed is essentially different.† And again while the passage from the Epistle refers to 'enemies of god,' the passage of the Gîtâ refers to the 'enemies of oneself.' On the latter part of the note on the passage, it is further to be observed, that in Matthew X. 36 only a sectarian or a mystic can see any reference to the 'lust which dwells in man.' Lastly as to the 'Christian doctrine of concupiscence' I do not see its bearing on the passage at all. On the fourth passage (IV. 4) it would be well to remember the sequel of the claim made by Jesus. The fifth instance of coincidence (VI. 5) is, I think, at the best only apparent and superficial. While Kṛishṇa is there speaking of the Transmigration of the Soul, Jesus has not the remotest conception of it in his words. The lengthy note on this passage, however, requires also a somewhat lengthy treatment. And first, Dr. Lorinser holds, of course without assigning reasons, that "the Avatârs all belong to the Purâṇs, hence to a post-Christian age." Now there are three assertions involved in this, two of which may or may not be correct, the third of which is certainly not correct, and all of which are without the slightest proof. It is *not*

---

* The question is discussed somewhat more fully in the sequel,

† See the notes on our translation of this passage,

proved (*pace* Prof. Wilson and others) that the Puráṇs are
post-Christian;[*] it is *not* proved that the 'Avatárs all
belong to the Puráṇs'; it is *not* proved that the Avatárs
are post-Christian, but on the contrary it *is* proved that they
are ante-Christian. Dr. Lorinser, after some remarks which
it is not necessary here to refer to, proceeds :—"In my opinion,
there can, at present, be no doubt whatever, that the incarnation of Vishṇu as Kṛishṇa, the only one represented
as a truly human incarnation of the person of the god, is
an imitation of the Christian dogma regarding the person
of Christ." Now so far is this from being correct, so far is
this 'imitation' from being beyond doubt, that the reverse of
it is now demonstrated. Vishṇu's incarnation as Kṛishṇa
dates from the time of Patanjali if not of Páṇini—in either
case, from before the time when the incarnation of Jesus existed, so to speak, as a fact; much more before it existed as a
belief; still more before it was transmitted to India as a belief. The allegation again, that none of the other Avatárs
except Kṛishṇa were 'truly human,' simply forgets Paras'u-
rám, and Rám, and I may add Buddha. Dr. Lorinser goes
on to state the reasons for his 'opinion.' The first, the similarity of the name Kṛishṇa to Christ is, I take leave to say,
a mere *ignis fatuus*, not worth very much more than that travesty
of philology where vowels interchange and consonants matter
not. The many coincidences in the legends, if they are of
much value in the investigation, are not more consistent with
the theory of imitation as propounded by Christian scholars
than with that theory read the other way. And more than
this, the latter, I think, is more likely to prove the more correct
view. Dr. Lorinser further adds, that the imitation " is pointed to, as may be specially shown, by the Bhagavadgítá itself."

---

[*] Compare our Introduction to Bhartṛihari. p, vii, *et seq.*

The only observation this calls for is—why in the world is it not shown? If it could be shown, it would almost, I might say altogether, decide the question. Why, I ask again, is it not shown? But to proceed. The sixth coincidence (IV. 8) Dr. Lorinser might have made more thorough by adding to the passage cited from the Gîtâ a portion which his translation omits—"for the destruction of evil-doers." On the other hand it should also be noted, that the Gîtâ says 'from time to time,' to which there is nothing similar in the Christian passages, yet it is of the very essence of the doctrine of the Gîtâ. On the eighth passage (V. 8) it is to be remarked that the first part of it certainly does not coincide with the passages cited by Dr. Lorinser. It has nothing to do with the glorification of God at all, it is only conversant with the question—what is the active principle in man? And the answer is—Not the soul. The latter portion is much nearer the meaning of the passages cited, but there is another passage which is nearer still, but which, strangely enough, Dr. Lorinser does not allude to either in this place or anywhere else. That passage is Gîtâ IX. 27. The next passage discloses a coincidence only if misunderstood. The passage from the Gîtâ is not so general as divorced from its context in Dr. Lorinser's citation it appears to be. But it is perfectly clear that it must be interpreted in connexion with its context, and thus interpreted, I do not think, that anybody will be able to trace the slightest coincidence. In the next passage (V. 16) there is again a mistake. There is no reference to "minds"* in the original of the Gîtâ; and without that, there is little to liken it to the passage cited from 2 Pet. I. 19. Even with that, the coincidence is of such a nature, that nothing can, in my opinion, turn

---

* Probably Dr. Lorinser has so misunderstood the word आत्मनः.

upon it—not to say, that the differences between the two
passages are perfectly obvious. The same remark applies
to the next passage (V. 23). Calling a thing a "temptation,"
and calling it the "agitation (for it is not exactly pressure)
produced by desire and anger," if they are one and the same
thing, are at least two different sides of it; and in fact the
difference of language seems to me to be only typical of the difference in the two points of view. What is the object of bidding
us in the note to compare I. Cor. VII. 40 " as to Sukhí Nara,"
is, I must confess, more than I can make out. What follows,
however, I can make out, and do certainly deny. Dr. Lorinser
says:—"The idea enunciated in this S'loka bears an entirely
Christian stamp." I say, on the contrary, that it is an essentially Hindu idea; and I do repudiate the claim put forward
by Dr. Lorinser on behalf of Christianity. I must own, too,
that the quotation from Chrysostom seems to me to be scarcely
relevant. The next passage (VI. 10) well exemplifies
the danger of wrenching passages out of their contexts for
purposes of comparison. The whole of the passage from the Gítá
shows the object of the "secrecy" to be the avoidance of
interruptions; and Ânandagiri says so expressly :—योगप्रतिबन्धकदु-
र्जनादिविभूरादेशो गृह्यते. Now what is the meaning of the passage in
Matthew ? Why, it is a warning against making a show and
pomp of piety. Do not, Jesus says, and if I may add it well
says, do not pray in public that you may be seen praying
and thus regarded as a pious man. Admirable advice! But
what has it to do with the admonition given by Krishna?*
The passages are entirely distinct in meaning. The word
'secret,' indeed, does occur in both ; but the meanings of the
two are not thereby brought nearer each other at all. Whether
there is a coincidence in the next instance adduced by Dr.

* Compare Sutta Nipata by Sir Mutu Coomar Syamy p. 106.

Lorinser (VI. 16) depends to a certain extent upon the true interpretation of the passage from Matthew. My own opinion is that Jesus's teaching allows much more liberty than Krishṇa's, and that there is but a very slight coincidence. This, however, only as far as Dr. Lorinser sets out the passages; when the other portions of the passage from the Gîtâ are considered, I think it will be found, that there is no reason for supposing any connexion between the two. In the next passage (VI. 39) I fail to see any coincidence. And it is beyond question that the circumstances are essentially distinguishable. Nor, I think, is there really any coincidence in the next passage adduced (VII. 1-2). Then again, as to the sixteenth passage, (VII. 14) there appears to me to be a very important distinction between the deliverances of Kṛishṇa and Christ. The former speaks of illusion, the latter of burden—a distinction, which again appears to me typical of the essential difference between the two. In the next passage, (VII. 15) again, I can see no coincidence except, indeed, it be that based on 'demoniac' in the one passage and 'devil' in the other. In the following two passages (VII. 16 and VII. 22) I can see no coincidences, when the passages in the Gîtâ are considered, as only they ought to be, in connexion with their contexts.* The translation of the second passage is not correct on the most vital point in the comparison. And it is also worth observing, that whereas Dr. Lorinser quotes Matthew XI. 28 against the passage at Gîtâ VII. 16 as well as against that at Gîtâ VII. 14, there is little coincidence between these two passages of the Gîtâ itself. This shows how exceedingly slight, to say no more, are the coincidences which sometimes satisfy Dr. Lorinser's mind.

---

* See our translation of the passage, and compare the sequel of it with the words 'every good gift and every perfect gift' in James I. 17.

In the next passage (VII. 26) I see a difference just as
clearly as a coincidence. In the twenty-first passage (VII.
27) the expression इदमोह is certainly misunderstood, and
the coincidence, besides being open to a remark already
made as to the addition of aversion to desire in the Sanskrit,
is also very slight. The next passage (VII. 28) contains
an even slighter coincidence, if it can be called a coincidence at all. In the next passage (VII. 29)* there
is a difference more remarkable than the alleged coincidence. The two passages from John, the one referred
to in the text and the other in the note, speak only of death,
while the Gītā speaks of old age also—and yet, Dr. Lorinser,
in the note, once more thinks it proper to dogmatize, and
although he produces not a single passage from the Christian
Scriptures referring to "liberation from old age," he under-
takes to say, that the idea "that taking refuge in Krishṇa
liberates from *old age* and death, is an idea so foreign to
Indian Philosophy that its origin can only be Christian".
Such reckless dogmatism,† for by no other name can it be
justly described, is not calculated to make converts to Dr.
Lorinser's views. Again मामाश्रित्य in the Gītā is certainly
very different from the expression "if a man keep my say-
ing" and not quite the same thing with the expression in
John XI. 26. Once more, the point of the two passages in
John is entirely different from that of the passage in the
Gītā, as may be seen from the remaining portion of the latter
which is not quoted by Dr. Lorinser. In the next passage

---

* It may be mentioned too, that मामाश्रित्य is not accurately rendered by 'have fled unto me.'

† If Dr. Lorinser had given but a moment's thought to the grand
old story of Buddha, he might have been saved from the error of
making this extraordinary statement. And see too Kaṭhopanishad
I. 12. 28. Pras'na V. 7. Mundak. II. 7.

again (VIII. 7) no coincidence can be traced. The idea of the father 'giving' is certainly not found in the passage from the Gitâ. And as to "casting out," that too has nothing answering to it in the passage cited. There is something nearer to it in Gitâ VI. 30. The passages in the note from John are to the effect that knowing or believing in Jesus is everlasting life. That is not the way it is put in the passage in the Gitâ; and the difference is again noteworthy, as showing the essential difference of the two systems. And this being so, the Christian trace "too clear to be overlooked" is nowhere. On the contrary I cannot but repeat here, that the idea appears to be eminently Hindu. The remark on "Karma Divyam" I must confess I do not understand.[*] And I may add, that the similarity which in Dr. Lorinser's eyes is so unmistakable between that expression and the verses from John referred to by him is perfectly obscure to my weaker vision. In the next passage (VIII. 9) there is some coincidence. In the next one after that (VIII. 22) there is much less, and St. Paul himself says his teaching is not novel but common to him with the Greek Philosophers. In the twenty-seventh passage (IX. 1) "with understanding" is a blunder in the translation, and the "mysteries of the kingdom of god" are something which differ *toto cœlo* from the "hidden knowledge" taught by Krishna.[†] There is some coincidence in the next passage (IX. 11). On the next passage to this (IX. 11, 12) the remark made before on "demoniac" and "the devil" fully applies. Beyond that, I see no coincidence between the two

---

[*] I may remark, that it is quite wrong to say that कर्मदिव्यम् is the 'designation' which "Krishna applies to his incarnation." But this is a minor point.

[†] Nor is there any such distinction in the Gitâ as that indicated in the passage from St. Luke.

passages cited. In the next passage, 'transient' is not a correct rendering of गतागत. There is some difference, too, between the 'law of the Ved' and 'the tenets of the Scribes
and the Pharisees.' The kingdom of Heaven' also, as understood by Jesus, is different from the 'Heaven' (स्वर्ग) spoken of
by Krishna in the foregoing portion of the passage cited. And
the most important point is, that whereas Jesus speaks of
righteousness, Krishna speaks of abandoning desires. In the
next passage (IX. 23) there is a misprint in the reference.
The verse is the twenty-third not the twenty-eighth. I do not
feel sure here about the meaning of Paul's words, but if
'ignorantly' has, as it seems to have, reference to the word
'unknown' in the sentence preceding, it seems to me that
there is no real coincidence in this case. In the next passage
(IX. 29), the contexts, I think, show that much of the similarity is merely apparent. In passage No. 33. (IX. 30) there is
really no coincidence whatever,* and it is further to be observed
that one word in the Gîtâ is not translated by Dr. Lorinser. And
yet it is of almost vital importance here. That word is the word
भाव. In the thirty-fourth passage (IX. 33 ; 23 in the original
is a misprint) there is some coincidence, but not very
much, I think. What is the coincidence in the next passage
(X. 1) or in that which follows (X. 3)? I own I see much
difference and little similarity. And when in passage No. 37
(X. 11) Dr. Lorinser quotes a sentence from Mark in
which the word 'compassion' is used, one feels tempted to
ask, what possible conclusion can such a comparison lead to ?
Dr. Lorinser apparently wishes the passage from 2 Cor. IV. 6
to be read together with that. But that, even if admissi-

---

* The passages cited in the note on this have a slight similarity,
but only a slight one, to one another. I can see nothing, however,
to connect them with the passage discussed in the text.

ble from the point of view of an "apologetic critic," is certainly inadmissible, more especially in such an inquiry as the present. Nor, I think, is the similarity exhibited even after so coupling the two passages, of any significance. The next passage (X. 14, 15) is again an instance where we have an unquestionably peculiar doctrine of Christianity which has no parallel in the Gitâ, while the similarity insisted on by Dr. Lorinser is a very vague one on an immaterial point. In the next passage (XI. 20) I see great differences. In passage No. 40 (XI. 22) there is nothing about belief in the Gitâ where the 'blessed ones' are mentioned as well as the 'devils'. In the next passage (XI. 52) I do not quite understand the quotation from Peter, but as far as I do understand it, I think there is very little in it to compare to the passage from the Gitâ. In the next passage (XII. 7) "the world of mortality" appears to me to involve an idea essentially distinct from "the body of this death," and it is simply allowing ourselves to be deceived by words to suppose any coincidence between them. In the next passage (XII. 8) there is, it seems to me, such an absence of coincidence, that the ideas of the Gitâ and the Epistle are in my opinion clearly and obviously distinct from each other. And the little appearance of similarity which there is, is based on a mistranslation of अनऋर्वैम् by 'on high.'* In the next passage (XII. 14) "bringing every thought to the *obedience* of Christ," seems to me a very different thing from "giving heart and understanding to me." In the next passage (XIII. 17) 'far from darkness is his name' is wrong. In the next passage (XIII. 17) the verses noted at foot appear to be nearer the passage in the Gitâ than the one cited against

---

* म'येन निर्वसिष्यसि also is inaccurately rendered by 'live *with* me.'

it. In the forty-seventh (XIII. 25) I can see no coincidence
at all; nor in the next one either, (XIV. 2) for whereas the
Gitâ in this passage refers to the doctrine of metempsy-
chosis, and indeed can be understood only with reference to
that doctrine, the passages from John and the Revelation, of
course, have no such meaning. How Dr. Lorinser can have
persuaded himself that there is a coincidence in the next passage (XIV. 14) passes my comprehension.* There is, I think, a
very important distinction between the drift of the next passage
from the Gitâ (XV. 15) and the sentence from John cited by
Dr. Lorinser against it. In the next passage (XV. 19) I
again fail to see any coincidence whatever, and in the next one
after that (XVI. 5) I see most important differences. Once more,
in the fifty-third passage (XVI. 9-11.) I do not see that there is
any coincidence. And in the fifty-fourth (XVI. 12, 15) there is
but a very superficial one. Dr. Lorinser indeed thinks it 'strik-
ing', but I altogether disagree with him. In the next instance
adduced by Dr. Lorinser (XVI. 24) there is some similarity,
but there is also considerable difference, and on the next
(XVIII. 46) it is again to be remarked that the passage from
the Epistle to the Corinthians there cited is also cited by Dr.
Lorinser against Gitâ V. 8 10, and if one reads these two stanzas
in connexion with Gitâ XVIII. 46, one will find it, I think,
very difficult to see what coincidence there is between these
two passages. Nor is it by any means easier, on the contrary
it is perhaps more difficult, to perceive any coincidence in the
next passage (XVIII. 55). As to the last citation (XVIII. 67),
the only coincidence appears to be that between a very
general precept and a very special case, but there is scarcely any perceptible bond of connexion between the passages.

* सर्वे प्रवृद्धे in this passage, is unquestionably not ' after his *nature*
is fully grown.'

After enumerating sixty different passages in this manner,
Dr. Lorinser adds that "several more might easily be added
to them." I of course accept this statement, though it might
have been better if references at least had been given to
guide us to these other coincidences. But this I am entitled
to say, that the coincidences which have not been set out
may very safely be taken to be very much less remarkable
than any of those which have been set out; and that being
so, after what I have said before, I do not think that they are
entitled to any weight in this discussion. Dr. Lorinser, then,
coupling the frequency of the coincidences noted by him with
what he is pleased to call "the specially Christian character
of the thoughts," comes to the conclusion that these are
" suspicious" circumstances. Upon the coincidences, we shall
presently see what their cumulative effect comes to, but as to
." the specially Christian character," I need say nothing more
than that it is the very thing to be proved. And although
Dr. Lorinser, and *perhaps* other Christian scholars also, may
think it superfluous to prove this, I contend that that proof
is indispensable. Dr. Lorinser next proceeds to " add the fact
that we can *prove* from other sources the influence of Christian
traditions on the development of the Krishṇa-cultus," and
finally infers that the "hypothesis of an external connexion"
is not " a very far-fetched one." On this I only remark,
that so far is this influence from being ' proved,' that it is
not even attested by strong evidence, and that there are
exceedingly powerful arguments against the supposition of
any such influence. I need not say more, because the question
has been sufficiently dwelt on already.

Before going on to the next class of passages adduced by
Dr. Lorinser, I think it necessary to state what I conceive
to be the aggregate result of Dr. Lorinser's numerous citations.

And I have no hesitation in saying that I consider it to be quite insignificant. Some of the coincidences turn upon the doctrine of faith as to which something will have to be said further on. Some of the doctrines on which coincidences are observable are such as will be seen to have been the property of Hinduism long before the birth of Christ. The omniscience of God, the duty of doing everything " in the name of the Lord," are doctrines which no theist need borrow from another. And that the Hindus were theists independently of Christianity cannot be gainsaid. As to the Avatârs we have already spoken, and the idea appears to me to be an original idea of Hinduism. To sum up, therefore, not only are most of these coincidences individually very slight; not only do they turn upon such points, that the inference of a "borrowing" by Hinduism cannot possibly arise from them; but taking them all together and examining their cumulative effect, I repeat that they come to very little indeed. And this is quite independently of the argument which has been already hinted at, but which cannot be too often repeated, that reasoning from these coincidences to a borrowing by Hinduism is most assuredly a *non sequitur*. True it is, indeed, that the cumulative effect of these passages has to be coupled again with the results yielded by the other classes of passages to be hereafter considered. But it is to be noted meanwhile, that unless some clearly appreciable force can be claimed by this class taken by itself, the mere coupling of it with the others cannot give greater support to the final conclusion.

Come we now to the next class of passages, those which, according to Dr. Lorinser, contain a " characteristic expression of the New Testament with a different application." These passages, however, need not detain us long, for they are in the strongest manner open to the observations made above with regard to the inferences drawn from comparisons of passages, not to say that the words "characteristic expression" seem to beg the whole question.* It may however be useful to direct attention to some points in connexion with this class of passages. I do not think there is more than a very deceptive verbal agreement in the first passage. And in the next (Gîtâ III. 23), I cannot help thinking, we have the search for coincidences run mad. In the passage from Gîtâ III. 31, 'blaspheme' is not by any means a correct rendering of असूया. That word means दोषारोपो गुणेष्वपि; and the rendering of it by the word 'blaspheme' appears to me a wresting of it out of its proper sense for pointing a similarity when none exists. To proceed. The next coincidence (IV. 9) has been observed upon before. And in the next passage but one following that, (IV. 37) it is absolutely impossible, I think, to insist on the coincidence. What similarity is there between eating "the nectar of the leavings of a sacrifice" (IV. 31) and "eating of his bread"? In the next passage (IV. 38) faith being unquestionably different from knowledge—the "characteristic expression" in which Dr. Lorinser sees a similarity is contained in the word "purify"! In Gîtâ VII. 18 गति is not, as Dr. Lorinser wrongly renders it, 'way,' but more nearly 'goal,' a modification which not only makes the two passages different verbally, but almost diametrically opposite to one another both verbally and really. In the next passage (VII. 28) 'sin is destroyed' appears to constitute an expression "cha-

---

* When Dr. Lorinser says, as he does in the sequel of this passage, that "the composer of the Bhagavadgîtâ, was very far from being a Christian, or understanding rightly the Christian doctrines, since he only used Christian maxims to illustrate his Indian Sânkhya and Yoga doctrines," he seems unwittingly to lay bare one very weak point in his theory.

racteristic" of the New Testament!* In the next passage
the word असूया occurs again, and 'royal learning' is not, I
think, an admissible rendering for राजविद्या. It means the
" prince of learnings," as the commentators render it.   In X.
9 'dead in me' is certainly an incorrect rendering.

It is unnecessary, however, to dwell any longer on this
class of passages, although there is extensive room for
criticism. And we therefore proceed to the next class
on which Dr. Lorinser lays greatest stress. Now on the
very first citation, it appears to me that there is no "agreement" between the two passages—certainly not in meaning—
and scarcely even in expression. In the first place सर्वशः
does not mean 'every day,' and 'steps' is scarcely an accurate rendering for वर्त्म. The passage means, I think,—as
the commentators correctly interpret it—that God confers
favours on men in a manner answering to the intentions and
motives with which men worship him ; but however men
may act, i. e., to whatsoever form of the Deity they may
in appearance address themselves, they really address themselves to Vishnu. This meaning appears to me derivable
from the words of the text, and one which fits in with what
goes before and what comes after the passage under discussion.   And taking this meaning, it appears to me to be impossible to see any "agreement" between this passage and
those from John cited against it. The next citation (VI. 5-6)
introduces us to a couple of passages neither of which is as
clear as it might be. In the translation of the Sanskrit
Dr. Lorinser again differs from the commentators, and not,
as I submit, to his advantage. In the last clause, " by its
hostility" gives a very different sense from the natural one

_____

* Remark, too, that the New Testament has the peculiar expres-
ison ' body of sin' to which we have nothing parallel in the Gítá.

of the locative शत्रुत्वे. Further the translation does not show how that clause explains the previous words 'it is also his foe,' which yet it is evidently meant to explain. Lastly, the clause as translated conveys no clear meaning at all. One other point is remarkable with respect to this translation. The blank is represented in the original by नात्मानमवसादयेत् , which in English would be " one should not cast oneself down." Now this is not only different from, but almost diametrically opposed to, a portion of the sentences from the New Testament which Dr. Lorinser adduces. Why was it omitted from the translation? As I have said, the passages from the Bible are not particularly lucid any more than that from the Gîtâ. But I understand them to mean, that whoever is desirous of the pleasures of this world must forego those of the other world and *vice versâ*. Now the meaning of the verses in the Gîtâ, I understand with the commentators to be this— that a man who does not keep his senses under control is an enemy to himself, whereas he who is self-restrained benefits himself. Of course, it is possible to trace a certain coincidence between the two precepts *at bottom*; but I do not think it comes to much, and after all the reduction of the one to the other is not a very direct process. I own that to my mind, both in expression and meaning, these passages present but a very slight agreement. In the next citation, there is an agreement to some extent, but for the essentially Christian idea of "my Father," the Gîtâ has nothing to show. अनर्थम् is rendered by 'above possession s.' The rendering is not inadmissible, but it also to a certain extent differentiates the two passages. And the coincidence which there is does not support the inference which it is sought to base on it. In the next citation (VII. 26) there is a coincidence, if 'see' is interpreted in the sense of 'understand,' and not otherwise; and the context seems

to make against this interpretation. But surely Dr. Lorinser
goes too far when he grounds a claim on behalf of Christianity to have lent ideas to Hinduism, on such a passage
as this, on a passage positing nothing more than the unknow-
ableness of God. In the next citation प्रत्यक्षावगमम् is *not* 'easy
to understand'; सुसुखंकर्तुं is not '*not* sweet to do.' Here again
even if the ideas are looked upon as *to a certain
extent* one *at bottom*, still the associations through which
they are conveyed are *essentially* different. And there can be no
doubt that the words really show no agreement at all. In
the next (IX. 18) the apparent agreement is the result of a
mistranslation. गति is *not* way, it is more accurately the 'goal,'
not that by which you go, but that to which you go. And
this mode of putting the matter, which is the only correct
one, shows the essential distinction between the two systems.
With the New Testament writers, Jesus is but a sort of guide
to the goal; with the author of the Gîtâ, Krishṇa is himself
the goal. What Dr. Lorinser renders by beginning and end,
again, is really and truly producer and destroyer or absorber,
so that the whole coincidence vanishes in an error of translation! In the next citation (IX. 19) there is almost an appearance of disingenuousness, and I am bound to say that I
was in the first instance deceived by what has been done.
The passage as given from Matthew by Dr. Lorinser appears
to me to convey an entirely different sense from that which
it would have if given in its integrity; and it is only by
omitting essential words that the appearance of "agreement"
is obtained. One is almost tempted to call this garbling,
but without going so far, I do think that the circumstance
requires explanation. In the next citation (VI. 30), I have
not understood the meaning of the passage from John,* and for

---

* As explained by Barnes, the meaning of it does not appear to

the essentially Christian idea contained in the words omitted by Dr. Lorinser what has the Gîtâ to show ? The next passage, also from John is no less mystical. And I do not think it can possibly yield the sense which is put by the commentators on the passage from the Gîtâ. The passage from Gîtâ X. 5. appears, to me, I confess, to show but little agreement with the passage cited against it. On the next citation (X. 8) we have again a somewhat obscure passage from the Romans, which, however, does seem to show some similarity to the passage from the Gîtâ. As to the two citations which follow, they do show coincidences, but it may be doubted whether they are of any value. In the next citation after these (X. 33) I cannot help believing that Dr. Lorinser has again missed the sense of the Gîtâ. "Among letters I am A" is not equivalent to " I am the beginning and the ending ;" and not only is it not equivalent to this, its meaning is wholly and entirely different. Krishṇa, in the passage of which the words cited form part, is describing the best things of every class, and identifying them with the Deity. And when he says 'I am A among the letters,' he understands 'A' to be the principal letter, as embracing all the " Vâñmaya" as the commentators say. The sense of the passage from the Book of Revelations is of course and evidently distinct from this. The next passage, (XVIII. 66) however, shows a real agreement. But upon a review of the passages which thus do show a real " agreement," how much do they really come to ? Are they really such as to give rise to the inference based on them ? I must confess, that I cannot so look on them. The real " agreements" are all on points of such a very ordinary description as God's being the creator of the

me to coincide with that of the passage from the Gîtâ against which Dr. Loriuser cites it, or even with Gîtâ IX. 29 which is somewhat more like it.

world, the forgiver of sinners, and so forth. Does Dr. Lo-rinser really think, that the Hindus must have gone to the New Testament for these doctrines? It appears to me so extravagant a supposition, that I think to state it is to refute it. And yet upon this set of passages Dr. Lorinser bases his case more particularly, and talks about the "bor-rowing appearing clearly" in them.

Thus have we gone through all the various passages adduced by Dr. Lorinser as exhibiting those coincidences with passages in the Christian Scriptures which appear to him to lead to the conclusion that the former must have borrowed from the latter. We have endeavoured to point out in the course of our investigation of these passages the various errors in the translations from the Gîtâ. We believe we have shown enough of these both in number and quality, to justify the remark, made at the beginning of this part of the investigation, about the danger of comparing translations and basing inferences on such comparisons. We have endea-voured further to show, that even in some of those cases in which the renderings are not incorrect, it is difficult to see any coincidence as alleged. We have also endeavoured to argue that in some of the passages where there is no error in the rendering and where there is some coincidence, that coinci-dence is so far-fetched, requires such a lengthened process of reasoning to arrive at, that it is impossible to maintain successfully the theory of "borrowing" on the strength of those passages. Lastly we contend that in the very small balance of coincidences remaining, the teaching of the Gîtâ refers to points on which it is not only unnecessary to adopt the theory of borrowing, but simply impossible to adopt such a theory. We may, perhaps, be permitted to add also, that in some cases, we have referred to passages in the

Gîtâ more nearly agreeing with the passages from the Bible cited by Dr. Lorinser than those referred to by him—in order that the true state of the case might be presented to the honest investigator, as far as it was in our power so to present it. What now is the total outcome? On fully considering the matter, I must say that I can come to but one conclusion—Dr. Lorinser's contention is not borne out by these passages. He has failed to show that the "agreements" between the two works are of such a nature as to give rise to the inference of a borrowing by the Gîtâ. He has failed to show, though he has asserted it with not a little strength of expression, that the coincidences are with regard to doctrines characteristic of the New Testament. He has failed—to borrow an appropriate expression of Professor Tyndall's—to look round the grand question before him. I believe that Dr. Lorinser's argument fails in many ways. It fails to furnish an adequate number of real coincidences. It fails to show that those coincidences are of such a nature as to give rise to the inference he seeks to draw. It fails to show that the 'borrowing,' if there was any, was on the part of the Hindu writer from the Christian. On the whole, I have come to the conclusion, that not only does the strong language of Dr. Lorinser find no warrant in the circumstances set forth by him, not only is there no "proof" of the theory he has propounded, there is not even any likelihood in favour of that theory. The circumstances will not support even a strong suspicion of a "borrowing" by the author of the Gîtâ.

Dr. Lorinser next proceeds to observe, in confirmation of what he calls "the results already won," that large "sections of the gospel narrative have been imitated in the Bhagavadgîtâ." And the first "section" referred to is that

of the Transfiguration of Christ. Now there is no denying
the fact, that there is a certain degree of similarity between
the two narratives.   At the same time, it must, I think, be
admitted that the similarity extends no further than the fact
of the transfiguration, if what occurred to Jesus ought really
to be called by that name.   The manner of the occurrence,
the details of the occurrence, the motive, so to speak, of the
occurrence, are all wholly and entirely dissimilar in the two
narratives.   And in describing the scene as exhibited 'at
Arjun's request,' and as showing Kṛishṇa's 'infinite divine
glory in which he comprehends the universe in himself,' Dr.
Lorinser himself appears to me to have indicated two important points of difference.   For Jesus's transfiguration consists in nothing more than an extraordinary addition to the
glory of his countenance, and is an act unsuggested
by the disciples. Again, the form assumed by Kṛishṇa is
represented as one which even the Gods are anxious to see, and
as one becoming visible only to those who have faith exclusively fixed on Kṛishṇa. Not so with the form of Jesus. It is
not regarded as anything to be striven after.   If anything, it
is rather used to confirm the wavering faith of the disciples. It
is not a reward for plenary faith already existing. The apparent
want of purpose also, the somewhat unconnected way in
which the narrative is given, are both points to be noted in
the gospel story, when it is alleged that the Twelfth Chapter
of the Gîtâ is a copy of it. Dr. Lorinser assigns, as one reason
for his view that the Gîtâ copied this scene from the gospel,
the alleged circumstance that other "characteristic and prominent incidents" in the life of Jesus are transferred to
Kṛishṇa. On some of these which have been mentioned before
we have already spoken, and we have only to add that talking of the "transference to Kṛishṇa" in those cases is itself

only a begging of the question.* Further confirmation Dr. Lorinser finds in an "expression," used in the Gîtâ on the occasion when this transfiguration is narrated, which Dr. Lorinser holds to be "borrowed from the gospel"—of course without showing that it is necessary to infer from the facts that the Gîtâ 'borrowed' from the gospel, and not *vice versâ*. Now in the first place, the rendering of the passage from the Gîtâ, contains one not quite unimportant error, for what is rendered by "suddenly" ought to have been rendered by "simultaneously." And secondly, as to the substantial matter of the comparison, there is really nothing to compare except the mention of the sun in both passages. In the Gîtâ, the glory of a thousand suns is spoken of, and said to be the only parallel to the glory of Krishna's whole form. In the New Testament, the comparison is between only the face of Jesus on the one side and only one sun on the other. Why should you suppose a 'borrowing' in such a case? And is the sun's brilliance such a recondite affair that the author of the Gîtâ could not have himself thought of it as a good simile? The passage cited from Gîtâ XI. 11 (II. is a misprint), is, I take it, meant to be regarded as 'borrowed' from the gospel words "raiment white as the light." But I confess I find it quite impossible to see even the flimsiest foundation for a theory of borrowing with regard to it. In the citations which follow, there is, as might be expected, a general coincidence of ideas, but there is really no coincidence, I think, in the modes in which the

* As to one of the 'incidents,' we may refer back to the view of Mr. Greg (citing Sir W. Jones) which we have adduced at p. xxix. note. *suprâ.* I am unable to see what parallel Dr. Lorinser has found in Krishna's story for "the washing of the feet at the last supper." If it is the occurrence at the Râjasûya Sacrifice of Yudhishthir, Dr. Lorinser is certainly in the wrong.

ideas are brought out in the two works. A wonderful—an
extraordinary—phenomenon being seen, it is only natural
that the person who sees should become ' astonished,' should
not feel himself quite at ease. The central notion in the
descriptions of such a scene must necessarily . be one and
the same. You can, therefore, draw an inference of ' borrowing' by the one from the other only by looking at the
way that central notion is drawn out. And I think there
is no room for doubt, that in this part of the matter the two
sets of passages cited do not show any such similarity as
alleged. I may add before closing this part of the matter,
that in the last passage adduced by Dr. Lorinser here from
Gîtâ XI. 50, "for the great spirit was merciful" is most
clearly a mistranslation.

To proceed. There is I think an extremely slight similarity
between the words of Kṛishṇa in Gîtâ X. 12 *et seq.* and
the passages from Matthew and John cited by Dr. Lorinser.
And not only that, but there are also very great differences ;
and I do not think that any inference can be drawn from
a comparison of them. Dr. Lorinser next proceeds to Arjun's
"apology" in which he traces an "unmistakable similarity" with
the "exclamation of Peter on seeing the miracles of the fishes." I
confess I can see no coincidence at all. Dr. Lorinser afterwards
says, that "although the words are different, the situation is
exactly the same." So that it appears the "unmistakable" similarity is after all not between the "apology" and the " exclamation" but between the "situations" in which the one and the
other are respectively made. And this is supposed to confirm the " result already won" that the Gîtâ has copied from
the Bible ! By the way, it 'ought to be remarked that the
rendering of मसमम् by 'eager' (in Gîtâ XI. 42) is entirely
erroneous.

Lastly we come to a "certain similarity which may be accounted for by an intentional imitation" between the conclusion of the Twelfth Chapter and the beginning of the Sermon on the Mount. The similarity here is between the repetition of 'such a one is dear to me' in the Gîtâ and the repetition of ' blessed are' in the Sermon on the Mount. Now even Dr. Lorinser's dogmatism will not venture to contend, that ' intentional imitation' is the only way of 'accounting' for this similarity. There is no doubt that this tendency to repetition is to be marked in all archaic writings, and it is worth noting that a similar repetition occurs in the stanzas of the Gîtâ II., 25 *et seq.* II. 55 *et seq.*, and again in Gîtâ XI. 28-29. In the teeth of these circumstances,* I think, it is a very bold proceeding to adopt the theory of " intentional imitation." And as to the eight beatitudes, it should be remembered, as Dr. Strauss observes, that they "consist from first to last of those Christian paradoxes by which the new Christian view of things comes into contrast with the traditional one both of Jews and Gentiles."† If so, shall we not be justified in applying here the theory of Professor Weber above referred to, namely that contained in the words—"There is a gap between the two which apparently nothing but the supposition of an external influence can account for"? What if we say that the external influence in this case was the influence of the Hindu Philosophy, and that the language used was the result of an intentional imitation of this passage of the Gîtâ?

In taking a comprehensive survey of the passages from

---

* And see too Kaṭhopanishad III. 5, 6. V. 9, 10, 12, 13, and the Vâsettha Sutta in Sir M. C. Swamy's Sutta Nipâta p. 133. The Uraga Sutta, the Khaggavinsa Sutta, and the Mahâmangala Sutta, indeed, take their several names from this very circumstance.

† See Vol. I, p. 277.

which the Gîtâ is thus alleged to have "borrowed," Dr.
Lorinser finds that " it is the Gospel of John in particular
from which the composer has taken the most important and
the greatest majority of phrases." This is an important
observation. For the result of the application of historical
criticism to the New Testament records has rendered it nearly certain that the Fourth Gospel was the very latest of the
Gospels, and the conclusion arrived at by Strauss, as has
been already stated, is that the Fourth Gospel "was not
known until after the middle" of the second century A. C.
The remark of Strauss which follows this is also of great
moment, in the consideration of this question of borrowing.
The Fourth Gospel, he says, "bears every indication of having
arisen upon a foreign soil, and under the influence of a
philosophy of the time unknown to the original circle in
which Jesus lived."* Now I do not profess to have gone
through the long and able controversies on the subject of
the date and authenticity of the New Testament writings.
But from what I have read of the recent works on that
subject, especially "Supernatural Religion" and the works
of Mr. Matthew Arnold, Mr. Greg, and others, I believe,
that the conclusion stated by Strauss is a conclusion maintained not merely by him but by most if not all those
who have applied the canons of historical criticism
to the writings of the New Testament. M. Renan, I be-

---

* The following remarks of Dr. Westcott are to be noted in connexion with this point. "Though it is unnecessary to degrade it
into a mere controversial work, it is impossible not to feel that it
was written to satisfy some pressing want of the age, to meet some
false philosophy which had already begun to fashion a peculiar
dialect and to attempt to solve by the help of Christian ideas some
of the great problems of humanity," (*On the Canon* p. 246). And
see Greg's Creed of Christendom, II. 38. See too *Quarterly Review*
(January 1875) p. 186.

lievc, at one time held a position inconsistent with this view,* but in his most recent work on the subject, he too seems to have come round to the general opinion.

I am unable to find out the result of modern criticism as to the dates of the other New Testament writings, except that, according to Strauss, the second epistle of Peter is not "earlier than the end of the second century after Christ."† It is sufficient for our present purpose, however, to know that the portion of the New Testament which is supposed to have supplied "the most important and the greatest majority of phrases" is held by eminent authorities to be much later than the middle of the second century A. C. See now how the case stands. Not to speak of the foreign influences under which the Gospel was written, for that is relevant only to another branch of our argument, Dr. Lorinser's theory requires us to suppose, that the Fourth Gospel which dates after the middle of the second century A. C. was brought to India by missionaries of Christianity; was either translated into one of the vernacular languages of the country, and studied in such translation, or studied in the original Greek itself by a learned Brâhman "holding fast to the traditional wisdom of his caste;" was drawn upon by him for some of the most important 'phrases' and tenets of a work which has always been regarded in its own country as containing the quintessence of orthodoxy; and all this, we are required to suppose, occurred within the compass of a century or thereabouts, at a period when the world progressed at the rate at which it did sixteen hundred years

* See Greg's Creed of Christendom, Vol. II. 119. Mr. M. Arnold's view may be seen in the *Contemporary Review* (March 1875) p. 515.

† Life of Jesus, Vol I. p. 66. Dr. Westcott says the purely historical evidence does not take it much before the end of the third century (*On the Canon* p. 213).

ago.* Taking into consideration all the surrounding circumstances, even taking those and those only which have a
bearing exclusively on this point and omitting those which
lead to a conclusion opposite to Dr. Lorinser's by a different
line of argument, I maintain that this theory is quite untenable. But we need not dwell here further on this point
as it has been already discussed before.

We may here remark, parenthetically as it were, on the
two passages adduced by Dr. Lorinser from the Book of
Wisdom to which he finds parallels in the Bhagavadgîtâ. In
the first there is, indeed, a certain slight similarity. But it
is obviously neither very remarkable, nor on a point of
such a recondite nature as even to suggest an inference of
"borrowing." And remember, too, that "ordering all things"
and "comprehending everything" are two ideas wide as
the poles asunder. A similar remark applies to the next
passage. That the body is a prison for the Soul; that to be
liberated from it is to rise to a much higher walk of life;
that the abnegation of the body is the way, and the only
way, to final absolution; these doctrines are essentially
Hindu doctrines. And to say that the Gîtâ borrowed them
from the Book of Wisdom is to say what I maintain cannot
be proved, and what most assuredly has not yet been proved
by Dr. Lorinser or by any one else.†

Before leaving this question of coincidences, it may be
just as well to draw attention to the fact, that these coin-

---

* I would quote here a passage which ought to have been quoted
at P. xxiv. Dr. Westcott says "versions of scripture appear to
be in the first instance almost necessarily of gradual growth. Ideas
of translation familiarised to us by long experience formed no
part of the primitive system" (p. 202).

† It need scarcely be remarked here that the translation of अप्रकाशगति
by invisible way is entirely wrong.

cidences are observable not merely between the Gîtâ and
the New Testament but between other works also. Thus,
as we have elsewhere pointed out, Mr. Lucas Collins at
the close of his excellent little volume on the Odyssey in
the series of "Ancient Classics for English Readers," draws
attention to numerous points of resemblance between the
Homeric narrative and the stories in the Old Testament.*
A rather different species of resemblance is that between
the Gîtâ itself and the Platonic Dialogues. Thus to
the doctrine of the Gîtâ with regard to birth and death, in
Chap. II. St. 27 we may find something like a parallel
in the doctrine of Socrates in the Phœdo (Jowett's Plato I.
416-7). Again in the passage in Chap. VI. 43 we may trace
something very like Socrates's favourite doctrine of remini-
scence.† And the comparison of the several bodies which
the soul animates in its earthly career to clothes, which we find
in the Gîtâ II. 22 corresponds to a very similar comparison
in Plato's Phœdo (Jowett I. 436). The idea, again, enunciated in the words "And when they have there received their
due and remained their time, another guide brings them
back again after many revolutions of ages" (Jowett I.
458-9), is, to a certain extent, similar to that at Gîtâ IX. 21.
Several more instances of such similarity might, I have no
doubt, be added. Some few on which I am able to lay my
hands just now are referred to in the note.‡ But however
remarkable some of these are, I do not think, that they furnish any fair ground for the inference, that Plato borrowed

---

* P. 129 et seq.

† See Jowett I. 418.

‡ Compare Gîtâ. II. 16 (and our note thereon) with Jowett II.
523; Gîtâ VI. 40 with Jowett I. 590. The description of a philosopher in the Theætetus (Jowett III. 398-9) may be compared with
Gîtâ II. 69.

from the Gítâ, or that the Gítâ borrowed from Plato. And by parity of reason I think in the case before us, that the coincidences pointed out by Dr. Lorinser do not support the inference which he bases upon them.

Dr. Lorinser here closes the main part of his investigation, but before finally concluding it, he attempts to answer "two objections which may be raised." The first is this—Upon Dr. Lorinser's theory, what explanation is to be given of the fact that some of the Upanishads have passages in common with the Bhagavadgîtâ? "As the Upanishads," says Dr. Lorinser, "which are considered parts of the Vedas have a relatively high antiquity ascribed to them, and are regarded as older than the oldest Christian records, the supposition that those expressions and thoughts (*viz.* those which are common, according to Dr. Lorinser, to the Gítâ and the Christian Scriptures) were borrowed from Christianity seems to be excluded."* One would expect that after this admission which is a full and fair one and involves an important objection to Dr. Lorinser's theory, we should have such a satisfactory reply to it as would leave the theory safe and sound. But there is a cruel disappointment in store for him who may form such an expectation. Dr. Lorinser is pleased to give only a "short statement of his view," of course without reasons for many of the propositions implied in it, and then he "leaves the further investigation to others." I humbly submit that this is not quite a satisfactory mode of disposing of an objection. However, let us examine this "short statement of my view," which is vouchsafed to us.

According to Dr. Lorinser, then, all the Upanishads referred

---

* P. 294*b*.

to here "reverence a system which like the Bhaga-vadgîtâ, seeks to unite the doctrines of the Sânkhya, Ve-dânta and Yoga schools." Now it seems to me, that this initial step is a thoroughly mistaken step. I do not think, that we can trace in the Gîtâ or the Upanishads in question, any "seeking to unite" those doctrines. True it is, of course, that there are, as we may say, scattered about in those works doctrines which now are labelled Yog, and Sânkhya, and Vedânta doctrines. But I cannot see how we are from this alone entitled to infer, without support from other circum-stances, that the works in question attempt to reconcile those doctrines into one integral system. On the contrary, it strikes me that the circumstances point the other way. My view is, that in the Gîtâ and the Upanishads, the philosophical part has not been consistently and fully worked out. We have there the results of free thought exercised on different subjects of great moment, unfettered by the exigencies of any foregone con-clusion or of any fully developed theory. It is afterwards, it is at a later stage of philosophical progress, that system-making arises. In that stage some thinkers interpret whole works by the light of some particular doctrines or expres-sions. And the result is the development of a whole mul-titude of philosophical sects following the lead of those thinkers, and all professing to draw their doctrine from the Gîtâ or the Upanishads, yet each differing remarkably from the other. One of the best examples of such a thing in the history of Philosophy is presented by the relations be-tween Socrates and the Socratic Schools. "Several Philoso-phers" says Cicero cited by Mr. G. H. Lewes in his History of Philosophy "drew from the conversations of Socrates very different results, and according as each adopted views which harmonized with his own, they in their turn became heads

of philosophical schools all differing amongst each other." *
Now this, I conceive, is really the correct view of the rela-
tionship between the Gîtâ on the one hand, and the Yog, the
Sânkhya, and Vedânta schools on the other. It is as much a
mistake to suppose that the Gîtâ endeavours to reconcile the
varying doctrines of those schools, as it would be to suppose
that the Socratic philosophy was the result of an attempt to
combine together into one harmonious whole the systems of
the Cynics, the Cyrenaics, the Megarics. As we have said before, the question in great measure depends upon the indications
afforded by the surrounding circumstances. If we simply
find a combination of doctrines belonging to two or three
systems in any work, it is not possible from that circumstance alone to conclude whether the systems flowed from
the book as a fountain-source, or whether they were the small
rills of which the book was, so to speak, the reservoir. In the
case before us it appears to me, that the points hinted at above
militate strongly against the view propounded by Dr.
Lorinser.

The next point taken by Dr. Lorinser is that the Upanishads in question "belong to the latest of the Vedas, the
Atharva, and in the case of none of them is there any convincing reason for looking on the hypothesis of their post-
Christian origin as impossible." Now I must draw special
attention to the first part of this sentence. What if these
Upanishads belong to the latest of the Veds ? The impression intended to be suggested is that *by reason of that circumstance*, these Upanishads are not unlikely to be of post-
Christian origin. But where is the ground for this sugges-

* Vol. I. p. 175, (3rd Ed.) Compare also Schwegler Hist. of Phil.
p. 53. (4th Ed.) and Prof. Ferrier's Lectures on Greek Philosophy.
I. 267-70.

tion? The fact of these Upanishads belonging to the Atharvaved has really nothing at all to do with their date as far as that is concerned in the present inquiry. On the one hand, even if they belonged to the Ṛigved, they might be later than the beginning of the Christian Era; and on the other hand even if they belonged to the "latest of the Veds," that would not necessitate the postponement of their date to a period after the beginning of the Christian Era. The truth is, that when we look at the facts, the remark proves to be almost irrelevant, and it receives the semblance of relevancy only because of the extreme want of precision with which the expression 'latest of the Veds' is used, so as to suit the necessities of the occasion. If the quite unbounded vagueness of that expression is removed, even as far only as we can remove it on the most irrefragable evidence, the correctness of our remark will become at once evident. For although it may be the latest of the Veds, the Atharvaved is older than the beginning of the Christian Era by many centuries. I have already pointed out elsewhere that the Atharvaved is mentioned in the Mahâbhâshya of Patanjali,* and in the Chhândogyopanishad,† both works, I apprehend, unquestionably older than the Christian Era.‡ I have also pointed out that Patanjali alludes to the Upanishads,§ and I contend that putting these two facts together, the result is that the suggestion of Dr. Lorin-

* As being, it may be added, even then 'ninefold' नवधा आथर्वणो वेदः. (p. 16. Introd.).

† P. 474.

‡ See "Was the Râmâyana copied from Homer?" p. 24 and references there.

§ P. 16 (Introd.) Banâras Ed. See too, Manu and Vâtsâyan in his commentary on the Nyâya Sûtras (Manu II. 145, 160; and Vâtsyâyan Bhâshya p. 3).

ser is the reverse of the conclusion to which the facts seem to point. And when Dr. Lorinser proceeds to say that there is no "convincing reason" for refusing to believe the post-Christian origin of the Upanishads, it becomes necessary to ask, what "convincing reason" is there for believing in their post-Christian origin—what but the necessity which Dr. Lorinser is under of making guesses to suit his foregone conclusions? I agree with Dr. Lorinser that there is nothing to prove the hypothesis to be " impossible." But what is there to prove the hypothesis of its being ante-Christian to be "impossible" ? The truth is that in the domain of history, impossible is a word which ought to be used very rarely if at all. The whole question in historical matters is a question of likelihood, of probability, and reasons must be found in all the surrounding circumstances of each matter for holding an opinion one way or the other regarding it. Now what are the surrounding circumstances here to render this post-Christian origin likely? The only thing adduced by Dr. Lorinser is a guess or rather a couple of guesses of Professor Weber, based on certain facts connected with one of the Upanishads enumerated, namely the S'vetás'vatar, which Dr. Lorinser pronounces to be "as I believe, the oldest of them." The first guess is one based on the names S'vet, and S'vetás'va and S'vetas'ikh, and S'vetalohit. On this, Professor Weber says "Perhaps, we have here a mission of Syrian Christians."[*] Of course, no further ground is assigned for this guess : nor are we instructed as to the connexion of ' Syrian Christians' with the Yog Philosophy ; nor further is any explanation vouchsafed as to how Syrian Christians came to be described as having ' white blood' and ' white hair.' In truth the whole thing is but a gratuitous guess. which calls to my mind the following weighty words of an eminent authority on historical matters. "The very minimum of presumptive evidence," says George Grote in a letter to his eminent friend Sir G. C. Lewis, "appears to those gentlemen enough to warrant both the positive affirmation of a matter as historical and the demand which they make upon opponents to produce counter-evidence and disprove it."* Perhaps these words are rather stronger than are fairly applicable to the matter before us. But with just a little toning down, the protest embodied in them by Grote against the methods employed by the Egyptologists and Assyriologists of his day appears to me to be strongly called for both in the present and other inquiries touching our ancient history. However let us proceed. Prof. Weber's second guess is founded upon a basis only less narrow than the basis for this one which we have now considered. This guess is based on the name S'vetâsya Râjarshi and on the fact of his having "raised his son to life again." I do not think this guess to be much more tenable than the last one. But even if it is more tenable, it is less relevant to the point before us ; for it is suggested by a story in the Mahâbhârat, and we are not now on any question connected with that work but with the S'vetâs'vataropanishad. It is useful to add that in the course of his statement of these guesses, Prof. Weber makes an observation, which shows how the comfortable old principle of " so much the worse for the facts" is impressed to do service here. After the sentence quoted above with regard to 'Syrian Christians', the Professor says :— " that their doctrines would be put by their Indian scholars into a Brahmanical dress, and that of Christianity only the monotheism would remain, is natural," I confess, I cannot concur in this. The enthusiasm of the renegade

---

* See Personal Life of Grote by Mrs. Grote p. 263.

against that which he has abandoned is proverbial. And it strikes me as very unlikely that the Indian scholars of Syrian Christians should have compromised the most essential peculiarities of Christianity out of the doctrines which they taught and recorded. But even waiving that, and admitting this abstract possibility for the sake of argument, what are we to say of a theory which first assumes a borrowing on the strength of nothing better than four names (which to say the least of them, are highly equivocal) and then assumes further that the most distinctive marks of the system borrowed from were flung away in the act of borrowing? Have we not here the veritable French Philosopher who said,—" If the facts do not suit my theory, so much the worse for the facts"?

Dr. Lorinser goes on next to refer, for what purpose is not quite evident, to the Granthopanishad, which he says, " is regarded by Weber as older." But here again Dr. Lorinser sees in the mention of Vishṇu and S'raddhá " the development of the Vishṇu-cultus under the modification of Christian ideas." Now I have not been able to get a sight of this Granthopanishad, and do not know in what context the name of Vishṇu occurs there. But I want to know what ground Dr. Lorinser has for connecting that name with any Christian influences. I can only see in this assertion one further instance of that amazing dogmatism, on which I have found it necessary to animadvert before, and which in its manifestations elsewhere has fallen under the lash of the late Professor Goldstücker who speaks of " the bold assertions and solemn affirmations with which some writers on Sanskrit matters are wont to represent the unreliable result of their speculations."* One answer to

---

* *Westminster Review* (April 1868) p. 383.

e assertion not to mention others, is the very strong one
at Vishṇu is mentioned over and over again in no less a work
an the Ṛigved.* The reference to S'raddhâ I pass over
r the moment; nor shall I dwell on the conveniently vague
nguage of Dr. Lorinser when he speaks of the "time at
hich the Vishṇu-cultus began to develop itself under
hristian influences" without specifying anything more definite
to this time. But I think it worth while to pause here a
ttle, in order to cast back a glance at what Dr. Lorinser has
sumed or asserted, and to consider how the various assump-
ons and assertions stand when put together. We find then
e following series—according to Dr. Lorinser—1. The New
estament; 2. An Indian Translation of the same; 3. The Gran-
opanishad composed under the influences of this transla-
on; 4. The S'vetâs'vataropanishad similarly composed at
later pariod; 5. The Bhagavadgîtâ similarly composed at a
ill later period; 6. The Commentaries on the Gîtâ—for
ere were some—preceding that of S'ankarâchârya;† 7. The
ommentary of S'ankar himself. Now omitting the first and
vo last numbers of this series, and conceding to Dr. Lorinser
e very utmost he can claim, we have the Indian translation
the Bible dating from the end of the first century A. C.,
id the Gîtâ probably from the third century A. C. Is this a
fficient interval?‡ Even taking these dates as certain, can
ybody who takes due note of the circumstances of the case

---

* See *inter alia* Mandal, I. 11. 61. R. 7. The question will be
mewhat more fully discussed below.

† See his Bhâshya p. 7. (Calc. Ed. Samvat 1927).

‡ Upon the view suggested above about the earliest possible date
a translation of the New Testament into an Indian language,
any such translation was ever made, it is almost needless to say,
at the series is much longer than could be reasonably compressed
ithin the limits which even Dr. Lorinser must accept.

be reasonably satisfied of the probability of the result the
arising? I can confidently challenge any one free from bia
to say aye to these question.

Dr. Lorinser next goes on to propound and answer anoth(
objection to his theory, based on supposed coincidenc(
between passages in the Gītâ and Thomas A. Kempis
Imitation of Christ. His answer to the objection is thre
fold. To take the last answer first. Dr. Lorinser suppos(
that the thoughts and sayings in Thomas A. Kempis mu:
have been current among "old Indian Christians;" t
conclusion being, I suppose, for Dr. Lorinser does not e:
press it, that the Gītâ borrowed those "thoughts and sa
ings" also from the "old Indian Christians." Really t]
force of bias and dogmatism could no further go! Wh(
there is a coincidence between the Gītâ and a work for whi(
Dr. Lorinser thinks he can claim a higher antiquity th(
the Gītâ, then the borrowing is by the Gītâ. When t]
coincidence is between the Gītâ and a work which even D
Lorinser cannot venture to place chronologically before t]
Gītâ, still this other work is not the work which borrows, b(
some non-descript tradition current among "old India
Christians" is to be imagined—without the slightest possib:
ground for so imagining it,°—and once more apparently† t]
conclusion is to be drawn that the Gītâ borrowed fro:
Christianity! Surely this is not very logical. Surely eve
the "theological bias" ought to pause before going suc

---

* Dr. Lorinser himself does not venture to categorically lay dow
the existence of these "thoughts and sayings among old Indian Chri:
tians." He only says, "we need not be surprised if they a:
found." But are they found?

† I say 'apparently,' because Dr. Lorinser does not expressl
state this conclusion, but, it seems to me, that the argument
worthless unless this conclusion is drawn.

ngths as these ! Surely, on this point at least, it would
ve been well for Dr. Lorinser to vouchsafe some slight
nsideration to the possibility of Thomas a Kempis having
rectly or indirectly borrowed from the Gîtâ.

The second answer which Dr. Lorinser makes to his own
jection is, that "Christian asceticism and Indian Yoga have
many things internal points of contact...... so that we
ed not assume any external influence." I entirely concur in
e principle involved in this answer; and indeed I maintain
at if Dr. Lorinser had acted upon that principle in dis-
ssing the coincidences of passages relied on by him, he
uld have found reasons to shake his full confidence in
; own theory. The answer, however, is not sufficient to
ally dispose of the objection here. What is the explanation
these points of contact themselves? When do they first
anifest themselves in the history of Christian asceticism?*
ie answers to these questions may have a most important
aring upon the value of Dr. Lorinser's mode of obviating his
jection. And here again the thought suggests itself, that
:. Lorinser might fairly have considered the alternative
iich his one-sided inquiry has entirely ignored, namely the
ernative of Christianity having borrowed from the Gîtâ. For
an extract from Prof. Weber's *Indische Studien* made use of
Dr. Lorinser at a former stage of this discussion, the possibi-
y of this alternative being in some measure correct† is hinted

As to Dr. Lorinser's other answer to the objection, it is not
e of great importance, and I confess that, in the case of some
the coincidences pointed out by him between the Gîtâ and

* These questions will appear particularly important when we
nember that asceticism was no part of Jesus's system, and that in
t he set his face against it. See Luke V. 33. Matthew XI, 19 (both
ed by Dr. Lorinser).
† *Indian Antiquary* Vol. II. 285a,

Thomas a Kempis, there is not much to distinguish them
either in kind or degree from the coincidences which he ha
pointed out between the Gîtâ and the New Testament.

Dr. Lorinser next proceeds to note certain other coinci
dences "of much greater importance" "with later Christia:
theological doctrines." And first he speaks of the "*lume
gloriæ.*" Now I own, I can see but little resemblance be
tween what occurs at Gîtâ XI. 8 and the passage quoted from th
Book of Revelations. I am afraid, that here again we hav
the wish which is father to the thought. However, I am cor
tent to take it, that there may be something in the "theolc
gians" more nearly resembling the doctrine of the Gîtâ ; sti:
nothing has been shown in the New Testament of whic
that can be said with truth ; and what occurs in the "theolc
gians" is, I think, of very little value on Dr. Lorinser'
side of the question. As to the division of moral acts int
thoughts, words, and deeds, suffice it to say that it occurs i
Kâlidâs, in Manu, and sundry old Indian works.⁕ And as t
prayer, fasting, and almsgiving, surely Dr. Lorinser must hav
made some strange error when he refers to Gîtâ XVII. 28 fo
that division. There is nothing about either fasting or prayer
there.‡ Lastly, leaving for future consideration the won

⁕ See Kâlidâs Raghu. V. 5. XV. 85. Manu has it in sever:
places (See I 104. II. 236). And see Sir M. C. Swamy's Sutt
Nipata pp. 91,101, and most of all p. 63. See also Yâjnavalkʒ
(Âchâr) Sts. 27,155 and elsewhere.

† Apparently Dr. Lorinser has understood यज्ञ and तप: to mea
prayer and fasting. I can only say, that if this is so, we have
further instance of the dangers to which a comparison of transl
tions is exposed, especially when the translator has a theory
support.

‡ It is to be noted too, that it is to a certain extent unlucky for D
Lorinser's theory that the passage from *Tobit* cited by Dr. Lorins
adds 'righteousness' also. What is the meaning of Dr. Lorinser's ol

lerful dogmatism of the note on S'raddhâ, what are we to say o the observation of Dr. Lorinser that "all these expressions and ideas"—namely the *lumen gloriœ*, the dogma *credo ut intelligam*, and the others mentioned by him—"existed n Christianity long before they can be pointed out in Christian writers"!! Once more I am tempted to say, he force of dogmatism can no further go. The sublime assurance with which the observation is made is simply amazing. Where did these "expressions and ideas" exist f not in Christian writers? Did they exist *in nubibus?* And how long before they can be pointed out in "Christian writers" did they "exist in Christianity?" What is their history in that period, and what are the sources of information about it? Surely all these questions ought in fairness o be answered. Surely it is not fair to take refuge under this ort of dogmatism, unsupported by any definite evidence n a question like the present. If I understand him aright, Dr. Lorinser intends to suggest—and if he intends to suggest it, I submit he ought to have stated it expressly*—that a the later Christian writers these "expressions and ideas" ome without any "external influence" from the floating ody of Christian dogma, and that from this floating body f dogma, the Gîtâ must have got those "expressions and leas." Now if the *facts* are; as they undeniably are, and s upon Dr. Lorinser's own implied admission they are, hat the first definite and fixed form in which these "expres-

---

ervation upon the words 'It avails not after death or here'? The *abitus caritatis* is not the same thing as the श्रद्धा which the Gîtâ peaks of. For the expression नचनत्प्रेत्यनो इह, compare Manu II. 9 II. 20, 143, 175 and several other passages, and Yâjnavalkya Áchâr) St. 87.

* I am not sure about this, however; I find it difficult to follow he exact sequence of ideas in the last sentence.

sions and ideas" occur is to be found in the Gîtâ, and tha
the earliest Christian *writings* in which they can be trace
are, and must be admitted to be, unquestionably later tha
the Gîtâ; and if further, as also Dr. Lorinser on his principle
must perforce contend, the coincidence is so great that n
other theory than the theory of borrowing will suffice to ex
plain it; then I say the irresistible conclusion upon thes
facts is that the Christian writings must have borrowed froi
the Gîtâ. This would be the conclusion, I submit, whic
would be drawn by anybody not tainted with the "thec
logical bias." Now if Dr. Lorinser wishes to escape froi
this, surely he is bound to adduce some more tangibl
grounds than the superlatively vague and indefinite state
ment that the "expressions and ideas" in question "existed i
Christianity long before they can be pointed out in Christia
writers"—a statement for which no authority has bee
adduced, and which I do not see that anybody is bound t
accept on the mere *ipse dixit* of Dr. Lorinser ; a statement, toc
which if I may allow myself the liberty of applying to
the strong expression of Dr. Lorinser, seems to me to " plaii
ly bear on its forehead" the stamp of being put forward ex
pressly in order to get out of an inconvenient conclusion.
own that to my mind this is one out of many passage
in this essay of Dr. Lorinser which convince me that l
has looked at the whole question under the overpowei
ing influence of "bias", and also, though perhaps unconsc
ously, with a violent desire to prove a foregone conclusioi
Indeed this unscientific frame of mind, if I may so say, :
betrayed by sundry passages in this essay, one of which occui
at the very outset, where Dr. Lorinser says, "Our aim hei
then must be to establish that the Bhagavadgîtâ may be attr
buted to a period in which it is not impossible that its con

oser may have been acquainted......with different books of he *New Testament*."◆ There, it appears to me, we have the key to the whole of Dr. Lorinser's argument. Dr. Lorinser has an "aim", and to that aim he has endeavoured to suit he facts which have confronted him in the course of his nvestigation. It will be said that this is verbal criticism. So it is, in a certain sense. But when it is remembered, hat the conclusion to which this verbal criticism leads is ne for which we have the strongest supports in the very ubstance and essence of the argument, I think that that criti-ism is entirely divested of its objectionable character. I may add here, that considering the peculiar circumstances of his case, I hold it to be important, and indeed necessary, to point out this pervading characteristic of Dr. Lorinser's argument.

I have now, I think, gone through all the points made by Dr. Lorinser, with a single exception. And that exception concerns the doctrine of faith as laid down in sundry pas-ages of the Gîtâ. As we have observed before, Dr. Lorinser iterates and reiterates his opinion that this doctrine of faith was borrowed by the author of the Gîtâ from Christianity, and f strength of language were any evidence of truth this pro-osition about the Gîtâ borrowing from Christianity would most ertainly be true. But to borrow a phrase of Professor Tyndall's bstinacy of assertion on Dr. Lorinser's part furnishes a by no means sufficient assurance that his assertions are objec-ively correct.† Let us then bring together to a focus, s it were, the various passages in which Dr. Lorinser ex-resses his opinion upon this point. And first he says in a

---

* See *Ind. Ant.* Vol. II. 283a.

† See the *Contemporary Review* for July 1874, p. 138.

note on Gitâ III. 34 :—* "There appears to be no doubt the
these ideas (scil. S'raddhâ and Bhakti) are not originall
Indian representations (as they are not found anywhere else i
heathendom) but that they have been taken over from Chris
tianity, as Dr. A. Weber among others (*Indische Studie
II. 398 ff.*) supposes and has partly demonstrated." Agai
annotating on Gitâ VIII. 7,† he says "these passages remin
one too clearly of the Christian doctrine of faith to overlool
the Christian trace." Once more, speaking about th
Grantha Upanishad,‡ Dr. Lorinser sees in the wor
S'raddhâ an indication of the "development of the Vishṇu
cultus under the modification of Christian ideas." Lastly
he says " I hold the idea of faith (*S'raddhá*) in this sense jus
as that of *Bhakti* (III. 31. IV. 10 and see Lassen *Ind. Al*
II. 1099; Weber *Ind. Stud.* II. 398.) as a representatio
adopted from Christianity, and doubt if S'raddhâ is used i
this sense in the earlier Indian works in which a Christia
influence cannot yet be pointed out."§ Now what does al
this really come to ? To this, I think, that Dr. Lorinse
maintains the opinion under discussion on grounds whicl
are stated by Professor Weber, to which he adds one furthe
ground, namely that the ideas of S'raddhâ and Bhakt
"are not found anywhere else in heathendom." Now, witl

---

* *Ind. Ant.* Vol. II. 286.

† *Indian Antiquary* Vol. II. 288*b* (note).

‡ *Ibid* 295*b*.

§ *Ibid* 296. Upon this last passage, one remark is necessary. Dr.
Lorinser ventures to suggest a meaning for S'raddhâ other than the
ordinary one. Why does he not state what that other meaning is, an
what authority he has for adopting it ? His declaration here is bes
described by a terse and vigorous expression of Lord Bacon—it i
"dogmatising in scepticism." As to Bhakti the last Stanza of the
S'vetâs'vataropanishad should be noted ; and see too Raghu. I. 90 ; II
22, 63; V. 14, 20.

regard to this last point, I think, that without going into any elaborate review of the "earlier Indian works," to which Dr. Lorinser refers, but which, I suspect, he has not carefully examined, it is possible to show clearly that Dr. Lorinser's statement of facts is entirely incorrect. I will give quotations from tolerably early works belonging to various classes, which will suffice, I think, to fully "demonstrate" to any unbiassed inquirer the reverse of that which, according to Dr. Lorinser, Professor Weber has "supposed and partly demonstrated." I refer first to the writings of Kâlidâs. According to my own view as to the date of this great writer, the testimony to be found in his works is of considerable value in the present discussion. But as the date is yet not settled, I do not claim the same weight for this part of the argument which I should otherwise have claimed. Nevertheless it is a matter which is worth mentioning. At Raghu II. 16 occurs the line श्रद्देव साक्षिदिधिनोगत्वा; and similarly in the seventh Act of the S'âkuntal Nâṭak occurs this stanza—

दिष्ट्या शकुन्तला साध्वी सदपत्यमिदं भवान् |
श्रद्धा वित्तं विधिर्घेनि विनयं तत्समागतम् ||

I think these passages show by implication the importance attached to S'raddhâ in the time of Kâlidâs. Let us now go on to a more ancient work, about the antiquity of which there can, I think, be no question, certainly none in its bearing on the point before us—I mean the Mahâbhâshya of Patanjali. There in the comment on Pâṇini, II. 2. 34. occur the following examples:—श्रद्धामेधे and श्रद्धातपसी.* Now when we observe, that these examples are given to illustrate the rule that in copulative compounds the more important term stands before the less important, it becomes clear that श्रद्धा

---

* P. 370 (Banâras Ed.)

was in the time of Patanjali regarded as a more important element in a religious life than even मंत्र and तपस्. If we go now to another class of works we find the doctrine of S'raddhâ laid down in Manu and Yâjnavalkya.* Going to a still older class, to the class namely of Upanishads, we find there also clear traces of this doctrine of S'raddhâ. The Chhândogyopanishad is, I believe, one of the oldest of these Upanishads, and in it we have the passage यदेव विद्यया करोति श्रद्धया उपनिषदा तदेव वीर्यवत्तरं भवति,† where we see the value ascribed to S'raddhâ. Furthermore, the quotations from the Taittirîya Brâhmaṇ, and the Vâjasaneyî Sanhitâ, contained, in the fifth volume of the elaborate work of Dr. Muir,‡ show that the Chhândogyopanishad is not the only one of the Vedic works in which a high rank is ascribed to this S'raddhâ. But going still further into antiquity, going to the very first of the Veds,§ we are still able to cite passages from it which show that the idea of S'raddhâ is not a new-fangled idea as Drs. Lorinser and Weber would have us believe. For some of these passages I am again indebted to Dr. Muir's book, but there are others which I have come across myself in my own very partial study of the Ṛigved. If opportunity should offer, I might discuss the history of this doctrine of S'raddhâ from the period of the Ṛigved to the beginning of the Christian Era. But the facts to which

---

* See Yâjnavalkya (Âchâr) Sts. 6 and 202 and Manu III. 202, 275. IV. 158. 226.

† See p. 23 (Biblioth. Ind.)

‡ See pp. 103 and 347. (2nd Ed. 1870)

§ See *inter alia* Ṛ. V. II. 1. 12. 5. (I give references on the Mandal division) II. 3. 26. 6. VII. 1. 6. 3. VII. 2. 32. 14 (which, it may be noted, occurs also in the Sâm Ved. See Benfey's Ed. I. 27). IX. 7. 113. 2. There are other passages of, perhaps, even greater value than these. But these are enough.

attention has been already drawn are, I apprehend, enough, if not more than enough, to satisfy any candid mind, that the doctrine of S'raddhâ existed in India long before the time when Christianity arose, still longer before it began to influence the thought of this country even upon the hypothesis of Dr. Lorinser. It is, of course, not at all unlikely that the doctrine underwent some development in India, that it did not originally come forth in the shape in which we find it even in the Bhagavadgîtâ. I have not thought it necessary here to consider the question from this point of view, but nothing could surprise me less than that this should be so. At the same time, it is scarcely necessary to point out, that this is very different from the theory propounded by Dr. Lorinser—that the Bhagavadgîtâ borrowed this doctrine from Christianity. Indeed it seems to me, that the fact, if it be one, of the doctrine being traceable in its gradual development in the extant Vedic literature would negative that theory even more strongly than the mere existence of traces of the doctrine in that literature.*

The question, however, as between the Gîtâ and Christianity does not rest there. Speaking of the "independent activity of the Original Christian Church." Dr. Straus says— "And the *doctrines of faith*, of the forgiveness of sins, of the true keeping holy of the Sabbath, which we find interoven with the narratives of the miraculous cures in the New

---

* I have thus far referred only to the orthodox Brahminical works. But in the Buddhistic Sutta Nipata also, we have abundant, I was going to say superabundant, evidence of the recognition of the value of faith in India. See Sir M. C. Swamy's Sutta Nipata pp. 21 25, 63, and sundry other places. And as to *credo ut intelligam* listen to the following from the same work (p. 49) "one who being diligent (and) wise *believes* in the law of the saints for attaining Nibbana will by listening constantly (to them) acquire knowledge.

Testament, the thought that death is but a sleep which we find brought out in those of the raising of the dead, are *nothing but so many Christian ideas breathed as a newer and better soul* into those narratives."* Considering only that part of this sentence which is pertinent to our present inquiry, I understand this to mean that the idea of faith was a doctrine added by Christianity to the old Jewish stock of ideas. Now if this is so, mark the conclusion according to Dr. Lorinser's principles. The absence of all trace of the ideas of S'raddhâ and Bhakti "anywhere else in heathendom" than in the Gîtâ, is urged by Dr. Lorinser as a ground for holding that the ideas "have been taken over from Christianity." Is it not then open to an opponent of Dr. Lorinser to contend, that as the doctrine of S'raddhâ is not found anywhere in Judaism, "there appears to be no doubt that it is not an originally Christian representation, but that it has been taken over from Hinduism?" I maintain, that as an *argumentum ad hominem* this argument is of great value. And not only so, but I think that even as a general argument, it is entitled to some weight—more especially in view of those considerations which I shall presently proceed to set forth. And this introduces me to the next very important question in this investigation.†

That question is one which has been already hinted at as having never received even a cursory glance from Dr. Lorinser, the question, namely, whether it is not possible that Christianity may have borrowed from Hinduism, and

* Life of Jesus I. 205.

† I do not know by what arguments "Dr. Weber among others has partly demonstrated" that the doctrine of S'raddhâ has been taken over from Christianity by Hinduism. I do not, therefore, say anything more about them than this, that I think those arguments, whatever they may be, are most likely put out of court by the facts to which we have drawn attention in the text.

not *vice versâ.* The question is undoubtedly a large one, and as important as it is large. I do not profess to have viewed it in all its bearings. I do not propose to discuss it here at any length. For, indeed, I do not consider it necessary or expedient to complicate the present question by such a matter, enveloped, as to a great extent it must be, in doubt. But as it has been strongly suggested to my mind by the method of argument which Dr. Lorinser has adopted, and as it has a very important bearing upon the central question, I think it necessary to offer a few observations upon it from my point of view.

The first general observation, then, to be made on this aspect of the question is, that every body must admit that philosophy was cultivated from very early times in India. Professor Wilson who expresses a 'shrewd suspicion' as to the originality of the Gîtâ admits the contention of Wilkins and Schlegel to that effect;[*] and it is, indeed, a matter beyond the reach of doubt. Now the known character of our people makes it, to my mind, much more likely, that in such intercourse as there was between them and foreigners, the latter carried away with them some knowledge derived from the former, than that foreign thought so far influenced the higher intellects in India as to leave its traces in their most orthodox works.[†] And if the Greeks and other peoples who came into contact with India did learn some things in the country, what more natural than that such new ideas as they learnt should go towards the formation of that system which arose soon afterwards? This seems to me to be ren-

---

[*] Wilson's Essays on Sanskrit Literature &c. Vol. III. p. 103.

[†] Professor Weber seems to question the truth of this proposition (*Indische Studien* Vol. II. 397 as translated for me by my kind friend Mr. S'ankar Pândurang Pandit) But his argument appears to me to be, in great measure, a *petitio principii.*

dered more likely by the fact, that about the time of Alexander's invasion, Buddhism was agitating Indian religious thought to its core; and such a new system (in which, by the way, several of the so-called characteristic doctrines of Christianity may be found anticipated) was very likely to leave some impression on the minds of the foreigners. Accordingly Dean Milman has said, that "it is by no means improbable that tenets which had their origin in India have for many centuries predominated in or materially affected the Christianity of the whole Western World."* In further confirmation of this view, we may refer to the accounts, not indeed well vouched for, but still much better vouched for than Professor Weber's imaginary journeys of Bráhmans to Asia Minor, and probably as well vouched for as the legends about St. Thomas and St. Bartholomew and all the rest of them, we may, I say, usefully refer to the accounts of Pythagoras travelling to India and learning there some of the doctrines of the Indian philosophers of the day.† The Essenes also, a sect flourishing at the time of Jesus, are supposed to have had some intercourse with the East, whence they are said to have partly derived their inspiration. And according to Dean Milman, the Jewish doctrine of inheritance of disease by children from their parents may be clearly traced to India.‡ These being some of the facts bearing upon this branch of our investigation, facts, too, admitted by a learned Christian historian, it appears to me, that the theory of Indian philosophy having borrowed from Christianity, based as it is upon the very slender and very deceptive grounds stated by Dr.

* Milman's Hist. of Christ. II. 31. And see also Wheeler's India III. 257; and Wilson's Vishnu Purán, Preface p. viii.

† See Colebrooke's Essays I. 419. Thomson's Gítá Introd. xxviii.

‡ Milman I. 153, 252.

Lorinser and others, is not only unproved but highly improbable. On the contrary, the conclusion to which the
facts and probabilities of the case seem to point as more
probable is one which the adherents of that theory have
not condescended even to glance at, namely, that it is Christianity which has borrowed from Hinduism, and not Hinduism which has borrowed from Christianity.

We now come to the last of Dr. Lorinser's propositions as
stated above. Dr. Lorinser evidently thinks, that there are
no means available for fixing a terminus before which the
Gîtâ must have been composed except the date of its commentator S'ankarâchârya. As to that date a few remarks
have been made already. But since the generally received date
is the eighth century after Christ, and since Dr. Lorinser
seems to expect that a later century may yet prove to be the
one in which S'ankar flourished, it is as well to draw attention
to the fact that the Kâdambarî of Bâṇabhaṭṭa does enable us
to fix a considerably earlier period as a terminus before
which the Gîtâ must have been composed. For in that
work one of the equivoques we meet with runs as follows :
महाभारतमिवानन्तगीताकर्णनानन्दितनरमृ॰—which may be thus rendered :—[The royal palace] in which people were gratified by hearing innumerable songs [was] like the Mahâbhârat, in which
Nar (Arjun) was gratified by hearing the Anantagîtâ.
Anantagîtâ clearly stands here for the Bhagavadgîtâ. Now
Bâṇabhaṭṭa flourished about the middle of the seventh century
A. C.† In his time the Mahâbhârat was looked upon with

---

* See p. 182. (Târânâth's Ed.).

† See Dr. F. E. Hall's Preface to his Vâsavadattâ p. 17. It will
there be seen that Bâṇabhaṭṭa's date depends on that of the great
Harshavardhan. And the date of that prince, though pronounced
by Mr. Fergusson (see J. R. A. S. (N. S.) Vol. IV. p. 93 and Indian
Antiquary Vol. II. 93a) to be " fixed within very narrow limits,"

almost, if not altogether, the same feeling of veneration, with
which it is looked upon in our own day. Of this work the Gîtâ
had already come to be regarded as a genuine portion. What
interval, then, must have elapsed between the composition
of the Gîtâ and the seventh century of the Christian Era?
But let us go on to a somewhat earlier period. I will not
refer to the quotation in the Panchatantra from the Bhagavadgîtâ,* for I do not agree with Dr. Kern about the value
of the Panchatantra in such an inquiry.† But we have exceedingly good warrant for holding that the Gîtâ is older
than Kâlidâs. And first let us look at the Raghuvans'a. Towards the beginning of the eighth canto of that work, we find
expressions and ideas which coincide remarkably with expressions and ideas to be found in the Bhagavadgîtâ. And the inference hence derivable is obviously much stronger than the
inferences which Dr. Lorinser has endeavoured to draw from
the coincidences, or supposed coincidences, on which he relies.
Similar coincidences may be found also in other parts of the
works of Kâlidâs. But the most important of all is to be
found in the Kumâr Sambhav VI. 67.‡ It is impossible, I
think, to mistake the allusion to the Gîtâ there. And taking all these passages together, it becomes, I think, quite

ought, according to the late Dr. Bhâû Dâjî, to be placed nearly a
century earlier (See J. B. B, R. A. S. Vol. VIII, 250) I believe that
Prof. Bhândârkar also, from a consideration of the Vallabhi and
Châlukya plates, is inclined to the view that the accepted date of
Harshavardhan should be reconsidered.

* See p. 104 (Kosagarten's Ed.). The quotation is not to be found
in the edition in the Bombay Series of Sanskrit Classics.

† See our Bhartṛihari, Introduction p. ix.

‡ See Mallinâth's commentary on this. Among the other parts of
Kâlidâs referred to in the text I would specially note Raghu, Canto
X. Stanza XXXI. of that canto, more particularly, should be compared with Gîtâ IV. 9 and III. 22, And see Dr. Lorinser's note at p.
238.

evident, that the Gîtâ must have preceded Kâlidâs by a considerable period. Now it is true that the date of Kâlidâs is by no means well settled, certainly not as well settled as that of Bâṇabhaṭṭa; still no scholar, I believe, now contends, that Kâlidâs lived after the sixth century A. C.; and even arguing upon the basis of that date, we are entitled to infer a considerable antiquity for the Bhagavadgîtâ. If any of the earlier dates proposed should prove correct,* Dr. Lorinser's theory will be at once put out of court.

There is another argument on this part of the question, which is not of great weight, but is, I think, entitled to some consideration. Bhaṭṭa Kumâril is said to have flourished about the close of the seventh century A. C.† A considerable period before him must have lived the author of the best known commentary on the Pûrva Mîmânsâ, namely S'abar Svâmî. A considerable period, again, must have elapsed between S'abar Svâmî and Jaimini the author of the Mîmânsâ Sûtras. The Mîmânsâ Sûtras on several occasions mention Bâdarâyaṇ, who is probably to be identified, and who by Colebrooke is identified, with the author of the Sûtras of the Uttar Mîmânsâ.‡ These Sûtras in their turn mention Jaimini, and the two works may therefore be taken as probably contemporaneous with one another. Now among the Sûtras of the Uttar Mîmânsâ, there are several which refer to certain Smṛitis as authorities for propositions which they lay

---

* See Bhartṛihari (Bomb. Series of Sansk. Classics) Introduction p. xii. and references there given.

† See Indian Antiquary Vol. I. 369. See also Windischmann's S'ankar.

‡ Essays (Madras Ed.) Vol. I. 296. I am bound to state, however, that I have not succeeded in tracing to the Brahma Sûtras any of the doctrines ascribed to Bâdarâyaṇ in the Mîmânsâ Sûtras. And Madhusûdan Sarasyatî's Prasthâuabhed shows that there were several Bâdarâyans.

down; and in the case of about five of these Sûtras, I have found that the commentaries of S'ankarâchârya and Madhvâchârya, and Râmânujâchârya, differing, as is well known, on the most fundamental points, agree in setting out passages from the Gîtâ as the Smṛitis referred to. We may from this infer, though I admit that the inference is not a strong one, that the Gîtâ was composed before the Brahma Sûtras. If so, then according to what is stated above, we have the Gîtâ prior to the Brahma Sûtras, the Brahma Sûtras contemporaneous with the Mîmânsâ Sûtras, the Mîmânsâ Sûtras prior to S'abar, S'abar prior to Kumâril, and Kumâril prior to the close of the seventh century A. C. And if this is so, I think the inference can very fairly be drawn, that the Gîtâ is sufficiently old to negative the theory of Dr. Lorinser. It may be added, that the expression ब्रह्मसूत्र occurs in the Gîtâ, but, according to all interpretations, not as standing for the Sûtras of Bâdarâyaṇ. I do not think, however, that any inference can be safely drawn from this circumstance.

As stated above, this argument is not of much weight. There is, however, an argument, based upon a slightly different series of Mîmânsâ authorities, which is, I contend, entitled to much more weight. Thus we have I. Kumâril Svâmî (seventh century A. C.) II. A considerable time prior to him, S'abar Svâmî III. A long time before him, Upavarsha, whom S'abar describes in his Mîmânsâ Bhâshya as "Bhagavân Upavarsha"[*] IV. A considerable time before him, the Brahma Sûtras, for as appears from S'ankar's commentary on Brahma Sûtra III., 3, 53, Upavarsha was the author of a work on the S'ârîrak Mîmânsâ[†] V. A considerable time

---

[*] P. 13 (Bibl. Ind.)

[†] See too Colebrooke Essays I. 332. Upavarsha is again mentioned by S'ankar at p. 291 of his Bhâshya. I do not know the grounds

before the Brahma Sûtras, the Bhagavadgîtâ. Upon this last item of the series a few more words may be added here. Under Brahma Sûtra I., 2, 6. S'ankar cites as the Smṛiti referred to Gîtâ XVIII. 61; Madhva cites X. 20 and XV. 13; and Râmânuj X. 15, 19 and XVIII. 61, 62—which is notable as combining the passages cited both by S'ankar and Madhva. On I., 3, 23 S'ankar and Madhva quote XV. 6, 12; and Râmânuj quotes XIV., 2. These two instances are of comparatively little moment. The three that follow appear to me, I own, all but conclusive to show that the Gîtâ was before the mind of the author of the Brahma Sûtras. Under II., 3, 45 all the commentators cite Gîtâ XV. 7, and the context seems to me to fully justify them. Again under IV., 1, 10. the commentators refer to the same passage, S'ankar and Râmânuj to Gîtâ VI. 11, and Madhva to VI., 13. Lastly under IV. 2, 22 all the commentators refer to the same passage, that at the close of Gîtâ Chap. VIII. In all three of these cases, the context seems to me to show clearly, that the commentators are perfectly right in considering the Gîtâ as the Smṛiti which the author of the Sûtras had in his mind. The inference, therefore, when one comes to look into the matter, is immensely stronger than I have described it above; for we have not to rest simply upon the commentators' authority on the point, though their concurrence would itself be a powerful fact.

In considering these arguments and their bearing upon the question before us, it must never be forgotten, that they lead us no further than the limit *after* which the Gîtâ could not have been composed. We get nothing positive, not even any hint, as to when precisely it was composed, nor even as to how long before the limit. While it does furnish

---

upon which Weber and Thomson have assigned the Vedânta Sûtras to the third century A. C. (See Thomson pp. xlvii. *et seqq.*)

us with a *terminus ad quem*, it has not even the tendency
to show us a *terminus a quo.* Professor Bhândârkar thinks,
that the style of the S'âbar Bhâshya belongs to nearly the
same period to which the style of Patanjali's Mahâbhâshya
belongs. As far as I have looked at the two works, I am
inclined to accept this opinion. And if it is correct, then upon
the foregoing argument the Gîtâ must have been composed
at the latest somewhere about the fourth century B. C.
Furthermore, we have also to remember, that S'ankar was
one of the later commentators on the Brahma Sûtras. Colebrooke states that a commentary on the Brahma Sûtras
is ascribed to the sage Baudhâyan,* though his work is
not now forthcoming. And this circumstance has also
to be weighed in the consideration of the question before
us. Nor must it be forgotten that even on the Bhagavadgîtâ itself, S'ankarâchârya, as stated before, was not the
earliest commentator. On the contrary, from the introduction
to his Bhâshya, it would appear that several writers before
him had interpreted the Gîtâ, and in modes which did not
coincide with his—a circumstance which would seem to indicate, that the sectaries had been, already before S'ankar's
time, at work upon the Gîtâ, in order to be able to claim
for their own opinions the sanction of that book. If so,
it becomes probable, that the Gîtâ had, long before S'ankar's
time, begun to be regarded as a work of very high authority;
and the interval between its composition and that of S'ankar's
commentary must have been even larger than the five
centuries which Dr. Lorinser reluctantly allows. However that may be, it appears to me to result from what
has been stated above, that Dr. Lorinser's position on this
last point is as untenable as his position on the other points,

---

* See Essays Vol. I. p. 332.

ınd that the indications which the evidence before us gives
are strongly against his final conclusion.

We have now finished the observations we have to make
upon the several propositions laid down by Dr. Lorinser with
regard to the Bhagavadgîtâ and upon the arguments by which
he has sought to fortify them. But before proceeding to the
few other points which we propose to notice, it may be advis-
able to consider what is said on our subject by Mr. Thomson,
to whom we are indebted for a very good English translation
of the Gîtâ. In his Introduction to that translation, and in
the notes which he has added to it, there are observations
interspersed which furnish a hint as to Mr. Thomson's opinion
about the age of the Bhagvadgîtâ. I am not aware, however,
that he has explicitly stated the chronological limits within
which he supposes the Gîtâ to have been composed in any
other passage than the following extracted from his Introduction. After stating that a "burning sun" and a "hot wind"
drove not only the Brâhmaṇ but also the Kshatriya to asceticism, and that "in virtue of the powers acquired" by such asceticism, the Kshatriyas attempted to wrest from the Brâhmaṇs the exclusive right to minister to the spiritual necessities
of the people, Mr. Thomson proceeds :—" The Brahmin trembled
at this new danger, and no longer able to seek support in any of
the other castes,⁰ had recourse to conciliatory means, and the
way was thus prepared for the teachings of the Bhagavadgîtâ.
Such however were not the only causes which gave rise to
the Karmayoga doctrines of our poem ; and a long interval of
perhaps several centuries must have intervened between the
Yoga of Patanjali and the new branch of that school. Indeed if we may place the probable date of the Yoga Sûtras
between 400 B. C. and 100 B. C., we must consider that of

---

* Mr. Thomson does not state why this was so.

the Bhagavadgîtâ to lie between 100 B. C. and 300 A. D
But this only by the way."*   As above stated, this is the
least vague passage on the subject of the date of the Gîtâ
which I have been able to find in Mr. Thomson's book. Let
us examine it. In the first place, I must take leave to
observe, that I am not quite satisfied with the arguments by
which Mr. Thomson makes out that the system of Patanjali
is posterior to the rise of Buddhism. But as it is neither
necessary nor desirable to go into that question on this occasion, I shall for the purposes of the present argument
proceed upon the assumption that that posteriority is made
out. But upon the other point, as to the priority of Patanjali's system to the Bhagavadgîtâ, I must join issue with
Mr. Thomson. The only reason which he has adduced for
his proposition is based upon that bit of Indian religious
history which is contained in the passage above set out. Mr.
Thomson says, indeed, that "there is every reason to believe"
the Gîtâ to be several centuries later than Patanjali.† But he
does not state any other "reason" than that above referred to.
Now that being so, the question arises—from what materials
has Mr. Thomson constructed this interesting historical narrative? I am not aware of any evidence which shows that
the Kshatriyas, as a body, had at any period of our ancient
history begun to encroach on the domain of the Brâhmaṇs, either in consequence of Patanjali's Yog system
or of anything else.‡ The case of King Janak is always
treated, so to say, as standing alone. And no less so

* Introd, p. xlii,

† P. lxxxii,

‡ Mr. Thomson's broad inference to this effect finds but a narrow
basis in Gîtâ III. 24 on which he rests it (see p. 25 of his translation note 27.)

s that of Vis'âmitra.* Those stories do not seem to
ne to show that "the Kshatriya was allured from the
oils of an active life to the enjoyments of profitable
epose"; while the manner in which they are treated,
whenever allusion is made to them, appear to indicate that
one main point marked about them was their exceptional
character. And when Mr. Thomson, in his graphic account
of the religious revolution he describes, speaks of "kingdoms
and principalities being abandoned to their own guidance
states left defenceless" and so forth, one is almost tempted to say that he is here evolving history out of his inner
consciousness. He certainly has shown no scrap of evidence,
valuable or otherwise, for that statement. As Mr. Matthew
Arnold says with regard to a somewhat similar matter in
connexion with modern Biblical criticism, Mr. Thomson's
narrative is at the best "plausible"; but it is, I submit,
quite impossible to allow a whole historic superstructure
like Mr. Thomson's theory to be based on such a plausible
which is, in other words, an excessively weak—foundation.
But I do not think, that we need rest content with merely
this negative argument on this subject. For I think that
we have some slight evidence which points the other way.
And first, a system called the Yog is mentioned several
times in the Gîtâ,† and in some places as distinguished from
what is there called the Sânkhya system. Is this Yog system
dentical with what we now know under that name, namely
the system of Patanjali? Commenting on Gîtâ II. 39 Mr.
Thomson says, that "undoubtedly the names by which the
two schools of philosophy were known are here intended,

---

* Mr. Thomson refers to this in the note at p. xlii. where
here is some misprint, I think. It may be remarked also that both
the stories are of very great antiquity.

† See, for instance, Gîtâ. II. 39, V. 4, 5 among other passages.

in the words Sânkhya' and Yoga."* This is not perfectly
clear; but if it means, that in the passage in question, the
systems of philosophy now known to us as Sânkhya and Yog
are referred to, that is not only not indubitable, but is, I
think, highly improbable. For if we consider the Sânkhya
doctrine as expounded in the verses preceding the verse
above referred to, we shall find it, I think, somewhat
difficult to identify it with any portion of the current Sânkhya
philosophy. And similarly the doctrine that the fruit of
action should never be regarded, that men should preserve
equability of mind whatever the results of their acts may be
—these are doctrines which are most prominent in the Yog
system as understood in the Gîtâ, yet I think, we shall search
for them in vain throughout the Sûtras of *our* Yog Philosophy,
namely the Sûtras of Patanjali. Again, when we are told
as we are in Gîtâ V. 4, 5, that he sees truly who sees no
difference between the Sânkhya and the Yog systems, I
think it is almost impossible to admit that the Sânkhya
and Yog here meant are identical with the systems now
known to us under those names. And if this is so, if it
is true, that *a* Yog system is mentioned in the Gîtâ, and
that system is different from the Yog system of Patanjali
what is the conclusion as to the relative dates of the Bhagavad
gîtâ and Patanjali which is hence derivable? Upon the
principle underlying some of the arguments of the late
Professor Goldstücker in his very elaborate and learned
work on Pânini, we may conclude that the Gîtâ must
have preceded the Yog Sûtras.† I must own, however

---

* P. 14, note 21.

† See Pânini p. 130. " Is it possible to assume " ask
Prof. Goldstücker "that Pânini could have known this sense of the
word Âranyaka, when he is altogether silent about it; and if h

that I am not quite satisfied with the soundness of the principle in question. I am unable to persuade myself, that the argument in the case before us, for instance, entitles us to conclude more than this—that when the Gîtâ was composed, the name Yog was probably not the name of Patanjali's system of philosophy.* Such an inference in the present case, would, I think, be somewhat strong, on account of the association of Sânkhya with Yog ; for these two words so intimately connected with each other in recent times would not have been used as they are used in the Gîtâ, if they had designated at the time of the Gîtâ the same things that they designate now. This inference, however, standing by itself, does not carry us very far in our search for the relative dates of the Gîtâ and Patanjali. Let us, therefore, look at another point in connexion with the two works. In Gîtâ VI. 34, 35 we have some observations on the unsteadiness of the mind and the means of making it steady. The same point is discussed in Yog Sûtras I. 12-16. Now I think, the difference between the two is one which lies upon the surface. And it is this. In the one we trace the age of systems ; in the other the age of poetry. In the one we have definition, division, a fitting in of the particular part into the rest of the system. In the other we have no such attempt at systematizing at all ; but immediately after

did not know it, that the works so called could have already existed in his time?" The *non sequitur* appears to me to lie at this last point of the argument.

* That this is not hypercritical may be seen from this that Vedântins (Goldstücker p. 150) were of old called Aupanishads. (See our Bhartṛihari Introd. p. vi.) Sânkhya was also called Samikshya (Mâgh. II. 59) and Nyâya is otherwise called Ânvîkshiki, and, perhaps, वाकोवाक्य also [see S'ankar on Chhândogya Upanishad p. 475 ; but also Kaiyaṭ on Mahâbhâshya p. 16 (Banâras. Ed.)].

a merely cursory hint as to this matter is dropped, the discussion branches off into a very different subject.　Having
regard to these circumstances, and to the fact, that with respect to its unsystematic and poetical character,* the Gîtâ is
one of a class of works—the Upanishads being of much the same
nature—I think it not quite unsafe to conclude that the Gîtâ
was probably older than the Yog Sûtras.　At all events, I
think the argument is perfectly good to this extent, that it
shows, that the priority of the latter over the former cannot
be taken, as Mr. Thomson seems inclined to take it, as a mere
matter of course.

There are sundry other passages in Mr. Thomson's work
referring to this point of the date of the Gîtâ.　In one place
he takes the last line of the 67th Stanza of Chapter XVIII.
to refer to the S'aiv sect; and says, that when the epoch of
their battles with the Vaishṇav party shall have been deter-
mined, "some approximation will have been made to the date
of the composition of the Bhagavadgîtâ."†　But in the first
place, I do not see the necessity of interpreting, as Mr. Thomson interprets, the 'me' in Chap. XVIII. St. 67 to mean specifically Vishṇu or Kṛishṇa.　It may mean the Supreme Being
without reference to any particular manifestation of Him; and
by His 'revilers' may be intended all godless people, not
necessarily people of any particular sect.　And in the second
place, this opinion of Mr. Thomson's is not easily recon-
ciliable with the opinion which he has also elsewhere pronounced, that the author of the Gîtâ was probably a contemporary of

---

* Compare as to this Thomson's Introduction p. xci. and also Muir
S. T. III. 175 note. It cannot be urged that there was no room for a
full treatment of the subject, for there is a very lengthy description
just before of the true mode of attaining the Yog.

† P. 121.

Kâlidâs.° For in Kâlidâs, at any rate, we have evidence not of sectarian quarrel, but of peace and amity.† And thirdly it may be observed—though in the present state of our knowledge the observation is not of much value—that the epoch of the battles between the S'aivs and Vaishṇavs is, I believe, generally placed at about the seventh or eighth centuries of the Christian Era, about the time in fact when S'ankar the great commentator on the Gîtâ flourished. Upon the whole, I think, we cannot safely accept Mr. Thomson's conclusion upon this point. In the same note Mr. Thomson also suggests, that "our poem must have been written either before or after the religious revolution of Buddha, at a period when the hierarchy were supreme in power, and science and philosophy were forced, as in the days of Galileo and the Inquisition, to creep in by stealth."‡ This is by no means very definite. Mr. Thomson afterwards speaks of the author as "probably warned already by the defeat of Buddhism." But what is the meaning of "the defeat of Buddhism?" From the time of As'ok to that of Harshavardhan, we have evidence to show that Buddhism flourished in India with scarcely any vicissitudes of fortune, and was, in some instances, patronized by Indian princes side by

---

* P. xlvi., and p. cxiv. At p. xlvi. Mr. Thomson speaks of the age of Kâlidâs as that in which "the elegant and measured S'lokas of a Vâlmiki were revived." What is the meaning of this, and what is the evidence for it?

† Compare Kumâr. Canto II. with Raghu. Canto X. and Canto I. St. 1 and see Kumâr. Canto VII. St. 44. Compare also Bhartṛihari (Bomb. Series of Sansk. Classics) Introd. p. xix.

‡ P. 121. To Gîtâ XVIII. 67, from which Mr. Thomson draws this inference, we have a parallel in Manu I. 103 which is, perhaps, even more narrow.

side with Brâhmanism.* I cannot, therefore, understand
to what period, according to this conjecture of Mr. Thomson's, the Gîtâ will have to be assigned. In another place,
Mr. Thomson again argues, that "this poem was composed
after the rise of Buddhism."† But here also, I think it
difficult to accept either his premises or his conclusion. He
again gives us a short historical narrative without so much as
referring to the evidence upon which it is based. And it is
further noteworthy, that whereas Mr. Thomson has said in
his Introduction‡ that the Gîtâ was composed when the
Kshatriyas were trying to wrest spiritual superiority out of
the hands of the Brâhmans, he talks here as if the Brâhmans
had already triumphed, and had compelled the Kshatriyas to
make common cause with them against the "growing power"
of the Vais'yas and the S'ûdras. Such are the contradictions
into which people run, when they leave the *terra firma* of
tangible evidence for the aerial ways, if I may so say, of
imaginative history. It is unnecessary, I humbly conceive,
to examine in detail Mr. Thomson's remarks in the passage
now under consideration. It is enough to say, in the first
place, that his statements of fact are without foundation;
and secondly, that the inference which he draws from the
passage of the Gîtâ does not arise from it at all.

We now proceed to a few points which appear to us to
be of some value in this investigation, but which have not
been considered by either Dr. Lorinser or Mr. Thomson.
And first, the metre of the Gîtâ in some of its stanzas calls

* Compare Kâdambarî (Târânâth's Ed.) pp. 133 and 384; and the
copperplates recently deciphered as to which see *inter alia* J. B. B.
R. A. S. Vol. X. p. 76; Indian Antiquary Vol. IV. pp. 107, 174.

† P. 67.

‡ See p. xciii of this Essay *suprâ*.

for a few remarks. If we take a rapid survey of the poetical portion of Sanskrit Literature, we shall find, I think, a certain development in respect of metrical regularity from the Vedic age to the age of what is called the classical literature. In the Veds, it is impossible to trace a rigid scheme to which verses of the same metre shall be found to adhere. There is, of course, a general similarity, and with the assistance of the *iyádipúrau*[*] and other metrical fictions, as they may be called, we can generally obtain the requisite number of syllables. But what we cannot obtain is the uniform collocation of the long and short syllables. A verse that is perfect according to the modern rigid schemes of the several metres, is not the rule but the exception. Now if we come to the Upanishads, we still find these same metrical irregularities, but they become, I believe, perceptibly fewer in number. Many of the Upanishad verses are perfectly regular according to the modern schemes, and may be very smoothly chanted in the manner in which classical Sanskrit verses can be chanted. But although the number of irregularities has fallen off, complete regularity has not yet been secured at this stage of metrical progress. Next after the Upanishads, or about the same time, come the Gîtâ and other works of that class. Here, too, we have irregularities, but very much fewer in number than those we meet with in the Vedic Sanhitâs, and perhaps, also fewer than those in the Upanishads. And if we look next at the whole body of classical literature, we find there the irregularities conspicuous by their all but total absence. This result, which we may obtain by a rapid review of Sanskrit Poetry will, I think, be found to be, in some measure, strengthened by the

---

[*] Compare Pingal Chhandas Sûtra III. 2, and Max Müller's Translation of the Rigved., Introduction *passim*.

testimony of the indigenous technical writers on Sanskrit Prosody. The chief, and indeed the only, writer to be consulted on this matter, is of course Pingal, whose Chhandas Sútras have been recently published with the commentary of Haláyudh in the Bibliotheca Indica. Now the fourteenth Sútra of the first chapter of Pingal is तौ which, according to the commentator Haláyudh, is an Adhikár Sútra—applicable, as the commentator says, throughout the "Sástra." And the meaning of it is, that when nothing specific is stated, long and short syllables may occur indiscriminately. Now as a matter of fact nothing specific is to be found till we come to Chapter IV. Sútra 15. In the metres mentioned down to that Sútra, therefore, there is complete freedom as to long and short syllables. Now Chapter IV. Sútra 8 says that thereafter the "laukik"—or as it may be called, classical—section begins; the Vedic metres having been treated of in the Sútras preceding it. And in the whole of that section the particular order in which the long and short syllables must occur is everywhere stated. We know, too, that these fixed schemes of the several metre are practically observed in the classical literature, as they are theoretically laid down, with great rigour.* And from all this, I think, it is not a very bold proceeding to conclude, that those works in which we observe any remarkable number of deviations from the fixed metrical schemes may be placed out of the pale of the classical literature, and consequently, I may add, some considerable time before the beginning of the Christian Era. For Pingal himself, is an author, of very respectable antiquity, as he is mentioned in the S'abar Bháshya† about which we have spoken a word before. And even in the

---

* Compare the verse आर्याच्छन्दसि पद् वृत्तेस्त्रिष्टुभ्‌ which is quoted in a different form by Mallinátha on Raghu. XIX. 23.

† P. 16. (Bibl. Ind. Ed.).

Manu Sanhitâ, we have a rigorous adherence to the metrical schemes which is far greater than that to be found in the Gîtâ.*

I may observe that the question of the metrical regularity of Vedic verses has been copiously discussed by European scholars of great note. It is not necessary, however, for our present topic to enter into that discussion. Nor have I studied the Vedic metres sufficiently to do so. It seems to me, I confess, that the irregularities which manifest themselves in different degrees at different stages of the post—Vedic literature raise a sort of presumption in favour of the existence of similar irregularities in greater abundance in the Vedic literature. And the discussion of the question of Vedic metres may, perhaps, be in some degree advanced towards a settlement, if the later literature is considered. I understand Prof. Max Müller's opinion to be in favour of holding, what is assumed in our argument above, that the irregularities in Vedic verses are not the result of mislections,† as some scholars seem to contend, but are genuine characteristics of Vedic verse.

If now we turn our attention to the style and language of the Gîtâ, we shall find, I think, further corroboration for the view which we have here taken of its antiquity. The style throughout impresses me as archaic in its simplicity. You have none of that exuberance of figure and trope which marks the classical literature. You have no long and involved compounds ; no puzzling syntactical constructions ;

---

* See the passages of Manu cited in the Digest of Hindu Law by West and Bühler Vol. I. Introd. p. xxix. and the older passages (also there cited) on which Manu's are based. With these compare the Stanzas in Gîtâ Chap. XI.

† Translation of the Rigved by Max Müller Vol. I. Introd. pp. xxvi. et seq.

no attempt at securing the jingle of like sounds.* We
have, on the contrary, those repetitions of single phrases
which have been noted before as characteristic of archaic
writings;† we have a few instances of inartificial grammatical constructions;‡ and once we find that particle§ इ,
which is well-known as occurring in the epic poems, and
in the Vedic literature in the form य, but which, I think,
never occurs in either form in the classical literature.
There are sundry words also, which occur in the Gîtâ in
senses other than those which they bear in the classical
literature.‖ Of course, this statement must be taken subject
to some allowance, as it is almost impossible for anybody
to say, that any given word has ceased to have a particular
sense attached to it at a particular stage of Sanskrit literature. Nevertheless, I believe I may say, that the following
words in the Gîtâ bear different senses from those which
they bear in the classical literature. संज्ञा (I. 7) मात्रा (II. 14)
अन्न (II. 16) माषा (II. 54) संग्रह (III. 20 and 25) गति (IV. 7)
व्यक्ति (IX. 14) धाम (X. 18; also IX. 5) ब्रह्म (XIV. 3) अकीलुन्दापु
(XVI. 2) संतित (XI. 1). Some other words might be easily
added to this list. But these will suffice to show the truth
of what has been asserted above. There is but one other
word on which, perhaps, a special remark deserves to be made.

---

* Mr. Thomson has noted one instance at VI. 23. A similar
instance is noted by Mr. Muir in the Rigved. See Muir Sanskrit
Texts Vol. V. p. 165.

† Suprâ p. lxi.

‡ See Gîtâ II. 59. X. 16, 19 among other instances.

§ Chap. II. 9 where, also, the repetition of उक्त्वा is inartistic.

‖ Compare the observations upon this point of the late Professor
Goldstücker in his Pânini p. 128.

¶ This, indeed, is altogether an anomalous word.

That word is वत It occurs twice in the Gîtâ, first in I. 39 and secondly in XIV. 9. Annotating on the latter stanza, Mr. Thomson writes:— "Lassen has a long irrelevant note on the force of वत, very useful in a grammar of the Vedas, but of doubtful value for a poem of the date of ours. Suffice it to say, that as he has shown, the fanciful explanation of the scholiasts must be rejected, and the common use of the particle throghout the 'Mahâbhârata,' and other works of like style and approximate date, be accepted, namely, that of a confirmatory expletive."* This is a rather remarkable note. In the first place, Mr. Thomson seems to think, that the Mahâbhârat belongs all to one age, a position for which very few, if any, advocates will be found in these days. But if he does not think so, it is somewhat difficult to understand the precise meaning of his final observation. "Like style and approximate date" to the Mahâbhârat means nothing unless any precise part of the Bhârat is specified. And if Mr. Thomson has no objection to the Gîtâ being considered as of "like style and approximate date" to the oldest parts of the Mahâbhârat, I have no quarrel with his remark. For I think Professor Goldstücker was perfectly right in contending that the oldest portions of the Bhârat are older even than the rise of Buddhism.† And when Mr. Thomson speaks of Lassen's note as "of doubtful value for a poem of the date of ours," he seems to forget that the subject of the note is one of the material elements in the consideration of the date of our poem, and cannot therefore be disposed of in that off-hand style. What we have to mark and consider is that वत appears to be used here as a conjunctive particle, as it is used in the Vedic literature, and not as a disjunctive

* P. 93. As to the 'fanciful explanation' Conf. West and Bühler Vol. I. p. xxx. Introd.

† Westminster Review (April 1868) p. 420.

which I believe, is the only use to which it is put in the classical literature.

A few words are necessary upon the grammatical structure of the language of the Gítá. Now it will not be by any means difficult to show, that there are several grammatical forms in the Gítá which are not used, and cannot correctly be used, in the classical literature, and which are not sanctioned by the precepts of the "grammatical saints." Thus प्रसविष्यध्वम् (III. 10) संयमनाम् (X. 29) श्रयय अहम् (XI. 54) हेसंखानि (XI. 41). प्रियायाईसि (XI. 44 dissolved into प्रियायाः अर्हसि)—these are some of the forms which occur in the Gítá, which would be quite un-allowable in the classical literature. And it may, therefore, be plausibly argued upon the strength of these forms, that the Gítá must be assigned to an epoch considerably older than that of the classical literature, and therefore many years prior to the Christian Era. At the same time, I must state, that while this is a favourite argument with European scholars,[*] it is not one which is quite satisfactory. My very able and learned friend Professor R. G. Bhándárkar is of opinion that the argument proves nothing. And he relies on the fact, that the Aitareya Bráhman, for instance, which is undoubtedly a very old work, is in its grammar scrupulously exact, and strictly ad-heres to the rules laid down in the Ashṭádhyáyí. Now this must be admitted to be a very remarkable circumstance, worthy of notice in considering the weight to be attached to the argu-ment from grammatical anomalies. We may further add that even in the admittedly later literature, we several times find grammatical forms often quite as anomalous as any that the Gítá or any other archaic work can show. Thus no less a writer than Kálidás has more than once the form आस,[†] which,

---

[*] See West and Bühler's Digest Vol. I. Introd. xvii. or Indian Antiquary I. 182.

[†] Kumár. I. 35, Raghu. XIV. 23.

according to Pâṇini II. 4, 52, cannot be correct. True the commentators,* as is their wont, resort to all manner of shifts in
order to explain the form. But there can, I apprehend, be little
doubt that Kâlidâs has there used a form which Pâṇini has
prohibited. The same form recurs, strange to say, even in
the S'ankar Vijaya of Mâdhavâchârya.† Kâlidâs has further the
following forms which are not allowable in the classical literature—कामयान and तस्थिवान् and जग्मिवान् ‡ And it would not, I think,
be very difficult to cull a few similar instances from other
writers. In Pâṇini V. 2 89, it is laid down that the word
परिवन्थी is used छन्दसि; yet the passages are numerous in which
we find modern poets using the word.§ In fact, the Siddhânta
Kaumudî shows several cases where the ingenuity of gram-
marians is very much exercised to explain what, according
to the established rules of grammar, would be errors.‖ And the
only explanation available in some cases is निर्ब्रूया: कवय:, or
कवयस्तु बहुलं प्रयुञ्जते,¶ or something to that effect. It would
seem, therefore, that the rule which has been commonly
adopted in this matter is one which fails both in the anvaya
and the vyatirek, as our native logicians would put it. The
induction is incorrect both ways. There are unquestionably
ancient works which scrupulously adhere to the rules of
grammar. There are unquestionably modern works which
deviate from those rules. It must be held, therefore, that

* See under Kumâr. I. 35.
† See Sarga III. Stanza 6.
‡ Raghu. XIX. 50; V. 61; V. 34. And see Siddh. Kaum. II. 364.
§ See Kâvya Prakâ's p. 271 (Ed. Mahes'achandra) परिवन्थिनी occurs
in the Mâlatî Mâdhav.
‖ Vide *inter alia* II. 245 (Târânâth's Ed.)
¶ See Siddh. Kaum. II. 364. In the Mahâbhâshya under Pâṇini
I. 4, 2 we find Patanjali saying छन्दोवत्कवय : कुर्वन्ति (p. 269 Banâras
Ed.).

grammatical anomalies, standing by themselves, are not
necessarily an index of the antiquity of the works in which
they occur. And it may be doubted, also, whether they are of
much value even when coupled with other considerations.

Turn we now to the contents of the Gîtâ to consider whether they afford anything that may prove of assistance in
this investigation. We have already referred to its mode of
treating its subject in some parts, and have argued that it
bespeaks an epoch previous to the epoch of cut and dry
systems. We have also referred to the use of the terms Sânkhya* and Yog, and contended that the Gîtâ was probably
composed before those systems came into existence. We
shall now proceed to draw attention also to a few other
points which are not, perhaps, of very considerable weight,
standing alone, but which all taken together may, I think,
be regarded as of some value. And first the Gîtâ mentions
only three Veds.† And of these it regards the Sâmaved as
the best,‡ therein agreeing with the Aitareya Brâhmaṇ, as we
have pointed out in our note on the passage. Now it is
remarkable, that in the Manu Smṛiti the Sâmaved appears to have
been ousted from this eminence,§ since we read in Manu IV.
124:—सामवेद: स्मृत: त्रिग्यस्समानस्याश्राचिर्धनि:; and based on this the
injunction in 123 सामध्वनावृग्यजुषी नाधियीत करदाचन. Further no

---

* By an oversight I omitted to refer to Gîtâ XVIII. 13 on this
point. I have failed to trace the " five conditions" there stated in any
work on what is now known to us as the Sânkhya Philosophy. We
must, therefore, adhere to the opinion expressed above, in spite of
Vijnân Bhikshu's contention the other way in the Introduction to his
Bhâshya on the Sânkhya Sûtras. See too Mr. Thomson's note at p.
115. It is also noteworthy that Sânkhya Sûtra I. 85 seems to run
counter to the theory of the Gîtâ as to action without desire.

† IX. 17.

‡ X. 22.

§ Cf. Muir S. T. Vol. III. Preface p. 9 (which I have since seen).

allusion is to be found in the Gîtâ to the Trinity which is referred to even by Bhartṛihari and Kâlidâs.ᵃ Indra is still described by implication as the chief of the Gods.†S'aṅkar too is described only as the chief of the Rudras.‡ And although undoubtedly Kṛishṇa is identified with Vishṇu, and both are identified with the Supreme Being, still in one place, Vishṇu is referred to as chief of the Âdityas.§ That no argument can be based on the high veneration paid to Vishṇu in the Gîtâ for holding it to be later than the Christian Era has been already stated.|| It is desirable, however, to make a few more observations upon this point. It appears to me to be clear from the evidence collected, with such fulness by Mr. Muir, that there are to be found even in the oldest of the Veds not a few passages which, if they stood alone, "might lead us to suppose that this deity was regarded by the Vedic Ṛishis as the chief of all the gods."¶ It is true, that Mr. Muir points out several circumstances which appear to him to lead to the conclusion, that Vishṇu "occupied a somewhat subordinate place in the estimation and affections of the ancient Ṛishis."¶ But although his argument is fairly open to an orthodox Hindu believing in the revealed character of the Ṛigved, it is at least a matter of doubt whether it lies in the mouth of a European Sanskritist of the present day to insist upon it. The circumstances on which Mr. Muir relies do not, I submit, justify the conclusion drawn from them. If we made a collection of

---

* See "Was the Râmâyana copied from Homer?" p. 46. note 101 and Bhartṛihari Introd. xix.

† X. 21.

‡ X. 22.

§ X. 23.

|| See p. lxxiii. *suprâ*

¶ Muir S. T. Vol. IV. (New. Ed.) p. 98.

passages from the classical Sanskrit Literature containing praises of various Deities, I think the collection would show many of the marks which Mr. Muir finds in the Ṛigved. We shall find now Vishṇu and now S'ankar, now Gaṇes' and now Devî, all represented as the highest Deity. We shall find likewise, that in some passages, the powers conceded to one of them are nevertheless stated to come from another of them. We shall find in hymns specially dedicated to one of them that all the others are clubbed together with the minor members of the Hindu Pantheon in one promiscuous crowd. I do not know that we should be entitled to draw from such a collection any inferences like those which Mr. Muir draws from the Ṛigved collection. Yet the cases are quite parallel. I admit that the fact of a comparatively small number of hymns being addressed to Vishṇu is worthy of note, and would seem to indicate that, in the age of the Ṛigved, Vishṇu had not been regarded as the highest divinity by a very large proportion of the ancient Ṛishis. Nevertheless it is obvious that the germ was there ; and I do not think that it would take all those centuries, which, according to European scholars, intervened between the Vedic age and the classical age, for that germ to develop into the later view of Vishṇu's divinity. And if this is correct, it is enough for the purposes of our present argument. For all we have to consider here is whether the eminence which Vishṇu occupies in the Bhagavadgîtâ is one to which he could not have risen from his position in the Vedic age, except after the lapse of the centuries which separate the Vedic age from the birth of Christ. I maintain that such a length of time is quite unnecessary.

It has been suggested, indeed, that the "Vishṇu of the Veds is in no way the Vishṇu of the mythologists."[*] But I under-

* Muir S. T. Vol. IV. (New Ed.) Preface p. x. note.

stand this to mean simply that some of the qualities and actions attributed to Vishṇu by the " mythologists" are not found attributed to him in the Veds. And if this is the only meaning of the assertion, then, I conceive, that it does not by any means affect our argument. Vishṇu as one of the Âdityas is alluded to, as pointed out by Mr. Muir himself, in the Atharva Ved and the S'atapath Brâhmaṇ.* So that upon that ground nothing can be said against the antiquity of the Gîtâ which also speaks of him as one of the Âdityas. Vishṇu as the Highest Being, also, is referred to as much in some of the hymns of the Rigved as he is in the Gîtâ. Whatever, therefore, may be the view of the mythologists, there is nothing in the Gîtâ to necessitate its being classed with their writings and nothing, therefore, in the view which the Gîtâ takes of Vishṇu's divinity, that in any way affects our conclusion.

Come we now to another point. At Gîtâ X. 35 we read मासा- नां मार्गशीर्षोहम्. The only commentary in which I have seen any explanation of this is Madhusûdan's.† He ascribes the position here assigned to this month to its merits as neither very hot nor very cold and so forth. But I think it more likely, as Lassen argues, that the reason for mentioning the Mârgas'írsha above others is that it was formerly the month with which the year commenced. Now Lassen points out, that according to Bentley, Mârgas'írsha was the first month of the year between 693 and 451 B. C.; and he adds that if that were correct, the age of the Bhagavadgîtâ would be indicated by this passage. I own, however, that I cannot yet accept this argument. For even in the time of Amar Sinha, apparently, Mârgas'írsha was still the first month of the year. That appears to me to be a safe inference from the

* Muir S. T. Vol. IV. 115.
† See it quoted in Schlegel's Gîtâ by Lassen p. 276.

fact, that in the enumeration of the different names of the months, Amar mentions the Mârgas'îrsha month first.* Now it is true that the date of Amar is not yet well settled, but tradition does not carry it further back than 56 B. C.; while Prof. Wilson is not quite certain as to whether that date or the fifth century A. C. is the correct date ;† and Prof. Kern seems to be quite decisive in favour of the latter date.‡ Whichever view is taken, however, the date of Amar does not fall within the limits stated by Bentley ; and the matter is one therefore which requires further elucidation. I am unable to throw any light upon it, and I must therefore leave it here.

Let us now proceed to another point. And let us compare the view of caste taken in the Gîtâ with that in Manu. The duties of a Brâhmaṇ are stated in the Gîtâ at Chap. XVIII. 42, and by Manu in Chap. I. 88. The former lays down as the duty of a Brâhmaṇ the acquisition of sundry moral and religious virtues, such as purity, straight-forwardness and so forth. The latter lays down the well-known six-fold division of a Brâhmaṇ's duties. Now I think that a comparison of these two views shows that the view of the Gîtâ is considerably older than the other. In fact it appears to me to take us back to the time when the differentia of the Brâhmaṇ caste was a living reality, and had not as yet petrified into a mere dogma. The doctrine of Manu appears to me to be the doctrine of a Brâhmanical priesthood, involving little, if any, responsibility, but conferring numerous valuable privileges. The doctrine of the Gîtâ is that of a class which is really superior in a certain sort

---

* See Kânda I. St. 15 (Kâlavarga) and Varâhamihir *ad finem.*

† Essays &c. Vol. III. 184. And see Goldstücker's Dictionary under अमरसिंह.

‡ See the Preface to his Bṛihatsanhitâ.

of intrinsic worth, and which does not desire that superiority to continue divorced from that worth.[*] The Gîtâ seems to me to belong to the age when the Brâhman still possessed that which had made him the head of Hindu society. The Manu Smriti seems to belong to the age when the Brâhman continued to enjoy the position of head, not so much because of his possession at that time of the virtues which had originally raised him to it, as because of the rules laid down with authority at a time when those virtues had not yet died away. Furthermore the generality of statement in the Gîtâ, contrasted with the specific hard and fast rules laid down by Manu, appears to me to show that Manu belongs to a later stage of religious development. If we now compare the duties of Kshatriyas as laid down in the two works, we still obtain the same results. The Gîtâ enforces the acquisition of those qualities which made the Kshatriya what he was—bravery, courage, the imperial dignity. That, like the rule about the Brâhman's duties, appears to me again to lead us back far into antiquity, when the difference of castes existed in its original form as a division of classes, consequent on a division of labour. Fight and conquer enemies; acquire booty and make presents out of the booty so acquired. That is the Kshatriya's mode of life. See now the view which Manu places before us. And first, protection of subjects. Compare that with the less specific imperial dignity, or bravery in war of the Gîtâ; it shows an advance on the state of society exhibited in the latter work. And next, sacrifices and study; that again shows a well-settled state of society, and one in which the Kshatriya's

---

* Mr. Thomson (p. 121), thinks that "our poet-philosopher" did not wish the Kshatriya and Vais'ya to be initiated in his doctrines except with great care. I do not think that Gîtâ XVIII. 67, from which Mr. Thomson draws this among other inferences, shows any such disinclination on the part of the author.

duties required him to call in the help of the Brâhmaṇ. In regard to the Vais'ya, there is much less difference between
the two views. The Manu Smṛiti adds sacrifices and study
to the list given by the Gîtâ, and therefore, it is here
open to the last remark made above with regard to the
Kshatriyas. The unfortunate S'ûdra is in precisely the same
position in the Gîtâ and in Manu. But taking the two pictures
thus presented to us, I think there can be little doubt,
that the Gîtâ mirrors a state of society considerably more
ancient than that which Manu presents to our view. There
is nothing in the Gîtâ corresponding to the laudation of the
Brâhmaṇ to be found in Manu I. 93 *et seq.* And perhaps also it
is not quite unworthy of note, that whereas the Gîtâ refers for
the origin of these duties to the Svabhâv,° the constitution or
nature of each class, Manu says it is laid down by divine
authority.

There is another passage in the Gîtâ upon which a question somewhat akin to the one we have now been discussing
may be raised. I refer to Gîtâ Chap. IV. 2-3. Mr. Thomson thinks the passage "curious......as giving to the
Kshatriya caste, the Râjarshis, the honour of its transmis-
sion, (*scil.* of the Yog system,) a sop offered to the offended
lion by the wary Brâhmaṇ." I cannot see what led
Mr. Thomson to propound this view of the passage. But
why, I would fain know, was the "lion" offended? It
will be remembered, that the Kshatriya has already figured
in Mr. Thomson's pages firstly as hankering after the "enjoyment of profitable repose;" and secondly as being compelled
"to join the Brâhmaṇ against the bulk of the populace."† He
now assumes a third character—not quite consistent with either
of the these two—standing forth as the "offended lion." And

° See too Gîtâ IV. 13.
† P. xliv. (Introd.) and p. 67.

all this, be it remembered, just about the period when the Bhagavadgîtâ appeared. I cannot reconcile these various views, nor can I discover the evidence for any one of them. And in this state, therefore, I will leave them. It appears to me, that the Kshatriya receives comparatively high honour in the Gîtâ, not only in the passage under consideration, but also in Gîtâ Chap. IX. 33, in which Mr. Thomson is again pleased to see a "lump of sugar thrust down the Kshatriya's throat."* That this is not so, that our view of these passages is more correct, appears to me to result, in some measure, from the view of caste generally, which, as shown above, is exhibited in the Gîtâ.

There is but one other point upon which we now propose to dwell. And that is that we find one whole stanza common to the Gîtâ and Manu, and several in which the ideas expressed coincide, though there is little or no coincidence of language. The one stanza which we refer to is Manu I. 73, which, with a few variations, is the same as Gîtâ VIII. 17. A comparison of these two stanzas appears to me to corroborate the view which we have taken above of the relative dates of Manu and the Gîtâ. In the first place, where the Gîtâ in the second line of the stanza substantially repeats the expression in the first line viz.: सहस्रयुगपर्यन्त, Manu substitutes for it तावती. Now if our view of repetition of expressions† is correct, this is one ground for putting the Gîtâ before Manu. Secondly, the passage in the Gîtâ does not define the duration of a Yug. The natural construction, therefore, would be that a human Yug was intended. In Manu, however, in the stanza just preceding, the Yugs spoken of are divine Yugs, and they are referred to in the stanza under discus-

* P. 67. The Bráhman, too, has to thank Mr. Thomson for finding "sops" and "lumps of sugar" for him in the Gîtâ, (p. 111.)

† See p. lxi suprâ.

sion by the words वेदे—words which, it is to be noted, are
not in the Gîtâ. Now as Mr. Muir points out, the theory that
the duration of the Yugs stated in Manu and other works is
reckoned not in human but in divine years, is a later re-
finement.° It may therefore, be regarded as a not very
violent assumption, that this difference between Manu and
the Gîtâ is an index of the chronological priority of the
former over the latter. In corroboration of the results drawn
from these arguments, we may also use a comparison of one
other passage of Manu with a corresponding passage in the
Gîtâ. In Gîtâ X. 25 we have the Jap described as the best
of the different forms of "Yajna." A similar opinion is expressed in Manu II. 86, but the distinctions there stated
with regard to this Jap may, I think, be fairly used,
as further showing the priority of the Gîtâ over Manu
There are a few other passages in Manu and the Gîtâ which
exhibit like coincidences. Some of them are noted in the
Notes and Illustrations. But I think it perfectly safe to
contend, upon the strength of the various arguments above
set forth, that the Gîtâ must have preceded the Dharmas'âstra
of Manu by a very considerable period of time.

"And now," to borrow the eloquent language of Professor Tyndall's splendid discourse before the British Association at Belfast, "and now the end is come. With more
time, or greater strength and knowledge, what has been here
said might have been better said, while worthy matters here
omitted might have received fit expression. But there would
have been no material deviation from the views here set
forth." Those views may be thus concisely stated. Dr. Lorinser's theory is utterly untenable, firstly because it is based

---

* Muir S. T. Vol. I. (2nd Ed.) 47 citing Prof. Roth.

on assumptions which have not been, and cannot be, proved. It is untenable secondly, because the coincidences upon which he relies are either really no coincidences at all, or are such as do not warrant the inference drawn from them. It is untenable thirdly, because even if it were otherwise unobjectionable, it would be quite incompetent to account for all the facts of the case. Lastly it is untenable, because it omits to take note of various circumstances which, as we have endeavoured to show above, completely negative it. We have shown that the internal evidence furnished by the Gîtâ would lead to the conclusion that it was composed prior to the Christian Era. We have shown that the evidence available enables us to put it chronologically before Kâlidâs and before the author of the Manu Smṛiti. We have shown that we may even hold provisionally, that it is older than the rise of Buddhism. We further argue that the date which Dr. Lorinser takes from Professor Lassen would, if accepted, lead to ulterior conclusions which must make us fall back upon the position that that date must be rejected. And in considering this point it must never be forgotten, that due allowance of time must be made not merely for the ideas to be borrowed, but for their settling down into the accepted ideas of the Hindu people. A right appreciation of these circumstances will enable us, I think, to see that Dr. Lorinser's theory cannot be correct. I maintain, that the foregoing investigation has shown by negative criticism that the grounds advanced by Dr. Lorinser for his several propositions are quite untenable. And I go further. I claim also to have shown affirmatively, that the Gîtâ belongs to a period when the "Christian influences" of which Dr. Lorinser speaks could not possibly have existed, and *a fortiori* could not have acted upon the Indian mind.

And now, I trust, I may allow myself here one general

remark, suggested not merely by Dr. Lorinser's essay, but by various writings of the most celebrated Sanskrit scholars of Europe. It appears to me that in these days, there has set in a powerful tendency in Europe to set down individual works and classes of works of our ancient Sanskrit Literature to as late a date as possible.° One of the greatest of living European scholars, for instance, has written as follows :—" I should like to see a possibility by which we could explain the addition, not of the Vâlakhilya hymns only, but of other much more modern sounding hymns, at a later time than the period of the Prâtis'âkhya." And once more :—"I say again that I am not free from misgivings on the subject, and my critical conscience would be far better satisfied if we could ascribe the Prâtis'âkhya, and all it pre-supposes to a much later date."† Now this outspoken naïveté is not by any means very common. Nevertheless there can be little doubt, that the above deliverances of Prof. Max Müller put into words a feeling entertained, more or less vaguely, more or less consciously, by the vast majority of European scholars. Yet I submit with all respect, but with very great confidence, that they betray a frame of mind which is the reverse of scientific. Prof. Müller has a right to his " misgivings ;" and not only has he a right to them, he is bound to express them whenever a proper opportunity arises. But what right, it may be asked with all deference to the learned Professor, what right has he to express or to feel " likings" and " satisfaction" regarding one explanation more than another ? Would it not be more correct, would it not be more scientific, to cease craving and hankering after the " possibi-

---

* Cf. Wilson's Essays &c, III. 182-3 and J. B. B. R. A. S. Vol. X. 82.

† Max Müller Translation of the Rigved. I. Introd, pp. xxxix,, xl.

lity" of escaping from a position presented by a " string-
ency of argument" which is " frightening ?" Would it not be
more correct, would it not be more scientific, to loyally accept
such a position, and endeavour to rectify the foregone conclusion with which it stands in irreconciliable conflict ? It
appears to me, I confess, that it is this reserve of "likings"
and "satisfactions" and "foregone conclusions," lying in
the back ground of most of the logical artillery which European scholars have brought to bear upon the chronology of
our ancient Literature, it is this that is temporarily doing
damage to its antiquity. Those foregone conclusions easily
throw these scholars into the frame of mind, in which, to
borrow the terse vigour of Chillingworth's language, "they
dream what they desire and believe their own dreams." And it
is against this frame of mind, and against the often "moist
light" of European Sanskrit scholarship of which it is the
source, that I feel bound to lodge my very humble but very
emphatic protest on the present occasion.

BHAGAVADGÎTÂ.

--◆--

Dhritarâshtra. What did my party and the Pâṇḍavs do,
    Oh Sanjaya! when upon the Holy Field
    Of Kurukshotra, longing for the fight,
    They met together?

Sanjaya.   Seeing then the host
Of Pâṇḍu's sons drawn up in battle array,
The Prince Duryodhan to his teacher went,
And thus began : " Look at this mighty host
Of Pâṇḍu's sons, Preceptor! well arrayed
By thy talented pupil—Drupad's son.
Here are brave men, and archers great, the peers
Of Bhîm and Arjun—he of the great car[*]
Drupad, and Dhṛishṭaketu, that bravo king
Of Kâs'î, Kuntibhoj, and chief of men—
S'aibya—Virât, Subhadrâ's son, the sons
Of Draupadî, Yudhâmanyu the brave,
The valiant Uttamaujas, Sâtyaki,[†]
And Chekitân—all masters of great cars.
Know, next, our own best men, chiefs of my host,
Whom, best of Brâhmans! I shall name, that thou
Mayst know—thyself, and Bhîshma, and Karṇa, and Krip

---

   * I have thus literally rendered the word महारथ here and elsewhere. Its technical meaning is stated in a stanza cited by Malli-
nâth under Raghu IX. 1. एको दशसहस्राणि योधयेद्यस्तु धन्विनाम् | शास्त्र-
शास्त्रप्रवीणश्च स महारथ उच्यते |

   † S'rîdhar Svâmî states that the name युयुधान which occurs in
the original text stands for Sâtyaki.

Victor in battles, As'vatthâmâ too,

Vikarṇa, and Saumadatti, heroes more

In numbers, who have for me laid down their lives,

Adepts at various weapons, all well skilled

In war. By Bhîshma our host defended thus

Is numberless, while theirs guarded by Bhím

Is but a small one. Therefore do ye all,

Standing in your positions as assigned,

Defend Bhîshma only. Then to his delight,

Roaring aloud as with a lion's roar,

His grandsire, oldest of the Kauravs, blew

His conch, heroic. Then were conchs and drums

Cymbals and horns played on at once ; their noise

Was great. Next seated in a mighty car

Drawn by white coursers, Kṛishṇa and Pâṇḍu's son

Their conchs celestial blew. The Lord of minds ◆

Blew the Gigantea,† while the Conqueror

Of wealth ‡ blew the Theodotes, and Bhîm,

The doer of fearful deeds, his mighty conch

The Arundinea. Then too Kuntí's son

Yudhishṭhir blew his Triumphatrix—conch,

---

* This is, of course, a very unsatisfactory rendering for हृषीकेश, as it is not quite literal, and does not *at once* suggest the idea attached to it, हृषीक being, according to Amar, synonymous with विषयान्द्रिय. Under all the circumstances, however, I have thought it sufficiently correct to be adopted for its terseness and suitability to verse. Madhusûdan Sarasvatî renders it by सर्वेन्द्रियप्रवर्तकत्वेनान्तर्यमी.

† This and the following names of the conchs are borrowed from Schlegel. They have been approved of by Prof. Wilson.

‡ Mr. Thomson renders धनंजय by "Despiser of wealth." I have preferred to follow the literal sense which has the sanction of the commentators.

Nakul and Sahadev their conchs then blew—
Dulcisona and Gemmiflorea.

That first of archers—Kâs'ya—Sâtyaki
The unconquered one, and he of the great car
S'ikhaṇḍí, Drupad, Draupadí's sons too,
And Dhrishṭadyumna, Saubhadra of large arms,
Virâṭ, and all their several conchs then blew,
Oh king of the Earth! That great noise rent the hearts
Of all thy party, causing to resound
Both Earth and Heaven. Seeing thy party then
For battle drawn, the clash of arms commenced,
Arjun, whose chariot's standard is the Ape,
Oh king of the Earth! in these words then addressed
The Lord of minds: "Oh undegraded one!
Between the two hosts let my chariot stand,
While I observe those who stand here to fight,
Whom, in the troubles of this field, I must
Do battle with. I would see those who are come
To fight, and do good to the wicked son
Of Dhṛitarâshṭra." "Offspring of Bharat!* then
Addressed by Arjun thus, the Lord of minds,
Stopping that paragon of cars between
The hosts, and face to face with Bhîshma and Droṇ
And all kings of the earth, said "Pṛithâ's son!
See these assembled Kurus." There he saw
Fathers,† grandfathers, and preceptors too,

---

* This expression, or one of its equivalents, occurs several times in
our poem. It refers to Bharat, the son of Dushyanta and S'akuntalâ,
from whom the Pâṇḍavs and Kauravs were said to have descended,
and after whom India is called Bhâratavarsha.

† The original is पितर:, fathers. It must be understood as including those in positions similar to that of a father, e. g. paternal
uncles and so forth. So too of the rest.

Uncles, and brothers, sons and their sons, friends,
And others more in either host. He saw,
And seeing all those kinsmen, overcome
By pity, thus he spoke, dejected : "Krishṇa!
Seeing our own men thus come here to fight,
My limbs droop down; my mouth is quite dried up;
My body trembles; my hair stand on end;
The Gâṇḍîv slides down from my hand; my skin
Intensely burns : I cannot stand ; my mind
Whirls round ; Oh Kes'av! omens bad I see;
Nor do I see in prospect good to come
By slaughtering in the fight my kin. Oh Krishṇa!
I want no kingdom, and no victory,
No comforts. What, Oh Govind! shall we do
With kingdoms, and with pleasures, even with life?
Even those for whom we wish for kingdoms, pleasures,
And comforts, stand for battle here, their lives
And wealth forsaking—teachers, fathers, sons,
Grandfathers, uncles, son's sons, relatives.
Oh slayer of Madhu! I wish not to kill
These, even though they kill me, for the sake
Of rule over all the three worlds, much less then
For this earth. Killing Dhṛitarâshṭra's sons,
What pleasure, Oh Janârdan! shall we feel ?
These felons* killed, but sin shall fall to us.
Therefore, 'tis not becoming that we kill
Our own relations—Dhṛitarâshṭra's sons.
For how, Oh Mâdhav ! shall we ever be
Happy by killing our own kinsmen ? Though

---

* The original is आततायिन: which is thus interpreted अग्निदो गरद.
धीर शस्त्राणिमैनाह: ॥ क्षेत्ररारावहारी च षडेते आततायिन: ॥

With consciences* by avarice defiled,
They do not see the evils that are caused
By the extinction of a family,
Nor see the sin in treachery to friends,
How should not we, Janârdan! who do see
These evils, turn off from such sinful acts?
The eternal rites of families extinct
Are lost on that extinction;† on that loss,
Impiety makes the family‡ its own .
And when impiety triumphs thus, Oh Krishṇa!
Then do the women of the family
Become corrupted; and on their corruption,
Offspring of Vrishṇi! comes mingling of castes.
That intermingling needs must send to Hell
The family and those that ruin it ;
For their ancestors, of their balls of food
And their libations then bereft, fall down. §
The eternal rites of families and castes
Are thus uprooted by such sins of men
Who ruin families, sins from which flow
Caste-interminglings. Oh Janârdan! those
By whom the rites of families are destroyed,‖

---

* Mr. Thomson renders वेन: by 'reason.' I prefer 'conscience' in the present context.

† As there is no one to perform them, women not being authorized to do so—Ânandagiri.

‡ The remaining members of it—Ânandagiri.

§ To Hell, that is to say. The lines following are taken by S'ridhar Srâmî as a resumé of what has gone before, and that seems the best way of construing this passage, which at its close is somewhat involved—perhaps, intentionally.

‖ The commentators take this to mean "those whose rites" &c., which is not inadmissible, but I think the rendering in the text leads more directly to the sense here required.

Are ever doomed, as we have heard, to live
In Hell. Alas! we are seeking to commit
A heinous sin, busying ourselves to kill
Our kinsmen, out of lust of the happiness
Of sovereignty. If Dhritaráshtra's sons,
Weapon in hand, should kill me in this field,
Me weaponless, not making self-defence,
The better for me." Arjun saying so,
Forsaking bow and arrow in the field,
Grieved to the heart, sat down upon his car.

Chapter II.

Sanjaya. To him cast down, by pity thus overcome,
(His eyes all turbid and suffused with tears)
These words spoke Madhu's slayer—" Oh Arjun! whence
Has this taint caught thee in this fearful place*—
This taint, unworthy of the wise, the source
Of infamy, excluding too from Heaven?
Be not effeminate, Oh Prithás' son!
It is not fit for thee, killer of foes!
Do cast off this mean want of heart! Arise!
Arjun. Oh slayer of Madhu! how shall I fight Bhishma
And Droṇ, with arrows in the battle-field,
Oh slayer of foes! both venerable men?
Not killing glorious elders, in this world
'Twould even be better on begged food to live;
But killing them, desirous though of wealth,
Blood-tainted pleasures I shall here enjoy.

---

* Mr. Thomson's rendering of this is not satisfactory to my mind.
I follow the commentators who are supported by the passages cited
in our note to Stanza 97 of the Nitis'ataka (Bombay Series of Sanskrit
Classics).

Which too is better for us we know not[0]—
That we should overthrow them or they us.
Against us stand even Dhṛitarâshṭra's sons,
Whom killing, we do not desire to live.
My mind about my duty quite confused,
My heart, too, by the taint of helplessness[†]
Tarnished, I ask, tell me with certainty,
What's better—thy disciple I—teach me
Who have on thy indulgence cast myself.
Having obtained a prosperous kingdom here
On earth, without a foe, or even the rule
Of Heavenly beings, I see not what will
Dispel the grief my body will dry up."
The Lord of sleep,[‡] destroyer of his foes,
Having so spoken to the Lord of minds,
Sat down in silence, saying then to Krishṇa,
"I will not fight." To him, between the hosts
Disheartened thus, offspring of Bharat! then
The Lord of minds spoke with a little smile.
" Thou grievedst for those for whom no grief should be,
And talkst the words of wisdom ; learned men
Lament not for the living nor the dead.
Never did I not exist, nor thou, nor these
Rulers of men, nor shall we ever cease
To be hereafter. To the embodied soul.[§]

---

* Madhusûdan understands the two alternatives to be " living on begged food " and fighting ; and Ânandagiri agrees with Madhusûdan. S'ridhar takes the alternatives to be those stated in the next line, and this construction I prefer.

† Mr. Thomson's rendering here again is not satisfactory to me. I follow Ânandagiri. Madhusûdan understands कार्पण्य to mean अनात्मविन्न.

‡ Thus the commentators interpret the name गुडाकेश which is applied to Arjun in the original.

§ I have thus rendered the word देही, which means literally " [the soul] which has [*i. e.* animates] a body."

As in this body infancy, and youth,
And old age, so the acquisition too
Of other bodies; a discerning man
Is not deceived by that. Oh Kunti's son!
The contacts of the senses* causing cold,
Heat, pain, and pleasure, do not long endure;
They come and go. Bear them, Oh Bharat's child!
That wise man, Prince of men! whom these harm not,
He to whom pain and pleasure are alike,
That man doth merit immortality.
Existence that which is unreal has none;
That which is real is never non-existent;
Those see the settled truth about them both
Who see the essence real. † That which pervades
All things, know thou, beyond destruction lies,

---

* The commentators, including S'ankar, interpret मात्रा by 'senses.' Mr. Thomson renders it by elements, I know not on what authority. Compare Chap. V. St. 22.

† The unreal, as remarked by the commentators, refers to the heat, cold &c. mentioned in the preceding verses. The real is the soul. The former are really non-existent as they 'come and go'; and only that which is in all time—that which is त्रिकालाबाध्य—really exists. The soul is such; and it cannot be destroyed. The word भूत has much exercised the European translators. Mr. Thomson renders it by end, which he next interprets as equivalent to object. This is scarcely correct. I agree with the commentators. The expressions सिद्धान्त and राद्धान्त may be compared. The meaning of the whole passage is this. Here are two things, the soul, which is indestructible, the feelings of pain &c., which are temporary. The true philosopher knows which of these is the really existent and which the reverse. He knows that soul alone exists, the others being the effects of delusion. The latter therefore ought not to be minded.

None can destroy it,   inexhaustible.
These bodies of the embodied soul eterne,
The indestructible and boundless one,
Are said * to be not lasting ; therefore fight,
Offspring of Bharat ! He who thinks this soul
The killer, and he too who thinks it killed,
Both these know naught; it kills not, is not killed. †
It is not born, it never dies, and never,
Having not been, is it to be again ;
Changeless, eterne, primeval, and unborn, ‡
It is not killed although the body be.
How can the man, Oh Prithâ's son ! who knows
The soul to be unchanging and unborn,
Beyond destruction, inexhaustible,
How and whom can he kill or get destroyed ?
As casting off old clothes, a person takes
Others and new ones, so the embodied soul
Casts off old bodies, goes to others new.
Nor weapons cut it, nor does fire burn,
Waters don't wet it, nor air dry it up ;
Impervious, and incombustible,
Not to be wetted, nor to be dried up,
Changeless, and all-pervading, § stable, firm
Eternal 'tis.   It has been said to be

---

* By those possessed of true discrimination—S'ankar.

† The original of this may be seen also in the Kathopanishad II. 19.

‡ *Ibid* II. 18. The epithets used here are not quite easy to distinguish. The commentators differ among themselves. S'ankar in
one place renders निर्त्य by विपरिणामरहित; in another he says यस्मान्न क्षियते
तस्मान्निर्त्य:.

§ Mr. Thomson renders this by 'capable of going everywhere.'
This is scarcely an accurate rendering of सर्वगत:.

Invisible, incapable of change,
Unthinkable, and therefore knowing it
To be such, 'tis not fit that shouldst thus
Lament it.   But if thou dost think the soul
Always now born now dead, Oh large-armed one!
Still shouldst thou not lament it ; for to one
That's born, death's certain, and to one that's dead,
Birth ; hence for things that one cannot avoid
Thou shouldst not grieve.   Offspring of Bharat! things°
Have sources unperceived, mid-states perceived,
Ends unperceived.   What's there for grief in them?
One sees the soul with wonder; so one speaks
Of it with wonder; and with wonder hears
Another; having heard none knows it still.†
Offspring of Bharat! the embodied soul
Is ever within the body of every one,
All indestructible, hence 'tis not fit
For thee to grieve for any living thing ‡
Seeing thy duty too, thou shouldst not thus
Falter, for to a Kshatriya nothing else
Is better than a righteous fight, Oh   Pârtha!
Happy indeed the warriors who thus
Find battle as an opened door to Heaven §

---

* S'ridhar Svâmî renders भूतानि by शरीराणि. S'ankar explains
it by पूर्वमित्रादिकार्यकारणसंघातात्मकानि, and Madhusûdan by पृथिव्यादिभूतमया-
नि शरीराणि. S'ridhar Svâmî also takes अव्यक्त in the Sânkhya sense
to mean प्रधान.

† Compare Kaṭhopanishad II. 7.

‡ The original here is again भूतानि. S'ankar renders it by भीष्मा-
दीनि and   Madhusûdan by स्थूलानि सुक्ष्माणि च भीष्मादिभावापन्नानि.

§ Compare Bhartṛihari's Nitis'ataka Misc. St. 2 and note on it
(Bomb. Sans Class. Ed.).

Come of itself! But if thou wilt not fight
This righteous battle, thou wilt come by sin,
Abandoning thy duty and thy fame.
Of thy everlasting infamy will tell
All beings too, and infamy to one
Who has been honoured is far worse than death.
Masters of great cars will think that through fear
Thou from the fight desistedst. Thou wilt then fall,
Having by them been highly thought of once,
To littleness.* Thy enemies will talk
Much talk unspeakable, and will cry down
Thy power—than that more galling what can be ?
Killed thou wilt Heaven obtain, and conquering
Thou wilt the earth enjoy. Therefore, arise,
Oh Kunti's son ! resolved upon the fight !
Looking alike on victory and defeat,
On gain and loss, on pleasure and on pain,
Be ready for the fight—so thou wilt not sin.
This doctrine told you is that of the Sânkhya,
That of the Yog now hear ; † and knowing this,
Arjun ! from action's ties thou wilt be freed.
No disappointment here in what's commenced,
No obstacles exist ; from dangers great
A little of this piety protects.

---

* The construction of the original here is not quite clear. Madhusûdan says येषामेव.. ••तं बहुमनो••न एव त्वां महारथाः भयादुपरतं मंस्यन्त
इत्यन्वयः | अतो भूत्वा युद्धादुपरत इति शेषः लाघवं••••यास्यसि...सर्वेषामिति शेषः|
येषामेव त्वं प्राग्बहुमतोभूस्तेषामेव तादृशो भूत्वा लाघवं यास्यसीति वा || S'ankar's and
S'ridhar's interpretations may be seen in their works.

† The commentators interpret सांख्य to mean आत्मतत्त्व, भौगनिरटगुह्य,
and the like. This is not a satisfactory meaning. See *infra* Chap.
V. St. 4. (lines 650 *et seq.*) See too our Introductory Essay.

There's here, Oh Kaurav! but one state of mind,
Which in a resolution fixed consists. *

Endless are those of the inconstant ones,
And many-branched. No resolution fixed
On contemplation can they have whose minds,
They being attached to pleasures and to power,
Are led off by that talk which inculcates
Specific acts for pleasures and for power,
Which promises the fruit of actions done
In former lives—the flowery talk, Oh Pârtha!
Which those unwise ones utter who are charmed
By Vedic words, and say there's nothing else,
Those who are full of wishes, and whose goal
Is Heaven. † 'The Veds do merely concern
The effects of the three qualities; ‡ but thou

---

* S'ankar says येयं सांख्ये बुद्धिरुक्ता योगे च वक्ष्यमाणलक्षणा सा—thus embracing both Sânkhya and Yog in the passage. S'rîdhar says इह ईश्वरा-राधनलक्षणे कर्मयोगे व्यवसायात्मिका परमेश्वरभक्तये ध्रुवं नरिष्यामीति निश्चयात्मिका. Madhusûdan says, इह श्रेयोमार्गे (so says S'ankar too) तमेतमिति वाक्ये वा. See the Notes and Illustrations at the end of this book.

† The effect of adhering resolutely to contemplation is stated in St. 53. The different interpretations of समाधि given by Madhusûdan may be seen in the Notes and Illustrations. 'Flowery' (पुष्पित.) S'rîdhar interprets by भावतो रमणीय which means pleasant only at first sight—on a superficial view—not "pleasant until it falls," as Mr. Thomson erroneously translates it. On 'Vedic words' S'rîdhar says वेदे ये वादा अर्थवादा:. In this the other commentators concur. Heaven is not the highest good being a merely temporary affair, see Chap. VIII. St. 16 and Chap. IX. St. 21 and comp. Bhartrihari Vairâgya-S'ataka St. 3 and note on it (Bomb. Sans. Class.) and also the Vedic text तद्यथेह कर्मजितो लोक: क्षीयते एवमेवामुत्र पुण्यजितो लोक: क्षीयते.

‡ त्रैगुण्य = संसार. S'ankar and Madhusûdan. S'rîdhar त्रिगुणात्मका:

Must be self-ruled, Oh Arjun ! free from them
And from the pairs of opposites,* and rest
Always in courage,† from solicitude
For acquisition and protection free.‡
In all the Veds, a learned Bráhmaṇ finds
As much good as is in a reservoir
Of water, where from all sides waters flow.§
With action is thy sole concern, with fruit
Never at all. Let not thy motive be
The fruit of action.   To inaction, too,
Have no attachment, Conqueror of wealth !
Actions perform, but on devotion resting,
Casting away attachment, on success
And failure equable ; equality

सकामा येभिकारिणसद्रिषया:. निस्त्रैगुण्य they all interpret by निष्काम. On the three Gunas see Notes and Illustrations.

* Heat and cold, pain and pleasure, and so forth, which are so often alluded to in the Gitâ.

† So the commentators except S'ankar who understands by सत्त्व here the quality of that name. He is consistent as निस्त्रैगुण्य is with him only निष्काम. But I prefer to render सत्त्व by धैर्य, as the other commentators do, that being one of the ordinary meanings of the word. I prefer this to Mr. Thomson's meaning also, viz. "eternal truth," as it better suits the context.

‡ योगक्षेम. I adopt the interpretation of the commentators which coincides with the ordinary sense of the expression. Mr. Thomson's rendering agrees in substance, but the sense from which he directly derives it appears to me to be itself probably derived from the one adopted in the text. And see too Mitâkshará on Yâjnavalkya I. 100 where योग is explained to mean acquisition of what one has not ; and क्षेम preservation of what has been acquired.

§ See Notes and Illustrations.

Is called devotion. / Action lower far
Than acquisition of devotion* stands.
In that devotion, Conqueror of wealth !
Seek shelter. Miserable are those to whom
Fruit serves as motive. He who has attained
Devotion, casts off here both merit and sin.†
Therefore work at devotion. That in acts
Is wisdom.‡ / Those wise men who have acquired
Devotion, casting off the fruit of acts,
And from the shackles of repeated births
Released completely, to that seat repair
Where no unhappiness is. / When once thy mind
Has crossed beyond the taint of ignorance,
Then mayst thou be indifferent to all

---

* This is my rendering of बुद्धियोग. बुद्धि S'ankar and S'rîdhar take
to mean समत्वबुद्धि, which may be rendered by 'devotion' as योग is.
S'rîdhar indeed also proposes another interpretation which Madhusûdan accepts, viz. बुद्धि (or आत्मबुद्धि as Madhusûdan has it)
साधनभूतो वा (scil. कर्मयोग:). But if we accept this meaning of बुद्धि
here, we ought I think to accept the same meaning in the next line
बुद्धौ शरणमन्विच्छ ; and then there is not a proper contrast between
that line and the last line of the Stanza—a contrast which is nevertheless obviously intended. I would therefore adhere to S'ankar's
rendering, and as to योग I would take it as the substantive corresponding with the adjectival form युक्त in बुद्धियुक्त. I think this makes
the passage clear enough.

† Merit has for its fruit Heaven, which, as we have seen, is regarded
as not much of a gain. Comp. also S'âriraka Bhâshya (Bibl. Ind. Ed.)
pp. 899, 1080 and elsewhere.

‡ I. e. wisdom consists in indifference to failure or success in what-
over one does. Mr. Thomson's translation is not, I think, correct.

That thou hast heard or wilt hear/ When thy mind,
Confused by what thou hast heard,* will stand firm,
In contemplation steady, then wilt thou
Acquire devotion.

Arjun. What, Oh Kes'av ! are
The marks of one whose mind is firm, and who
In contemplation is assiduous ?
How does one speak who is of steady mind,
How sit, how move ?

Krishna, When one, Oh Pṛithâ's son !
Abandons all the wishes of one's heart,
Pleased in and by oneself, then is one called
A steady-minded person. One whose heart
Is not dejected in calamity,
And who in comforts feels no joy, from whom
Affection fear and wrath have fled, is called
A steady-minded sage. One who without
Attachments anywhere, feels no delight
And no aversion at the various sweets
And bitters† coming has a steady mind.
When as the tortoise draws in all his limbs
From all sides, he off from their objects draws
His senses, then is his a steady mind.
Objects of sense recede, not so the taste
For them, from one who lives in abstinence.
And even the taste recedes when the Supreme
Has once been seen.‡ The senses, Kunti's son !

---

* About the means for the acquisition of desirable things—
S'ankar.

† The original शुभाशुभ is rendered by अनुकूलप्रानिकूल by S'ridhar
and सुखहेतु and दुःखहेतु by Madhusûdan.

‡ This interpretation doubtless makes the construction a very

Boisterous, distract the minds even of the wise
Who try to make a stand, by force. All these
Having restrained, one should devote oneself
To me alone ; for steady is his mind
Who has his senses under his control.
He who over sensuous objects ponders still
Forms an attachment to them ; from this flows
Desire ; and from desire wrath ; from that wrath
Want of discernment; and from this want flows
Confusion of the memory ; and thence
Flows demency ; and from this utter ruin.*
But he who, with his heart in his control,
Senses restrained and from affections free
As well as from aversions, does perceive
Their objects, he tranquillity obtains.
When there's tranquillity, his miseries
Are all destroyed ; for he whose mind's at peace
Is soon possessed of steadiness. Whoe'er
Has no devotion† has no steadiness

---

irregular one. But the meaning is certainly that given in the text
on the authority of the commentators. Mr. Thomson's rendering is
not satisfactory to my mind.

* The first two stages are easily understood. From desire grows
wrath when the desire is baulked of its object. From wrath follows
the state of mind in which one cannot discern right and wrong ; from
that a forgetfulness of what has been learnt before—शास्त्रानायाँत.
देशादितसंस्कार says S'ankar. The rest is again clear enough.

† The original word here is अयुक्त which the commentators render,
I think correctly, by 'one who does not restrain himself.' I have
rendered बुद्धि in the original by 'steadiness' here. The commentators
explain it by आत्मस्वरूपविषया. Substantially, there is not much
difference, for steadiness means steadiness in contemplation of the

And no self-knowledge.* But no peace of mind
Is his, who has no knowledge of himself ;
And whence can one bereft of peace of mind
Find happiness ? The obedience of one's mind
Unto the rambling senses takes away
One's judgment, as the wind carries a boat
Astray upon the waters. ⁄ Therefore he,
Oh large-armed one ! whose senses are restrained,
And from their objects are on every side
Withheld, possesses steadiness of mind.
The man of self-restraint remains awake,
When for all creatures it is night ; and when
All creatures are awake, that is the night
Of the right-seeing sage.† He into whom
All things of sense enter as waters do
The ocean, which still filled still keeps its bounds
Unmoved, obtains tranquillity ; not he
Who wishes for those things of sense.   That man
Who all desires abandons, and remains
Free from affections and from " I " and " mine, " ‡

---

true nature of the soul. My interpretation is based on a reference
to the previous Stanza

* More accurately, according to the commentators, perseverance
in the work of knowing oneself. The text, however, is, I think,
practically right, and अभावयत: Madhusûdan renders by आत्मज्ञान-
मकुर्वन्:.

† As to spiritual pursuits, the run of men can see nothing there,
the whole thing is as dark as night to them ; while in worldly
pursuits they are ever wide awake. With the sage the case stands
exactly the other way.

‡ निर्मम, the second word means indifferent to his possessions and
things.   The first निरहंकार means either free from egotism, or better,
from a mistaken notion of what is the ego ; see Chap. III. St. 27.

Obtains tranquillity. Oh Pṛithâ's son !
This is the state divine;* at this arrived,
One's not deceived, and being in this state
In one's last moments too, one does attain
Assimilation with the Deity.

Chapter III.

Arjun. Janârdan ! if devotion is by thee
To action far superior esteemed,
Then why, Oh Kes'av ! dost thou still direct
Me to this fearful deed ? My mind by words
Ambiguous thou seemest to confound ;
Do tell me now one thing and certain, whence
I may attain salvation

Krishna.   Sinless one !
I have already said, that in this world
There is a two-fold path†—that of the Sânkhya—
Pursuit of knowledge, and that of the Yog—
Pursuit of action. One does not attain
Freedom from action, ceasing to perform
Acts merely, nor does one perfection reach
By mere renunciation.‡ For no one

---

* ब्रह्मह्रणेनावस्थानम् says S'aṅkar.

† निष्ठा S'aṅkar renders by स्थिति, S'rîdhar by मोक्षपरता. The word
in the text would seem to suit both renderings well enough. S'aṅkar
takes पुरा 'already' to mean 'at the beginning of the creation.'
S'rîdhar and Madhusûdan take it to mean in the last chapter
which seems preferable.

‡ नैष्कर्म्यं, which we have translated by freedom from action, S'rîdhar renders by ज्ञान 'knowledge,' and S'aṅkar says निष्क्रियात्मस्वरू-
पेणावस्थानमिति यावत्. Renunciation is what is technically called सन्यास,
which without ज्ञान or knowledge is inefficacious. According to

Even for a moment ever does remain,
But does perform some act; the qualities
Born of his nature* force him (of himself
Not master) to some work. He who restrains
His active senses, yet thinks in his mind,
Maddened, of sensuous objects, he is called
A hypocrite. But he, Oh Arjun ! who,
Having restrained the senses by the mind,†
Without attachment action still pursues
With the active senses, is superior far.‡
Action prescribed perform, for action is
Superior to inaction ; nor by this
Canst thou obtain subsistence for thyself.
This world is fettered by all acts but those
Spiritual.§ In these, Oh Kunti's son !
Do thou engage, attachment casting off.
Having made men, first, with the sacrifice,
Said the creator "Propagate with this ;

S'ankar कर्म or action is necessary as a stepping-stone to नैष्कर्म्यं or
freedom from action.

* The three qualities together constitute the प्रकृति or nature. As
to the power of this प्रकृति here stated, compare Chap. XVIII. 59-60.

† I. e. concentrating them on God, says S'ridhar.

‡ I. e. to the hypocrite says S'ankar. S'ridhar takes it to mean,
"He attains knowledge by means of purity of mind."

§ यज्ञ र्थे. The commentators interpret this expression by the light
of a Vedic text यज्ञो वै विष्णु:. Mr. Thomson renders it by "which has
worship for its object." The यज्ञ spoken of here appears to me to be
that which is spoken of in the next Stanza. The creator having
created men and the sacrifice said that men should perform sacrifice.
Nothing that is done in pursuance of this direction is an obstacle in
the way of salvation.

And may this be the giver of your desires.
Please* you the gods with this, and may those gods
Please you; each other pleasing, you will obtain
The highest happiness. The gods will give,
Pleased with your rites, the enjoyments you desire;
And he's a thief who, not returning them
What they have given, enjoys himself." The good
Who eat the leavings of a sacrifice
Of all sins are absolved. The sinful ones,
However, who for themselves alone prepare
Their food, are caught by sin. From food are born
Creatures; from rain too is the birth of food;
Rain is produced by sacrifice; and this
Is the result of action; action, know,
Has its source in the Veds; the source of these
Is the Indestructible.† Therefore the Veds,

---

* भावयन्त संवर्षयन्त तैर्यतेत्यर्थ: says Madhusúdan. As among the
Greeks, the offerings at the sacrifice were supposed by the Hindus
to be what the gods fed on. Compare Kumár. II. 46 or Mádhav's
S'ankarvijaya I. 34.

† I have followed the commentators here. Mr. Thomson says that
ब्रह्म means Ved "in later Sanskrit but never in our poem." But the
result of not accepting that sense here is that ब्रह्माक्षरसमुद्भवम् is interpreted by Mr. Thomson to mean "The Supreme spirit is co-existent with the indivisible." I know of no authority for taking समुद्भव
to mean co-existent. Besides, in the Fifteenth Chapter to which Mr.
Thomson refers, the word ब्रह्म, as he says himself, does not occur,
but instead of it we have परमात्मा. Again when Mr. Thomson says that
ब्रह्म has not the meaning of Ved in our poem, though he admits that
it has that meaning in what he calls later Sanskrit, I do not know
what ground there is for saying so. True it is, that no other use of it
in this sense occurs in the book. But no more do we see any other

Pervading all, are at the sacrifice, *

At all times. Whoso causes not to revolve

This wheel thus turned, he is of sinful life,

His senses humouring, and all in vain

He lives, Oh Prithâ's son! But† then the man,

Self-satisfied, who with himself alone

And in himself is pleased, has nought to do.

He has no interest in what is done,

Nor in what is not done,‡ nor yet does he

Depend on any creature for his wants.

Therefore § without attachment ever perform

Thy duty, for the man who acts performs

Without attachment, reaches the Supreme: ‖

By acts alone did Janak and the rest

---

example of the sense in which the same word ब्रह्म is used at the beginning of Chapter XIV.

* S'ankar says "Although they are all-pervading as elucidating all matters, they are always at the sacrifice, as the rites of sacrifice are their main subject." S'rîdhar takes सर्वगतं ब्रह्म as different from the ब्रह्म in the line preceding, and equivalent to अक्षर, and then says यज्ञे प्रतिष्ठितं यज्ञोपायभूतेन प्राप्यते · · · · उद्यमस्था सदा लक्ष्मीरिनिवत्. He also gives another meaning मंत्रार्थंवादि: सर्वेषु भूताथीख्यानादिषु गतं स्थिन-मापि वेदाख्यं ब्रह्म सर्वदा यज्ञे तात्पर्येण प्रतिष्ठितमतो यज्ञादि कर्म कर्नंख्यमित्यर्थः. In this Madhusûdan concours, and it is practically the same as S'an-kar's explanation.

† Here, according to S'rîdhar, he states that the man of know-ledge has nothing to do with कर्म or action.

‡ No good or evil accrues to him from anything he does or omits to do—S'ankar.

§ Arjun, says S'rîdhar, is told to perform action, as freedom from it is only for the man of knowledge. To that stage, it is impli-ed, Arjun has not risen.

‖ By means of purity of mind, say the commentators,

Attain perfection. Thou too shouldst perform
Acts, looking to the universal good.
Whatever a great man does, that do the rest,
And men at large follow what he respects
As of authority. I, Prithâ's son!
Have nought to do in any of these three worlds,
Nothing to gain that I have not gained; still
I do engage in action. Should I not
Engage assiduous in action, then
From all sides men would follow in my path,
Oh Prithâ's son! And should I not perform
Acts, ruined then those worlds would be, * and I
Of caste-comminglings should the author be,
And should destroy all people. As the unwise,
Offspring of Bharat! with attachment act,
So should the wise, desiring to advance
The general good, without attachment act.
A wise man, actions with devotion doing,
Should not distract† the ignorant, attached
To action, but should set them to it. One,
By egoism demented, thinks oneself
The doer of those acts which are performed
Throughout by nature's qualities.‡ But he,
Oh large-armed one! who knows the truth about

---

* As the rules of action, by which the world is carried on, would be broken—लोकस्थितिनिमित्तश्च कर्मणोभावात् says S'ankar. धर्मग्लानिर्न नश्येयुः says S'ridhar.

† Literally "shake their convictions" i. e. wean them away from the path of action.

‡ Compare Chapter V. St. 8. 9. The active principle is nature, or प्रकृति, The soul or पुरुष is only the looker-on and the enjoyer.

The difference from qualities and acts, [*]
Forms no attachments, thinks that qualities
Do deal with qualities.† But then those who
By nature's qualities are all confused,
To their works‡ from attachments. Such dull men,
Who know not all, the wise should not distract.
Devoid of hope, devoid of "mine", on me
Throwing all acts,§ the Adhyâtma pondering,‖
Fight, freed from mental anguish. Even those men
Who act on this opinion of mine,
Always with faith, not carping, they are freed
From action. Know, however, that those who carp
At my opinion, and do not act
Upon it, are demented, and confused
In knowledge of all kinds, to all good lost.
After his nature¶ even a wise man acts;
All creatures follow it, what can restraint

---

* The difference of soul from the qualities, and its difference from acts. The words refer to him who believes that he is different from the collection of the qualities, and who believes that he is not the active principle—नाहं गुणात्मकः न मे कर्माणि says S'rîdhar.

† I. e. Qualities (senses) deal with qualities (objects of sense). So the commentators. Mr. Thomson understands it differently.

‡ The workings of the qualities, namely, what are commonly known as man's actions.

§ I. e. Convinced by means of true discrimination that you are doing all for God.

‖ अध्यात्मचेतसा is explained by S'ankar as equivalent to विवेकबुद्ध्या; by S'rîdhar and Madhusûdan as equivalent to अन्तर्यामिमयीनां कर्ता इति दृष्ट्या. It means remembering the real relation of the individual and Supreme Soul.

¶ This is explained to be the पूर्वकृतभर्माधर्मादिसंस्कारो वर्तमानजन्मा दावभिव्यक्तः.—(S'ankar)—the effect of the virtuous and vicious acts done in a previous birth.

Effect? Towards its objects every sense
Has its affections and aversions fixed,
To them none should submit, for they are his foes.°
One's duty ill-performed is better far
Than that of others well performed; † even death
In one's own duty is to be preferred.
Fearful is that of others.

Arjun.   But by whom
Is man driven on to sin against his will,
Offspring of Vṛishṇi! as by force compelled?

Krishna. Desire it is, 'tis wrath, whose birth is from
The quality of Rajas—ravenous he,
And very sinful. Know that in this world
That is the foe.   As smoke envelopes fire,
As soilure does a mirror, as the womb
The fœtus, all this‡ he envelopes so.
Knowledge's enveloped by this constant foe,
Oh Kunti's son! of wise men, who can take
What forms he will, who's like a fire,§ and who

° This, says S'ankar, is in answer to the difficulty that the S'âstras
are useless if nature is so potent as described. The answer is, that nature can only work indirectly by means of those affections and aversions, and if one withstands their force, one is then at liberty to follow
the S'âstras. When they are succumbed to, the force of nature
irresistible.

† This, according to S'ankar, is in answer to one who acts under
the guidance of "affections and aversions," and who might say, that
since all duties are equally prescribed in the S'âstras he might do
whichever he chose.

‡ Explained, according to S'ankar and the other commentators,
by what follows. They understand it to refer to knowledge. Mr.
Thomson understands by 'this' the universe.

§ The commentators take अनल literally, as "that which never
has enough."

Is never filled. The senses, and the mind,
And steady resolution, have been said
To be his seat.° With these, he men confounds,
Covering up knowledge. Therefore first restrain
Thy senses, foremost of the Bhârats! next
This sinful thing do cast off, which destroys
Experience and knowledge.† It is said,
"Great are the senses, greater is the mind,
Greater than that is resolution, that
Which is above this is that same."‡ Thus know
That which than resolution higher is,
And by thyself restrain thyself, and kill
This foe, Oh large-armed one! who can assume
What form he will, and who is hard to tame.

---

* Since the operations of the senses and the rest give rise to desire. The mind is the faculty which thinks, and doubts, and so forth: the 'steady resolution' is the faculty which resolves and finally determines. संकल्पविकल्पात्मकं मन: | निश्चयात्मिका बुद्धि:.

† Knowledge is that learnt from books or teachers. Experience is that which is acquired by personal perception and so forth.

‡ This Stanza is evidently taken from that in the Kaṭhopanishad III. 10. There we have no reference to desire, and this is one of the circumstances which lead me to accept the meaning which the commentators put on स:, namely परमात्मा, in preference to that of Mr. Thomson, namely 'this passion of desire.' According to the meaning of the commentators, Krishna tells Arjun to understand the Supreme Soul who is higher than the principles in which desire is seated, and then with that knowledge to destroy the foe by means of self-restraint.

Chapter IV.

Krishna, This lasting system of devotion, I
Told to the Sun, to Manu he declared,
And Manu to Ikshvâku. Thus by steps
Obtained, this system royal sages knew;
That system, slayer of foes! has now been lost
By lapse of time. I have to-day told thee
That same primeval system, since thou art
My devotee and friend, for 'tis the best
Of mysteries

Arjun.   Later is thy birth, the Sun's
Is prior. How then shall I understand,
That thou didst first tell him ?

Krishna.   / Many have been
Our births, Oh Arjun! thine as well as mine.
I know them all. Not so, Oh slayer of foes!
Knowst thou./Unborn, and inexhaustible,
Lord of all creatures, as I am, I am born
By my delusion, taking the control
Of Nature to myself. ⁰/ I do create
Myself, whenever piety languishes,
And when impiety's rampant. I am born
In every age the sinful to destroy,
To establish piety, to protect the good.
My birth and work divine whoever thus knows

---

* A certain distinction is here drawn between प्रकृति and माया. The
S'vetâs'vataropanishad, however, has a line which runs thus, मायां तु
प्रकृति विद्यान्मायिनं तु महेश्वरम्. But here, माया means more specially
the divine power, knowledge, omnipotence and so forth; प्रकृति
refers to the material which goes to the formation of the body
taken by the Deity when " born."

Rightly, Oh Arjun! casts this body off,
Returns not to be born, but comes to me.
Freed from affection, terror, and from wrath,
By knowledge-penance ° made immaculate,
Thinking of me alone, and on me resting,
Many have come into my essence. † I
Favour men as they come to me; my path
Men follow from all sides, ‡ Oh Pritha's son!
Success in acts desiring, people here
Worship the deities, for in this world
Of mortals, swiftly is success obtained
By action. § I created classes four,
After the apportionment of qualities
And works. ‖ But though I am their maker, know
I am not their maker, ¶ inexhaustible.
Actions defile me not, I have no desire
Of fruit of actions . He who knows me so
Is not tied down by action.$ Knowing this,₩

° ज्ञानमेव तप: सर्वकर्माश्रयहेतुत्वात् says Madhusûdan. S'ridhar takes it to mean knowledge and penance.

† That is, attained salvation, the assimilation with the Brahma.

‡ This line occurs before but in a different sense. See line 439.

§ S'ridhar says न तु ज्ञानफलं कैवल्यं दुष्प्राप्यत्वाद्ब्रह्मणस्य.

‖ See Chapter XVIII. where this is explained at length.

¶ मायासंव्यवहारेण कर्ता परमार्थेनाेकर्ता says S'ankar. The explanation of the paradox seems to be contained in the next Stanza.

$ Since, as S'ridhar says, he who knows that the cause of God's not being affected by acts is his freedom from egoism and desire, will himself get rid of his own egoism &c.

₩ S'ankar says that this means नाहं कर्ता न मे कर्मफले स्पृहेति ज्ञात्वा— which is unexceptionable ; अहंकारादिरहितेन कृतं कर्म बन्धकं न भवतीत्येवं ज्ञात्वा says S'ridhar—which is less unexceptionable. Mr. Thomson

Those men of old who for salvation wished,
Action performed. Therefore do thou perform
Action^o alone, as by the men of old
Was done before thee. Even learned men,
Upon the question what is action, what .
Inaction, are confused. Therefore I will speak
Of action to thee. Knowing that, thou wilt
Be freed from evil. Action one must know,
Action prohibited, inaction too,
Abstruse is action's essence.† He is wise
'Mongst men, he is devoted, he performs
All acts, who in inaction action sees,
And in action inaction. Him the wise
Call learned, all whose action by the fire
Of knowledge is burnt down, whose every act
Is all from fancies and desires divorced.‡
Forsaking all attachment to the fruit
Of action, independent,§ at all times ·

---

takes the sense back as far as Stanza 13, casting a suspicion on the
genuineness of Stanza 14. I do not think his reasons either sound
or adequate.

    *   Not an action, as Mr. Thomson translates it, but action gene-
rally, as contrasted with भक्तर्मं. Comp. Chap. III. St. 20 (line 429).

    † The commentators render गति by तत्त्र, Mr. Thomson translates
it by 'path' but gives no explanation. Action, as the commentators
rightly say, stands here for all three. What the abstruseness is is
stated in the immediately following lines.

    ‡ Fancies are the cause of desires—S'ankar. Compare Chap. II. 62
and VI. 4 and 24. S'ridhar says काम: फले तत्सकल्पेन &c. Madhusûdan agrees with S'ankar, but interprets संकल्प by अहंकरोमीति कर्त्-
त्वाभिमान:.

    § Independent : lit. without support; support S'ankar explains to
mean that thing, resting on which one wishes to accomplish an end.

Contented, even engaged in action, he
Does nothing. All belongings casting off,
Restraining mind and senses,[*] free from hope,
And action merely for the body's sake†
Performing, he comes not by sin.   Content
With earnings not sought after, far above
The pairs of opposites, from envy free,
Unmoved on failure and success, he's not
Tied down, performing actions. All the acts
Of one without attachment, wholly free,‡
Of one whose mind is fixed on knowledge, who
Performs spiritual actions,§ are destroyed.
Brahma is the oblation; with Brahma it is given;
Brahma is in the fire; and by Brahma it is thrown;
And Brahma too the goal, to which he goes,
Who meditates on Brahma in the act. ‖

---

* आत्मा must here be rendered by 'senses'; Madhusûdan says बुद्धी-न्द्रियसहितो देह:.

† Madhusûdan takes शारीर to mean शरीरस्थितिनिमात्रप्रयोजन. He and S'ankar have a long discussion as to whether it does not mean शारीरनिर्धि and decide against it. S'ridhar, however, adopts this interpretation, which would seem to be preferable, having regard to the next Stanza. See also Chap. III. 7 and 8 (line 383 *et seq*).

‡ S'ankar renders the original मुक्त by निवृत्तधर्मादिवन्धन, S'ridhar says रागादिभिमुर्क्त, and Madhusûdan has कर्तृत्वभोक्तृत्वाद्यभिमानशन्य. Mr. Thomson's suggested emendation to युक्त is a very good one.

. § Comp. Chap. III. 9. Here S'ankar renders यज्ञाय by यज्ञनिवृत्त्यर्थम्.

‖ This identification of every thing with Brahma, furnishes according to S'ankar, the explanation of the 'destruction of acts' mentioned just before.   'With Brahma' means with the Juhû and other sacrificial implements.   The last line is thus explained by S'ridhar ब्रझण्येव कर्मात्मके समाधिधिर्नैकात्यं यस्य.

Some devotees the sacrifice divine *
Practise, and others in the fire of Brahma
The sacrifice offer up by itself. †
The sense of hearing and the rest some throw
Upon the fires of self restraint. ‡ And some
Again upon the sense-fires offer up
Their objects—sound and others. Others still
Offer up the functions of the internal winds,
As well as of the senses, in the fire
Of self-restraint by knowledge kindled up. §
Others there are whose offering is wealth,
Penance, devotion,‖ study of the Veds,
Or knowledge; others still of rigid vows—
The Yatis.¶ Some offer the upward wind
Into the downward, and the downward one
Into the upward, and restraining next
The motions of them both, are still engaged

---

* *I. e.* that in which the Gods are sacrificed to.

† S'ankar takes यज्ञ or sacrifice to mean आत्मा. S'ridhar says यज्ञेन ......ब्रह्मार्पणमित्याद्युक्तप्रकारेण यज्ञमृजुह्वति यज्ञादिसर्वंकर्माणि प्रविलापयन्तीत्यर्थः;, which is more satisfactory.

‡ *I. e.* practice restraint of the operations of the senses. These, according to S'ridhar, are नैष्ठिका ब्रह्मचारिण:. Those described in the words immediately following are correctly said by him to be those who are विषयभोगसमवेदनासक्ता:.

§ That is to say, says S'ridhar, concentrating the mind properly on the thing to be meditated on, and confining the mind to it, they stop all the workings of the senses &c.

‖ This is here taken in the sense of Patanjali (not that of the Gîtâ). viz. चित्तवृत्तिनिरोध 'concentration of mind.'

¶ This is taken as a separate class by Madhusûdan. He says व्रतयज्ञा इत्यर्थः. And see line 862.

In stopping up the lifewinds.ᵒ Others yet,
Eating but little, offer up the winds'
Into the winds.† Knowing the sacrifice,
All these have their sins by the sacrifice
Destroyed. Those go unto the eternal Brahma,
Who eat the leavings of the sacrifice,
Ambrosial.‡ Best of Kurus! not this world
Is theirs, who do no sacrifice perform;
Whence then the other? Thus out of the Veds,
Come sacrifices of these various sorts;§
From action‖ know them all to be produced,
And knowing thus, thou wilt salvation reach.
The sacrifice of knowledge, slayer of foes!
Is better than the sacrifice of wealth;
For each and every action, Pritha's son!
In knowledge ends. By salutation that,
By service, and by questions, learn. The wise
Who see the truth will knowledge teach to you.
That learning, Pandu's son! thou wilt not be

---

* These are the ascetic practices prescribed in the Yogas'ástra; the operations are technically known as Pûrak, Rechak and Kumbhak.

† S'ankar says यस्य यस्य वाधीर्जेयः क्रियंते इतरान्वायुभेदास्तस्मिञ्जुह्वति ने तज्ञ प्रविश्ट इव भवन्ति. S'ridhar takes प्राणान् to mean 'senses.' With this Madhusûdan agrees and cites Patanjali.

‡ Compare Chap. III. St. 13 (line 407).

§ The commentators say, that this means "They are all ordained by the Veds," and S'ankar quotes a passage as an instance. Mr. Thomson renders the words otherwise, but I do not know that there is much propriety in the sense he adopts.

‖ That is to say, according to the commentators, they are not the soul's doing. They are, says S'ridhar, यज्ञ:कायननिनाः, but आत्मसद्वसंसर्गौरहिता:.

Again confounded thus, and through it thou,
Without exception, wilt all creatures, see
First in thyself, and next in me.*, And then,
Even if thou art of all sinful men
Most sinful, still wilt thou cross over all sins,
By means of the boat of knowledge. As a fire
Kindled, Oh Arjun! burns all fuel down
To ashes, so the fire of knowledge burns
All action down to ashes. † Nothing is
Like knowledge pure; and that one in oneself,
Perfected by devotion, finds in time.
One who restrains his senses, who has faith,
And is assiduous, knowledge obtains;
Obtaining knowledge, then without delay,
Reaches supreme tranquillity. But one
Who has no faith, no knowledge, who's in doubt ‡
Is ruined. Neither this world, nor the next,
Nor happiness, are for the sceptic. Acts,
Oh Conqueror of wealth! shackle not him,
Who by devotion has all acts renounced,
Who has destroyed by knowledge all his doubts,
And who's himself. § Therefore, Oh Bharat's child!
Destroy this doubt, produced from ignorance,
And in thy heart residing, by the sword
Of knowledge. Have devotion, and arise!

---

* *I. e.* you will perceive the unity of myself and yourself and all
the world—that is to say, got rid of dualism.

† Compare Chap. IV. St. 19 (line 557).

‡ He who has no faith—*scil.* in what the preceptor teaches. He
who is in doubt, *scil.* as to whether his endeavours will be successful
or not—S'ridhar.

§ आत्मवन्तम्, the original, is explained to mean प्रयत्नम् in the commentaries. Compare too Chap. II. 13.

Chapter V.

Arjun. Renunciation of acts thou dost praise,
Oh Krishna! and also their pursuit,* tell me
For certain, which is better of the two.
Krishna. Renunciation and pursuit of acts
Are sources both of happiness; of them,
However, pursuit of acts is more esteemed
Than their renunciation.† He who's free
From likes and dislikes should be known to be
The true renouncer; for, Oh large-armed one!
He who's above the pairs of opposites,
Is freed with ease from bonds. 'Tis children talk
Of Sânkhya and Yog as different, not the wise;
Pursuing either well, one gets the fruit
Of both. ‡ The Yogs go to the selfsame seat,
Which by the Sânkhyas is obtained. He sees
In truth, who sees the Sânkhya and Yog as one.
'Tis hard, without devotion, large-armed one!
To reach renunciation; but the sage
Having devotion soon the Brahma attains.
Devoted, pure, one who restrains his mind,
Who rules his senses, and identifies
Himself with each and every creature, he,
Performing action, is untainted still.

---

* S'ankar renders कर्मयोग by तेषाम् (*scil.* कर्मणाम्) अनुष्ठानम्. It may also be devotion by means of them. In substance the two meanings coincide.

† Compare Chap. XVIII. 2 *et seq.*

‡ As S'ridhar says, by the Karmayog, one obtains purity of mind, and, by means of that, obtains salvation through right knowledge. By the Samnyâs, he also obtains the same indirect effects of the Karmayog practised before. This is stated in the next Stanza.

He thinks, who hath devotion, knowledge real,
That he, does nothing, when he sees, hears, sleeps,
Touches, smells, moves, eats, breathes, talks, takes, or gives,
Raises or drops the eyelids, but believes
The senses with their objects deal. ° He who performs
Action, and offers it to the Supreme, †
Without attachment, is not touched by sin,
Like to the lotus-leaf by water. ‡ Men
Who are devoted, from attachment free,
Action perform for purity of soul,
With the mere body, mind, or resolution,
Or even the senses. § The devoted man,
Abandoning the fruit of acts, obtains
Lasting tranquillity. ‖ He who's attached
To fruit, without devotion, is chained down
By action. The embodied soul at ease
Within the city of nine portals ¶ lies,
Not doing nor causing, ⁋ self-controlled, all acts
Forsaking by the mind.§ 'Tis not the Lord
Actions or agency creates 'mongst men,

* Compare Chap. III. St. 28 (line 455). Our rendering of which is supported by this passage.

† Compare Chap. III. St. 30 (line 461).

‡ A very common simile in our ancient literature.

§ With the body, bathing and so forth; with the mind, meditation and so forth; with the faculty of resolution, the ascertainment of the truth; with the senses, the hearing and celebrating of God's name and so forth—S'rídhar.

‖ Compare Chap. II. 70-71 (line 357 et seq).

¶ नेत्रे नासिके कर्णौ मुखं चेति सप्त शिरोगतानि भगोगते द्वे पायूपस्थएते.

⁋ I. e. not causing anything to be done.

$ Compare III. St. 30. Here S'ankar takes मनसा to mean अध्यात्म चेतसा, which he interprets there to mean विवेकबुद्ध्या.

Nor yet does he connect action and fruit,
But Nature only works.* The Lord receives
The sin or merit of none. † Knowledge is hid
By ignorance, thence do all beings err.
Knowledge, however, to those who have destroyed
By it their ignorance, shows like the sun
The Being Supreme. And those who in their minds
Have Him alone, whose soul is one with Him,
Who firmly rest on Him, whose final goal
Is He, they go—go never to return—
Their sins destroyed by knowledge. On a cow,
An elephant, a dog, a Chândâl too,
And on a Brâhman of humility
And learning wise men look alike.‡ Even here
They have conquered the material world, § whose mind
Is equable. They are with the Supreme;
For the Supreme is equable, above
Defects. He who has knowledge of the Brahma,
Whose mind is steady, who is not confused,

---

* S'ridhar and Madhusûdan say that this is an answer to
the difficulty.—How can man get rid of acts, when he is
but a dependent agent in God's hands? स्वभाव, the word used in the
original text, and translated by 'Nature,' is rendered by प्रकृति, in
S'ankar's commentary.

† S'ankar renders प्रभु by ईश्वर. Madhusûdan says प्रभुरात्मा स्वामी.

‡ According to S'ankar and Madhusûdan, the Brâhman has the quality of Sattva or Goodness, the cow that of Rajas or Indifference, and
the elephant and the rest that of Tamas or Badness. S'ridhar says,
the Brâhman and the Chândâl are instances of a difference as to
acts ; the elephant &c. of difference as to class.

§ सर्ग, the original word, is paraphrased by जन्म 'birth' in S'ankar's
commentary, and by संसार in S'ridhar's.

And who is with the Brahma,[*] does not feel
Delighted, finding pleasures, nor is grieved
Coming by ills. One who to external things
Is unaddicted, feels the happiness
That's in oneself; and by devotion joining
His own soul with the Brahma, he obtains
Eternal happiness.† Oh Kuntis' son !
Enjoyments which out of the touch arise
Of the senses‡ are a certain source of ills.
They do begin and end ;§ a prudent man
No pleasure in them feels. He who can bear,
Even here, ere he is from this body freed,
The agitations which desire and wrath
Produce, he is devoted, happy he.
He who within himself feels happiness
And pleasure, and the light of knowledge finds,
That devotee, one with the soul Supreme,
Attains the Brahmic bliss. The sages, too,
Whose sins have perished, and whose doubts destroyed,
Who do restrain themselves, who are intent
On universal happiness, obtain
The Brahmic bliss. To those ascetics, who
Restrain their minds, and keep themselves aloof
From anger and desire, who know the soul,
At hand‖ is the Brahmic bliss. He who excludes

---

* *I. e.* who has renounced all acts—S'ankar.

 † This follows the commentators, and that is the best sense to be got out of the passage as it stands. Mr. Thomson mentions an emendation, which, if adopted, would make it much clearer.

 ‡ The original is simply "from the touch." It means from the touch of the senses and their objects. Compare Chap. II. St. 14.

 § Compare 'they come and go' in Chap. II. St. 14 (line 170).

 ‖ The commentators say 'on both sides'—before and after death. At hand is also admissible, I think.

The objects of the senses, 'twixt the brows
Centres his vision,* making the upward wind
And downward even, does within the nose
Confine their movements, who restrains his mind,
His senses, and his faculty as well
Of fixed resolve,† the sage whose final goal
Is mere salvation, who is free from fear
Desire and anger, he is ever saved.
One knowing me attains tranquillity,
Me—the great God of all the worlds, the friend
Of all things living, me who do enjoy‡
All sacrifices and all penances.

Chapter VI.

Krishna. He who, regardless of the fruit of acts,
Performs his duty is the devotee,
He the renouncer, not he who discards
The sacred fire, nor who no acts performs.
That which is called renunciation, know,
Oh Pându's son! to be devotion, since
None can become a devotee, unless
All fancies § he renounces. Action's said

---

* The power of seeing; the original is चक्षु: which must be thus interpreted here. Compare Chap. VIII. St. 10. (line 1037). Mr. Thomson says 'confines his gaze to the space between the eyebrows'. But how can that be done?

† The same word which has been rendered before by 'resolution' or 'steady resolution.'

‡ S'rîdhar suggests an alternative rendering 'protect,' which is also admissible.

§ These, as said before, give rise to desires; see Chap. IV. St. 19 (line 558) and note there.

To be a means to that wise man who wants
To rise up to devotion ; and to him,
When that is reached, tranquillity is said
To be a means. Then is one said to have reached
Devotion, when all fancies casting off,
One ceases to attach oneself to things—
The objects of the senses—or to acts.
One should raise oneself by one's mind, nor cast
Oneself down,* for one's friend as well as foe
Is one's mind only. To him who has restrained
Himself † even by his own mind, is his mind
Friendly ; but then to one without restraint,
One's own mind like an enemy behaves,
Injurious He who has restrained himself,
And who is tranquil, has a soul intent
Wholly upon itself, ‡ in cold and heat,
In honour and dishonour, pain and joy.
He who restrains his senses, satisfied
With knowledge and experience, § who unmoved
By aught, looks on gold, sod, and stone alike,
Is called a devotee. He's most esteemed,
Who thinks alike of good and sinful men,

---

* The words for self and for mind in this and following lines are
the same. But the meaning is to be distinguished as above. ' Raise'
scil. out of this mortal world. ' Mind' means according to Madhusûdan ' discrimination.' ' Cast down,' Madhusûdan renders by
' Merge in the ocean of this world.'

† Here आत्मा or self must mean, I think, the ' senses &c.' as in St.
10 (line 770).

‡ समाहित: is rendered by आत्मनिष्ठ: in S'rídhar's, by साक्षात्कर्ममात्रेन
वर्तेने in S'ankar's, Commentary.

§ See above Chap. III. St. 41 (line 495).

Of friends, acquaintances, and enemies,
Of the indifferent, those that side with both,
Of relatives, and those that merit hate.
Devoid of hopes, restraining mind and sense,
Alone, without belongings,° and retired,
Seating himself with firmness in a place,
Tidy, and not too high nor yet too low,
With cloth and skin and Kus'-grass covered over,
A devotee should in devotion still
Engage. There, fixing on one point his mind,
The workings of the senses and his thoughts
Restraining, sitting in his seat, he should
Practise devotion for self-purity.
Firm-seated, holding body neck and head
Unmoved and even, looking at the tip
Of his own nose, not looking round about,
Tranquil at heart, devoid of fear, the vows
Of celibates † observing, and his mind
Restraining and concentering on me, he
Should sit devoted, given up to me.‡
Thus practising devotion, and his mind
Restraining constantly, a devotee
Arrives at that tranquillity which leads
At length unto salvation, and attains

---

* Compare Chapter IV. 21. आत्मा (sense) = देह —Commentators.

† The original is ब्रह्मचारी, which may be conveniently rendered by celibates. It is the stage before a man becomes a Grihastha, or married householder, and in which he lives with his preceptor to learn with him.

‡ As distinguished from 'with mind concentrated on me,' 'given up to me' must be taken, as it is by S'ridhar, to mean 'to whom I am the final goal.'

Assimilation with me. Neither he,
Oh Arjun! who eats too much, nor yet who
Eats not at all, not he who is disposed
To too much sleep, nor he who's ever awake,
Attains devotion. He who takes due food
And exercise, at work toils duly, sleeps
And rises duly, the devotion gets
Destructive of all misery. When the mind
Restrained, is steadied on the Soul alone,
Then he who is indifferent to all
Objects of longing is " devoted" called.
As standing in a windless place, a light
Moves not, that is the parallel employed
About a devotee, who has restrained
His mind, and in devotion ✿ is engaged.
That break of all connexion with all pain
Is called devotion, one should understand,
Wherein the mind ceases to work, restrained
By practice of devotion ;† where one sees

✿ The original word here rendered by "devotion" is still 'योग' but with the addition of आत्मनः. The same remark is to be made on Stanzas 10 and 15 and 28 (lines 774-786-833). What is meant here is concentration of mind.

† Mr. Thomson renders योगसेवा, the original expression, by "worship in devotion." That is certainly wrong. This definition of 'devotion' sins against one of the logical rules of definition, by including the word योग itself in a definition of योग; but this is only apparent, I think. The word योग defined means, I think, the union of the individual with the Supreme Soul—परमात्मनि क्षेत्रज्ञस्य योजनं योगः, as Srídhar says. The other word devotion, that to which this note is attached, means the stopping of all workings of the mind—the चित्तवृत्तिनिरोध which Patanjali speaks of.

Oneself by oneself, * and is satisfied
Within oneself; where one attains that joy,
Transcendent, knowable by the mind alone,
Beyond the senses; which attained, one never
Swerves from the truth; and which acquired, one thinks
No other acquisition higher still;
Fixed in which, one cannot be shaken off
Even by the greatest misery. With fixed mind,
And undespairing heart,† should be attained
This same devotion. Casting off desires,
Without exception, of the fancy born,‡
Restraining all the senses on all sides
With the mind only,§ one should by slow steps
Become unmoving,‖ with a firm resolve
Coupled with courage,¶ and upon the soul
Steadying the mind, should think of nought. Wherever
The active and unsteady mind breaks forth,
There should it be restrained, and held confined
Upon the soul alone. Then happiness
Supreme comes to this devotee, whose mind
Is fully tranquil, who is free from sin,
Who his Indifference$ has tranquilized,

---

* आत्मना समाधियरिशुद्धेनान्त:करणेन आत्मानं परचैतन्यम्—S'ankar.

† Mr. Thomson's translation here, which follows Schlegel's, is not at all satisfactory to my mind. The explanation given by the commentators is not only admissible, but makes perfectly clear and good sense.

‡ See above St. 4 (line 749).

§ Compare Chap. III. St. 7. (line 390).

‖ Comp. St. 20 (line 808).

¶ धैर्येण युक्तया is S'ankar's paraphrase of the original. This, to a certain extent, explains St. 23 (line 818).

$ The Second of the three qualities about which see Notes and Illustrations.

And merged himself into the soul Supreme.

Thus practising devotion constantly,

The devotee, free from all sin, obtains

With ease the highest happiness, the touch*

Of the Supreme.   And the devoted man,

Regarding all alike, sees in the soul

All beings, and in all beings sees the soul. †

He who sees me in every thing, as well

As all things in me, him I never forsake,

And he forsakes me not.‡/ That devotee,

Who worships me existing in all beings,

Convinced that all is one, exists in me,

However living. §   Arjun ! he is thought

The greatest devotee, who looks on all

Pleasure and pain alike, comparing all

With his own‖

Arjun.   Slayer of Madhu! I see not

How this devotion (which thou hast declared)

Through equanimity, can be sustained

Firmly, because of fickleness ;¶ for, Krishṇa!

The mind is fickle, turbulent, and strong,

And obstinate; and its restraint, I think,

Is difficult as the wind's.

Krishna.   Oh large-armed one !

Doubtless the mind is difficult to restrain,

---

* Comp. Chap. V. 7 (line 659) and other passages.

† S'ridhar says this means साक्षात्कार. Ânandagiri takes it to mean तादात्म्य, which would appear to be the closer interpretation.

‡ *I. e.* He always sees me, and I always look favourably on him.

§ Even abandoning all action, says S'ridhar.

‖ *I. e.* Who believes that pleasure and pain are liked and disliked by others as they are by himself.

¶ *I. e.* the fickleness of the mind as shown in the next line.

And fickle too; but then, Oh Kunti's son !
It may by practice and by unconcern,°
Be still restrained. Devotion, I conceive,
Is hard for one devoid of self-restraint ;
But for one, who restrains himself, and makes
Efforts, 'tis possible to achieve by means
Of measures apt

Arjun.   Oh Krishna what's the end
Of one, who's not a Yati,† who has faith,
Whose mind is from devotion shaken, and who
Has not attained it fully ?   Does he go
To ruin like a broken cloud, being lost
To both, deluded, on the Brahmic path‡
Unsteady, large- armed one ! Krishna, be pleased
This doubt of mine entirely to remove,
For none except thee can remove the doubt.

Krishna. Nor here, nor in the next world, Pritha's son !
Is ruin for him, for none, dear friend ! who does
Good deeds, comes to an evil end.   A man
Fallen from devotion goes into the world
Of Holy Beings, dwells there many a year,
And then is born into a family
Of great and holy men ; or even he's born
Into a family of devotees
Of talent ; for more difficult to obtain
Is such a birth in this world.   Then he comes

° वैराग्य means indifference to worldly good.

† शिथिलप्रयास: says S'rídhar—one who does not keep up his exercise of devotion. य.तं is interpreted to mean one who is assiduous. See too line 590.

‡ 'Both' refers to Heaven the fruit of action, and emancipation the fruit of devotion. 'The Brahmic path' is the path which leads to the Brahma.

In contact with that knowledge which belonged
To him the previous birth,* and then again
Offspring of Kuru! for perfection works.
For even reluctant,† he is led away
By that same former practice, and transcends
The word divine,‡ although he only wish
. To learn devotion.   Devotees, however,
Who work with might and main,§ whose sins are cleared,
Reaching perfection after many births,
Attain the goal supreme.   The devotee
To the ascetic is superior deemed,
Superior to the man of knowledge‖ too,
Superior to the doer of mere acts,
Therefore, do thou become a devotee,
Oh Arjun! And among all devotees,
He is by me the most devoted deemed,
Who, with his inmost soul upon me fixed,
And being full of faith, doth worship me.

---

* The knowledge about the Brahma.

† So S'rídhar interprets अवशः. He says कुनश्चिद्न्तरायादनिच्छन्नपि.
This meaning may be derived from its original meaning ' not
master of oneself.' Comp. Chap. III. 5 (line 384).

‡ He rises above the fruits of the actions prescribed in the Veds—
S'ankar and S'rídhar. He becomes fit for the Juán stage and rises
above the Karma stage—Madhusúdan.

§ As contrasted with the other who might be said to work half-
heartedly. S'ankar renders the original here thus :—प्रयत्नाद्यप्ययनमानार्-
भिकतरं यनमान इत्यर्थ: (?).

‖ According to the commentators one who is learned in the S'ás-
tras and their meanings.

Chapter VII.

Krishna.   And listen now, Oh son of Prithâ! how,§
With thy mind fixed upon me, and on me
Resting, and practising devotion, thou
Mayst without doubt fully know me. I will speak
To thee of knowledge and experience* too,
Exhaustively.' That known, nothing remains
For thee to know. Thousands of men among,
'Tis only some that for perfection work.
And even 'mongst those that do work for and reach
Perfection, some alone do truly know me.
Earth, water, fire, air, space, mind, fixed resolve,
And egoism, my Nature's thus eight-fold
Divided.† This a lower form; but know
Another and a higher Nature, which
Oh large-armed one! is animate,‡ and holds
This world. Know that these§ are the womb of all
Existences· I am as well the source.

---

* Compare Chap. III. St. 41 (line 495) and VI. 8 (line 765).

† Compare Chap. XIII. St. 5 (line 1663). For 'my nature' comp. Chap. IV. St. 6. This is in accordance with the Sânkhya Philosophy. Chap. I. Sûtra 61 of the current Sânkhya Aphorisms says in one part पृथिव्यापस्तेजोवायुराकाशमनोबुद्धिरहङ्कार-श्चेत्यष्टधा, where प्रकृति is identical with शक्ति in the text; the Tanmâtras are subtle rudiments of the earth and so forth in our text; and the first of the अष्टधाप्रकृति is the ' mind ' in the Gitâ.

‡ जीवभूताम्, say the commentators, the power which sustains the material world.

§ The commentators take 'एते' to refer to both the forms of Nature mentioned. Mr. Thomson takes it to refer only to the latter. I prefer the rendering of the commentators, as being supported by Chap. XIII. 26 (line 1733).

As the destroyer of the Universe.

7 Oh Conqueror of wealth! nothing exists
Besides, superior to me. In me all
Is woven as pearls in numbers on a thread.

8 I am the taste* in water, Kunti's son!
I am the light in both the sun and moon;
I am the "Om" in all the Veds; I am sound
In space; and manliness in human beings;

9 I am the fragrance in the earth; I am
Refulgence in the fire; vitality
In every creature; I am austerity †

10 In the ascetic, and Oh Pṛithâ's son!
Know me of all existences the seed
Eternal. I am the intellect of those
Of intellect; the glory I of those

11 Glorious; ‡ and of the strong the strength untouched
By fondness or desire; § love too I am,
Prince of the Bhârats! in all living beings,

12 To piety unopposed.‖ All states of mind,
Or by the quality of Goodness caused,
Or of Indifference or Badness, know

---

* रस: पुण्यो मनुरस्नन्मावह्दः सशीसामपां सारः कारणभूनों योप्सु सर्वरवनुगन: Madhusûdan. रसन्नमात्रवह्रया निभर्त्त आश्रयत्वेनात्सु स्थितः S'ridhar. So with the rest also.

† *I. e.* the power to bear the 'pairs of opposites'—S'ridhar and Madhusûdan.

‡ प्रागल्प is the synonym for तेजस् given by the commentators. Madhusûdan adds परामिभवसामर्थ्यं परेधानमिभास्यत्वम्

§ Desire is the wish to obtain what has not been obtained. Fondness is the wish to retain what has been obtained.

‖ Mr. Thomson, who speakes of the 'egregious error' of his predecessors, has not rendered this expression accurately in translating it by "which is prevented by no law."

To be from me alone ; not I in them*
But they in me exist. This universe
By these three states, (born of the qualities),†
Deluded, knows not me, greater than they,
And inexhaustible. Because divine
Is this delusion of mine, the result
Of the qualities, and difficult to transcend,
Therefore those only this delusion cross,
Who rest on me alone. Not those bad men,
Sinful and foolish, to the ways inclined
Of demons, who through this delusion are
Deprived of their discernment, ever do rest
On me.   Oh Arjun! men of classes four,
Doers of good, it is, that worship me—
He that's distressed, and he too who desires
Knowledge, Prince of the Bhárats! he who wants
Wealth, and he who has knowledge.‡   And of these,
The man of knowledge, who's devoted still,
Who worships me alone, the highest stance.
For to the man of knowledge, I am dear
Above all things, and he is also dear
To me. Good are they all, but I regard
As my own self the man of knowledge, who
With soul devoted me alone accepts—
Me the goal unexcelled.   After the close
Of many lives, the man of knowledge, knowing

* They do not dominate over me, but I dominate over them.
† गुणमये:, the original, is rendered by गुणविकारि:. वदयें: (S'ankar.) and भावे: स्वभावै: (S'ridhar.)
‡ Here the commentators interpret ज्ञानी as meaning ' one who has knowledge of the soul' not as in Chap. VI. St. 46. (line 891).

That Vâsudev is all, looks up to me.°

Such a high-minded man is hard to find.

Those who of their discernment are deprived

By various desires, to other Gods

Look up, performing various rites, controlled

By their own nature.† Whosoever desires

With faith to worship, as a devotee,

Any one form, ‡ his faith to that alone

I render firm.   With that faith furnished, he

That form seeks to propitiate, and thence

The pleasant things he wants receives, yet sent

By me alone.   But that fruit, thus obtained

By these men, undiscerning, perishes.

Those who the Deities worship go to them,§

My worshippers to me. / The ignorant

Think me unseen possessed of form, not knowing

My inexhaustible, high, unexcelled

Essence. ‖ / 'Tis not to all I am known, concealed

---

* प्रपद्यते is explained to mean भजति by S'ridhar and Madhusûdan; प्रतिपद्यते by S'ankar. And see XV. 4 (line 1860).

† 'Rites'—literally 'regulations'—S'ridhar instances fasts and so forth. 'Nature' is here again explained to mean the ज·मान्तरार्जितसं-स्कारविशेष, or as S'ridhar puts it, पूर्वाभ्यासवासना.

‡ *Scil.* of the Divinity.

§ And the Deities are not eternal, but as S'ridhar says अन्तवन्त:. Therefore the fruit these worshippers obtain is but ephemeral.

‖ भाव is interpreted to mean स्वरूप by the commentators. Mr. Thomson observes on this passage, that ' our philosopher would seem to be cutting his own throat on this ground,' but I am not sure that that is so. The true meaning seems to be, that the ignorant think the Divine essence of Vishnu to be no higher than is manifest in the human incarnation, and that gives them no idea of the purity and eternity of the happiness to be enjoyed by propitiation

By the delusion of my mystic power.*
This world, deluded, knows not me unborn
And inexhaustible. Oh Arjun! I
Know things that have been, things that are, and things
That shall be; me, however, nobody knows.
Oh Bharat's child! killer of enemies!
All creatures, when created, are confused
Through the delusion, by the pairs produced
Of opposites, arising out of likes
And dislikes./ Men of meritorious acts,
Whose sins have reached their close, firm in their vows,†
Worship me, freed from the delusion caused
By these pairs. Those who for release from death
And old age‡ strive, resting on me, know well
The Brahma, the Adhyâtma, and all acts.
And those who know me with the Adhibhût,
And with the Adhidaiv, the Adhiyajna—

---

of Vishnu. This, says Krishna, is wrong. Men ought not to confine
their view to the human form, which, for a special purpose, I have
assumed, but look to my real essence, which is far higher, and
judge from that. Compare Chap. IX. St. 11. (line 1136).

* Compare Kaṭhopanishad III. 12. S'ankar thus explains
योगमाया. योगो गुणानां युक्तिपटनं सैव माया योगमाया; S'ridhar says योगो युक्तिमि-
दीय: कोप्यचिन्त्य: प्रज्ञाविलास: स एव माया; Madhusûdan says योगो मम सं-
कल्पस्तद्द्रावनिनी माया. I follow S'ridhar as being supported by Chap.
IX. St. 5. (line 1114) "My mystic power creates a veil around me
which not every one can pierce through."

† S'ankar says एवमेव परमार्थितत्त्वं नान्यथेत्येवं सर्वगरित्यागात्रतेन निश्चितविज्ञाना
दृढव्रता वर्चन्ते. S'ridhar says एकान्तिन:; and Madhusûdan सर्वथा भगवानेव
भजनीय: स चैवंरूप एवेति प्रमाणजनितप्रामाण्यश्रद्धान्यविज्ञाना:.

‡ Mr. Thomson proposes to read जन्ममरण for जरामरण, which
might, perhaps, be a good suggestion, but for its breaking the metre.
And see too Chap. XIII. St. 8. (line 1671) and Chap. XIV. St. 20
(line 1823).

Those men, possessed of minds devoted, know
Me also at the time they hence depart.*

Chapter VIII.

Arjun. What is that Brahma, what the Adhyâtma, what
Those acts, Oh best of Beings! what is called
The Adhibhût, and what the Adhidaiv?
And slayer of Madhu! who's the Adhiyajna,
And how within this body; and how too
Art thou known by the men of self-restraint,
When they depart hence?

Krishna.   Brahma is the Supreme,
The Indestructible; its change† is called
The Adhyâtma; and the offering which is
The cause of the production of all things
And their development—that is called act.‡

---

* All this is explained in the next Chapter.

† स्वभाव. S'ridhar says स्वस्यैव ब्रह्मण एवाशतया जीवरूपेण भवनं स्वभाव:. S'ankar says परस्य ब्रह्मण: प्रतिदेहं प्रत्यगात्मभाव: स्वभावो इति स्वोभाव: स्वभाव:. Madhusûdan says ब्रह्मस्वरूपमेव भात्मानं देहमविक्रत्य भोक्तृतया वर्तमानमध्यात्म-मुच्यते. I do not think that Mr. Thomson's translation is satisfactory, but his explanation follows that of the commentators. 'Change,' too, is not an unexceptionable rendering; but it is better than 'nature,' as showing that स्वभाव is used in a somewhat unusual sense here.

‡ देवतोद्देशेन चरुपुरोडाश्यादे: सस्य द्रव्यस्य वितरणम्—S'ankar. From the offerings to the Gods are produced all things. Compare Chap. III. St. 14. (line 411). This is meant, says S'ridhar, as only an indication, an example, of all acts. The rendering 'production and development' is according to S'ridhar. S'ankar says भूतानि भावी भूतभावस्तस्योद्भवो भूतभावो-द्भवस्तं करोतीति भूतभावोद्भवकरो भूतवस्तूत्पत्तिकर इत्यर्थ:.

The Adhibhût is all things perishable.*
The Adhidaivat is the Primal Being.†
Best of embodied ones ! the Adhiyajna
Is I myself—I in this body here.‡
And he who at the time of death departs,
Abandoning his body, of me alone
Thinking he does into my essence come,
Without all doubt. Likewise, whichever form
He thinks on, when this body he forsakes
At last, to that, Oh Kunti's son ! he goes,
Having been used to think upon it.§ Hence
Always remember me and fight, thy mind
And steady resolution on me fixed,
Thou wilt come to me alone, there is no doubt.
For he, Oh Prithâ's son ! who with his mind,
Of the devotion of repeated thought‖

---

* I follow the commentators here also. Mr. Thomson takes the words here to mean "(my) own indivisible (*sic.* it should be divisible) nature," but there is no word answering to ' (my) own' in the text. भात means ' things,' and I think the sense given by the commentators admissible. And see, Stanzas XIX., XX., XXI. (lines 1067 *et seq.*), and also Chap. XV. St. 16. (line 1905). धरिभाव: may also be taken as answering to स्वभाव: above. See further Notes and Illustrations.

† वैराज: सूर्यमण्डलवर्तां says S'ridhar, following S'ankar here as elsewhere.

‡ *I. e.* as Krishna. On all these terms Mr. Thomson's note may be usefully consulted. They refer to the various manifestations of the Brahma.

§ S'ankar says तदिमन्भावस्तद्द्वार: स भावित: स्मर्यमाणतयाभ्यस्तो येन. S'ridhar has the following तस्य भावी भावनानुचिन्तनं तेन भावितो वासिताचित्त:. Madhusûdan states and agrees with both of these interpretations which, indeed, are not very different from one another.

‖ Devotion here again should be understood as meaning समाधि

Possessed, and steadied on one only, thinks
Of the Supreme and Heavenly Being,° goes
To him. He who doth meditate upon
The ancient sage, the ruler, more minute
Than the minutest atom, the creator
Of all, of form incomprehensible,
Like the sun brilliant, and removed beyond
Darkness, with faith, and with a steady mind,
And with the power of devotion, well
Concentering his breath between his brows,
At the hour of death, goes to that Being Supreme,
Divine. I will speak in brief to thee about
The seat, which those who know the Veds do call
The Indestructible, which those who wish
Practice the life of celibates,† and which
Ascetics enter, from affections free.
He who all paths‡ stops up, and in the heart
Confines the mind,§ shuts up the breath within

---

or concentration of mind, as in Chap. IV. St. 28 (line 588). So says
Madhusûdan. S'ridhar understands by योग a means, उपाय. S'ankar
does not explain the word. Compare Chap. XII. St. 9 (line 1609).

   ° S'ankar says on the word अनुचिन्तयन्, शास्त्राचार्योपदेशमनुपाय-
न्निर्येतत्, and he takes the next stanza as going with this—तमनु-
चिन्तयन्यातीति पूर्वेणैव संबन्ध:. S'ridhar says पुनरप्यनुचिन्तनीयं पुरुषं विशिनति
कविमिति द्वाभ्याम्. With this Madhusûdan agrees.

   † See note on Chapter VI. St. 14 (line 784.).

   ‡ द्वाराणि is explained to mean इन्द्रियद्वाराणि by S'ridhar and Madhusûdan, and apparently S'ankar also. May it not refer to the नवद्वाराणि
referred to in Chapter V. St. 13. (line 677)?

   § ब्रह्मविषयस्मरणमप्यकुर्वन्नित्यर्थ: says S'ridhar. With this agrees Madhusûdan, and also S'ankar, I think, but he says simply नि:प्रचार-
तामापाद्य. It describes the state in which, as Wordsworth says,
'Thought is not.'

The head,* adopts a firm devotion, utters
The single syllable "Om"—the Soul Supreme,†
And thinks of me, and goes abandoning
The body thus, reaches the goal supreme.
To him, Oh Pritha's son! who meditates
Always on me, with mind not elsewhere moving,
And without break, and who's a devotee
Devoted still, I am easy of access.
The high-minded ones coming to me, do never
Return to life—transient, a house of woes—
Having attained supreme perfection.   Worlds
Oh Arjun! up to that of Brahmâ, all
Are fated to return, but Kunti's son!
Coming to me, there is no birth again.‡
Those who a day of Brahmâ know, which ends
After a thousand ages, and a night
Which ends after a thousand ages, are
The men who know both day and night.§ All things

---

* Compare St. 10 (line 1035) *suprâ.*

† *I. e* signifying the Supreme Soul ब्रह्मणोभिन्नानभूनम् says S'ankar. Comp. Chap. XVII. St. 23 (line 2075).

‡ That is to say, persons, who go to any of the worlds up to and including the world of Brahmâ, are destined to be born again. Only those who reach Vishnu's abode are rid of birth and death for ever.

§ S'ankar says, that this explains why the abodes of Brahmâ and the others are held to be not everlasting. The reason is, that they are limited by time; they are not beyond time. S'ridhar says, that the intention is to show how the higher worlds are superior to the 'three worlds' so called, and thus to explain those texts in which the attainment of those other worlds is stated as something excellent, a doubt arising about their value from what has just been said about their not being everlasting. Madhusûdan agrees with S'ankar. S'ridhar's note on the 'Yugs' may be here epitomised. A human year is a day and night of the Gods. 12000 years made up of days of this duration make up the 'quaternion of ages.' A thousand such 'quater-

Perceptible are born from "The Unperceived"
Upon the approach of day; and they dissolve
In that same thing, called "The Unperceived," upon
The approach of night.° This mass of entities,
Also, produced once and again, dissolves
Upon the approach of night; and Pṛithâ's son!
Upon the approach of day, devoid of power,
It is sent forth.† There is an entity,
However, unperceived, apart from this
Which is perceived, above it, and eterne,
Which perishes not, though all these entities
Do perish—it is called The Unperceived,
The Indestructible; the highest goal
They call it; that attained, none ever returns.
That's my Supreme Abode.‡ Oh Pṛithâ's son!
This Highest Being, who all this pervades,
In whom live all existences, can through
Devotion undivided be attained
The time, Prince of the Bhârats! I will tell thee,
When devotees that go, go to return,
Or never to return. The flame of fire,
The day, the light half-month, and the six months

nions' make up a day of Brahmâ, and a similar one his night. Of such
days and nights Brahmâ has 100 years as the measure of his life.

　* Compare Chap. II. St. 28. (line 267). S'ankar says अव्यक्त means
प्रजापतेः रात्र्यादर्थां. The same idea as here may be seen in Kâlidâsa's
Kumâr Sambhav II. 8.

　† अनश is said to mean भरवतन्त्र by S'ankar. S'ridhar says कर्मादि-
परतन्त्र : सन्. See Chap. III. St. 5. (line 384). It means, 'having no will
of its own'.

　§ Compare Chap. XV. St. 6. (line 1870). धाम, which means abode,
also means 'glory;' and hence S'ridhar takes it here to mean स्वरूप.
The line may then mean ' That is my supreme and glorious form.'

Of the northern solstice—those who know the Brahma,
And die in these, repair unto the Brahma.*
The smoke, the night, the dark-half, the six months
Of the southern solstice—in this period
The devotee reaches the lunar light,°
And then returns.† These two paths, light and dark,

---

* The commentators endeavour very strenuously to reconcile this
with the Vedántic propositions on the subject. (See these expounded in
the Sáriraka Bháshya Chap. IV, Páḍ 2, Sútras 17 et seq., and Páḍ 3,
Sútras 4-6.) They understand all the different things mentioned here
as standing for the Deities appertaining to them. Thus Fire means the
God of Fire and so on. Sankar also suggests an alternative interpretation for the first two, Fire and Hume, namely that they both
signify Deities presiding over time. But this I do not quite understand. The whole interpretation presents this difficulty, that the passage purports to state the time in which one dying returns not to the
world. Srídhar gets over this by explaining the whole passage as
follows :—अत्रि-कालाभिमानिदेवतोपलक्षितः मार्ग उच्यते उत्तरायणादि.........यत्रकालेन
प्रयाताः योगिनः यान्ति ब्रह्म ब्रह्मविदो जनाः। The sub-
stance of this is that 'the time when' means 'the path, indicated by
a Deity presiding over time, by which.' It is somewhat difficult to
accept this interpretation. And Sankar's remarks under Brahma
Sutra IV, 2, 21 evidently show, that he thought the passage ought
to be taken to refer to 'time,' although he hints at a different
interpretation. One difficulty still remains, however; what is the
meaning of 'fire' when the question is about 'time?' Srídhar
says that the word 'time' is used here, having regard to the large
number of words signifying parts of time, although 'fire' itself
has no connection with time. अग्न्यादीनां कालावयवबहुत्वात् कालत्वेनाभिधानमेतत्-
स्थलबोधकानां शब्दानां बाहुल्यादुपचारात् कालपदेनोक्तम्। I own, I have no clear notion of the meaning of the word 'fire'
here. The difficulty almost tempts me to accept even the meaning
given by the commentators to the whole passage.

† Mr. Thomson thinks, that this whole passage has a metaphorical
force, and that it is the Philosophers of the Uttar Mímánsá school,
who have made the mistake of interpreting it literally. I think
the passages in the Chhándogyopanishad, which seems to be
the original of the passage in the Gítá, cannot be understood

Are deemed to be eternal in this world.*

Taking the one, one goes never to return,

By the other comes again. No devotee,

Oh son of Pritha! knowing these two paths,

Is ever confounded;† therefore, Arjun! be

Possessed at all times of devotion. This‡

Knowing, the devotee rises above

All the holy fruit laid down for penances,

For study of the Veds, for giving alms,

For sacrifices; and he does repair

To the transcendent, the primeval, seat.

Chapter IX.

Krishna. Of knowledge and experience—mystery

Supreme—I will speak to thee who dost not carp.

Knowing that, thou from evil shalt be freed.

Of sciences and secrets, 'tis the chief,§

---

metaphorically, but must be understood in the sense which the commentators attach to it. Besides, I cannot see why there should be much difficulty in accepting the lunar world as a place for enjoyment of an inferior sort. After all, what is the Heaven which the Gîtâ speaks of in Chap. IX. St. 21, but something like the moon? As to the *ground* for saying that the moon is a place for enjoyment, that is an entirely different question, which might be pertinently asked of several other 'superstitions' than this one.

* *I. e.* as S'ridhar says, for those who are fitted for the paths of knowledge or action.

† *I. e.* says S'ridhar, does not desire Heaven as giving happiness, but is steady in devotion to God; because, I take it, he sees that any other course would not free him from repeated birth and death.

‡ *I. e.* All that is stated in this Chapter—S'ankar.

§ This according to the commentators. The rendering 'kingly mystery' is scarcely satisfactory. See 1 Siddhânta Kaumudi 432.

The best of purifiers, not opposed
To law, directly knowable, not hard
To practise, and imperishable. Those
Who on this holy doctrine place no faith,
Oh slayer of foes! obtain not me, but come
Back to this mortal world. By me whose form
Is imperceptible, is all this world
Pervaded.   All existences in me
Live,* but not I in them. Nor yet do these
Existences live in me.   See my power†
Divine. Supporting and producing all
Existences, my spirit stands not in them.
Know, as the mighty air, pervading all,
Always remains in space, so in me stand
All these existences. Oh Kunti's son!‡
Upon the expiry of a Kalpa, all things
Into my Nature§ go, at the opening
Of the Kalpa, I send them forth again. I send
Now and again this mass of entities,

---

* Compare Chapter VII. St. 12. (line 936). Things live in him, he
being their cause and their support. He lives not in them, because
he is untainted by anything, like space, say the commentators.
From this last standpoint, follows the next assertion that the
things do not live in him. Mr. Thomson's explanation makes the
passage quite clear.

† The word used here is योग, and S'ankar here interprets it
thus, पश्य मे योगं युक्ति: घटनं मे ममैश्वरं योगमात्मनः ईश्वरच्येदमैश्वरं महात्म्य-
मित्यर्थं:. Compare. Chap. VII. St. 25 (line 980).

‡ On this S'ridhar says असंश्लिष्टयोरेव्याभारात्रेयभावं दृष्टान्तेनाह. As space
is untainted and unaffected by the air which yet remains in it, so
I am unaffected by all things which yet are in me. मयसंश्रयेणेव स्थितानि
says S'ankar.

§ Once more we have 'my Nature.' Compare Chap. VII St. 4
(line 910).

Entire, devoid of power,* by means of the power
Of Nature, taking its control myself.†
But not these actions, Conqueror of wealth!
Shackle me,‡ standing like one unconcerned,
And to them unattached. Nature gives birth
To immoveables and moveables, through me
The supervisor, and in consequence
Of this,§ Oh Kunti's son! the world moves on·
Deluded people of vain hopes, vain acts,
Vain knowledge,‖ who towards the natures tend¶,
Delusive, of Asurs and Rákshases—
Fatuous, they disregard me as I am
Invested with a human form, not knowing
My highest nature as great Lord of all·\$
But the high-souled ones, Oh son of Prithâ! who
Tend to the nature of the Gods, do know

---

* Compare Chap. VIII. St. 19. (line 1068).

† Comp. last note but one and line 519. We have 'my nature' here also.

‡ भूतग्रामं निपमं विदधतस्तन्निमित्तमपि धर्माधिमांभ्यां संबन्ध: इत्यादितीदमाह says S'ankar.

§ *I. e.* this supervision—भनेन मदाधिष्ठानेन हेतुना says S'ridhar. S'ankar agrees with this.

‖ Hope—that some other Deity will give them the fruits of their acts. The acts are vain, because they are not offered up to the Supreme Being. The knowledge is vain, as abounding in various foolish doubts and puzzles. So says S'ridhar. Madhusûdan says :— The hope is that their acts will yield them fruits independently of God. As to the other two, Madhusûdan is quite at one with S'ridhar.

¶ It is rather difficult to render श्रिन properly. 'Adopt' signifies an act voluntarily done. Mr. Thomson has ' incline,' and following him I take 'tend' as the best word I can find. Mr. Thomson is in error in translating मोहिनी by deluded. It means ' deluding.'

\$ Compare Chap. VII. 24 (line 979) and our note there, which is supported by this passage,

Me inexhaustible, and source of things,
And worship me with minds not elsewhere turned.
Always devoted, they do worship me,
Singing my glories constantly, in vows
Steady, and working,° and saluting me
Devotedly.† And others worship me,
The sacrifice of knowledge offering up,
As one, as separate, as pervading all,‡
Variously.§ I am the Kratu, I the Yajna.‖

* Working for knowledge of God's greatness, according to S'ridhar ; for an idea of his real nature, according to Madhusûdan ; for self-restraint and such other acts of piety, says S'ankar.

† भक्ति is the original which means devotedness. The commentators render it by पदं प्रेम—intense love.

‡ विश्वतोमुख lit. having faces towards all sides, is rendered by विश्वरूप by S'ankar ; and by सर्विक by S'ridhar ; and by सर्वात्मन् by Madhusûdan.

§ The sacrifice of knowledge means, according to S'ridhar, the sacrifice (यज्ञ) consisting in the knowledge that Vâsudev is all. The last words are thus explained by S'ridhar :—'as one' means with the feeling of all being one ; ' as separate' means with a feeling of difference—oneself being servant of God ; 'as all-pervading' is clear. 'Variously' is taken to refer to the different forms in which the Supreme is held before the mind, as Brahmâ, Rudra, &c S'ankar's interpretation is slightly different. The first ' as one' is explained as by S'ridhar ; the second by ' with a feeling that the sun, moon, &c., are really Vishnu in different forms' ; the third by ' with a feeling that the Supreme exists variously.' बहुधा is explained by बहुप्रकारेण—[worship] in a variety of ways. Madhusûdan says, the three stages are these. In the first, the man identifies himself with the Supreme (For this he cites the Upanishad text सं वाहमसिम भगवो देवते भहं वै त्वमसि). In the second, he takes the several " Pratiks" stated in Vedic texts (आदित्यो ब्रह्मेत्यादिश: &c). In the third the man worships another Deity altogether.

‖ Kratu is that laid down in S'rutis ; Yajna that in Smritis, say S'ankar and the other commentators.

I am the libation to the manes, I
The product of the herbs;* the sacred verse
I am; the sacrificial butter I,
I am the fire, I am the offering,
I am the father of this Universe,
The mother, the supporter, the grandsire,
The purifier, the thing to be known,
The Om, the Rik, the Sâm, the Yajus too,
The goal, and the sustainer, and the Lord,
The supervisor, and the residence,†
The asylum, and the friend, the source as well
As the destroyer, the receptacle,‡
And the support, the imperishable seed.
Heat I do cause, and showers I pour down
And stop. Oh Arjun! I am nectar, I
Am death, I am that which is, and which is not.§
Those who do study the three Veds, and who
The Som-juice drink, who of their sins are cleared,
Performing sacrifices for me,‖ pray
A passage into Heaven, and attain
The holy world of Indra, and there in Heaven
Enjoy the Heavenly pleasures of the Gods.

---

* The food produced from vegetables. S'ridhar says, it may also mean 'medicine.'

† Supervisor *scil.* of all the acts and omissions of living creatures : (S'ankar) residence, is the place of enjoyment (S'ridhar and Madhusû.dan).

‡ लयस्थानम् says S'ridhar. Madhusûdan says निर्जीयने कालान्नरो. पभोग्यं वरश्चदिमन्निति.

§ That which is gross and that which is subtle (S'ridhar). According to S'ankar, they mean the effects and the causes—कार्यकारणे.

‖ *I. e.* sacrifices given to me in the form of Indra and others.

Having enjoyed that great celestial world,
Their merit being exhausted, they return
Into this mortal world.* Those who adopt
The Vedic ordinances, for things of sense
Desirous, in this manner go and come.
To those who meditate on me alone,
And worship me, and who are constant, I
Give and preserve what's given.† Those also, who
Being devotees of other Gods, imbued
With faith, do worship, worship me, Oh son
Of Kuntî! but not as they ought.‡ For I,
Of every sacrifice am both the lord
And the enjoyer.§ But they know me not
Correctly, therefore do they fall.|| The men
Who to the Gods make vows¶ go to the gods,
And those who make vows to the manes go
To them, the worshippers of the Bhûts, too, go
To them, and those who worship me to me.
Whoever with devotion offers me
Leaf, flower, fruit, water—that from that pious man,
Brought on out of devotion, I accept.

---

* Compare Brahma Sûtra III. 1. 8. (p. 753) and Gitâ line 1088.

† Constant means always given up to me. 'Give and preserve'—the expression is योगक्षेम for which compare Chap. II. St. 45 (line 274).

‡ Compare Chap. XVI. St 17 (line 1978). In worshipping the other Deities, they worship Vishnu in effect, but not directly, and not with the knowledge that they worship Vishnu. S'ankar says अविधिरज्ञानम्. S'ridhar has मोक्षप्रापकं विधिं विना. Madhusûdan follows S'ankar. What follows explains these words.

§ Comp. Chap. V. St. 29 (line 734); lord=giver of the fruit.

|| *I. e.* return to this world.

¶ Compare Chap. VII. St. 23 (line 975). S'ankar says देवेषु व्रतं नियमो भक्तिश्च येषां ते.

Whatever thou dost, whatever thou eatst, whatever
Thou sacrificest, and whatever thou givest,
Whatever penance thou performst, Oh son
Of Kunti ! do as offered unto me.*
Thus shalt thou be released from ties of acts
In good or ill resulting, and possessed
Of this devotion, this abandonment,†
Freed, thou shalt come to me. I am alike
To every creature, none is odious
To me, none dear. But those who worship me
Are in me, and I am in them.‡/ Even though
An ill-conducted man should worship me,
None other worshipping, he must be thought
A saint, for he has well resolved.§/ He soon
Becomes a pious man, and then attains
Endless tranquillity. Oh Kunti's son !
Be thou assured,‖ never is my devotee

---

*Compare Chap. III. St. 30 (line 461) and other passages.

† संन्यास—The word which has been rendered by ' renunciation'
before. This mode of action is at once devotion and renunciation.
It is renunciation, because it is offered to another ; it is devotion, because, in such a case, he cares not for the fruit of the acts. Compare
VI. 2 (line 741-2). Mr. Thomson takes संन्यास and योग as two
different things here, and the whole as a Dvandva Compound. I prefer the commentators' view supported by the passage just cited.

‡ ' They are in me' by their devotion ; ' I am in them,' as giver of
happiness to them (S'ridhar). Comp. Chap. VI. St. 30 (line 840).
S'ridhar says यथाग्ने: स्वसेवकेष्वेव तम:शीतादिदु:खमपाकुर्वन्नीव न वैरम्यं यथा
वा कल्पवृक्षस्य तथैव भक्तश्रद्धानिनोपि मम वैषम्यं नास्त्येव किन्तु मद्भक्तेरेवायं महिमा.

§ Namely, that the Supreme Being alone should be worshipped.

‖ The commentators take प्रतिजानीहि in the ordinary sense ' de-

Ruined.   To me resorting, even those,
Oh Pritha's son!   who are of sinful birth,°
Women, and Vais'yas, S'údras too,   attain
The goal Supreme. / What needs then to be said
Of Holy Brâhmaṇs, and of royal saints
Devoted.   Having come into this world,
Transient, unhappy,† worship me.   On me
Steady thy mind ; become my devotee ;
Worship me ; bow to me ; and thus engaged
Still in devotion,‡ making thy resort
Me only, thou shalt surely come to me.

Chapter X.

Krishna. Once more, Oh large-armed one ! hear thou my words,
Important, which, solicitous for thy good,
I speak to thee delighted.§   Not the hosts
Of gods, nor mighty sages know my source ;

clare,' and add 'among persons who may raise disputes about it.'
This is not inadmissible, but it is rather farfetched, and on the
other hand, our meaning is not the usual one.

* S'ankar takes Vais'yas &c. to be specific examples of this.
S'ridhar takes it to refer to अन्त्यादय: and to mean निकृटजन्मान::
S'ankar says पापानि योनिर्येषां ते.

† Comp. Chap. VIII. St. 15 (line 1053).

‡ Compare Chap. VI. St. 19 (line 805) and note there.

§ Mr. Thomson translates the word here by ' whom I love.' I prefer
the rendering of the commentators, for which अनसूयवे in Chap. IX.
St. 1 (line 1102) furnishes a good parallel. प्रीणानि means ' pleases' as in
प्रीणानि य: सुच्चरितै: गिनरं स पुत्री &c., and the passive of that would
mean ' to be pleased.' परम (important) =परमात्मनिष्ठ S'ridhar.

For I am the origin of all the gods
And mighty sages.   He among all men
Who, undeluded, knows me as unborn,
Without beginning, the great Lord of the world,
Is from all sins released.   Intelligence,
Knowledge,* and freedom from delusion too,
Patience, truth, self-restraint, tranquillity,
Pleasure, and pain, birth, death, and safety, fear,
Contentment, equability, besides
Austerities, harmlessness, glory, shame,
Alms-giving—all these tempers different
Of creatures flow from me alone.† The seven
Great sages, and the Manus, the Ancients four,
Whose off-spring are these people in the world,
Partaking of my powers, all were born
From my mind.‡ He who rightly understands
My emanations and my powers§ thus,
Attains unmoved devotion, there is no doubt.

---

* S'ankar says बुद्धिरन्तःकरणस्य सूक्ष्मार्थविबोधनसामर्थ्यं......ज्ञानमात्मा-
दिपदार्थानामवबोधः.

† The words used in the original do not always signify 'tempers' or states of mind. But the 'tempers' answering to the si-
gnifications must be understood. Compare Chapter VII. St. 12.
(line 936).

‡ "The ancients four," means Sanak, Sanandan, Sanâtan
and Sanatkumâr. S'ankar would *seem* to take चत्वारो as going with
मनव : and adds सावर्णी इति प्रसिद्धाः. But the Manus are fourteen. 'From
my mind'—S'ridhar says संकल्पमात्राज्जाताः.

§ योग. Compare Chap. IX. St. 5. (line 1114). On विभूति see this
Chapter *passim.*

The wise, being full of love,* do worship me,

Thinking that I am the source of all, that all

Moves on through me. They rest contented, pleased,

Fixing their minds on me, and offering

Their lives to me,† speaking of me, each other

Teaching. To these, devoted constantly,

Who with love worship, I communicate

That knowledge‡ by which they do come to me.

And 'tis of such men only I destroy,

Being within their hearts, the darkness born

Of ignorance, by means of the bright lamp

Of knowledge, through compassion for such men.§

Arjun. Transcendent Brahma thou, the final goal,

The Holiest of the Holy, too, thou art.

All sages call thee the Eternal Being,

Divine, the first of Deities, Lord, Unborn.

So say the sages, so the sage divine—

Nàrad—so Asit, Deval, and so Vyàs;

And so, Oh Kes'av! thou tellst me thyself.

I do believe all that thou sayst is true.

For Oh great Lord! nor god nor demon knows

Thy incarnation,‖ thou alone dost know

---

* So S'ridhar. S'ankar interprets the original word to mean, परमार्थेनत्स्वाभिनेवेंश. Comp. सर्वभविन Chap. XVIII. St. 62 (line 2320).

† S'ankar says मय्युपसंहृनकरणा इत्यर्थः अथवा मद्गतजीवना:. S'ridhar agrees; मर्यार्पितजीवना is the alternative he gives.

‡ बुद्धिस्वं योगमुपायम् says S'ridhar. बुद्धि: सम्यग्दर्शनं तेन योग: says S'ankar; with this Madhusûdan agrees.

§ आत्मनो भावान्त:करणाश्रय: says S'ankar. बुद्धिवृत्ती स्थिन: says S'ridhar. There is a slight difficulty about आत्म on this construction.

‖ व्यक्ति is प्रभव, according to S'ankar; आभिव्यक्ति, according to

Thyself by thyself, Best of beings! Lord
Of the Universe! Maker of all that is,
And master! God of gods! Oh be thou pleased
Thy glorious emanations to describe,
Fully, by which thou permeatest all
These worlds. Oh glorious one! how shall I know
Thee, fully meditating at all times?
In what forms of existence, Oh great Lord!
Should I upon thee meditate? Once more
Janârdan! tell me of thy powers at length,
And of thy emanations; for to hear
This nectar, I feel no satiety.

Krishna. Well, first of Kurus! I will describe to thee
My emanations glorious, but the chief
Alone, for there's no end to my extent.
I am the soul, Oh Lord of Sleep! in the hearts
Fixed, of all creatures. The beginning I,
The middle, and the end of every being.
Amongst the Âdityas I am Vishnu. I
Among the shining bodies am the Sun
Beaming. I am Marichi 'mongst the winds.
The Moon among the Nakshatras I am.
Among the Veds I am the Sàm-ved.† I
Among the gods am Vàsav. I am the mind

S'ridhar who says देवा अस्मदनुग्रहार्थमियमभिव्यक्तिरिति न जानन्ति दानवा-
श्चास्मान्निग्रहार्थमिति न विदुरेव.

* योगो नामैश्वर्य तदस्यास्तीति योगी, says Ânandagiri, which seems to be
justified by the context. Otherwise it might be taken as equivalent to
योगेश्वर.

† Compare Aitareya Brâhmaṇ. III. 23. p. 68 (Haug's Ed.).

Among the senses. I am consciousness*
Among all creatures. S'ankar too I am
Among the Rudras, and I am the Lord
Of wealth among the Yakshas, Rakshases.
Among the Vasus I am Fire. Among
Mountains hightopped I am Meru. Know, Oh son
Of Prithâ! I am Bṛihaspati, the chief
Of priests domestic. Generals among
I am Skanda. I am ocean amongst reservoirs
Of water. And among the sages great
I am Bhṛigu. I am the single 'syllable Om
'Mongst words. Among all forms of worship I am
The Jap. Amongst the firmly-fixèd ones
I am the Himâlaya. Of all trees I am
The As'vattha. Sages divine among
I am Nârad. And among the Gandharvas
I am Chitrarath. Among the perfect ones
I am the sage Kapil. Among horses know
Uchchais's'ravas I am, through the nectar found.†
Airâvat I among great elephants.
A prince 'mongst men. I am the thunderbolt
'Mongst weapons. And among all cows I am
The cow Kâm-dhenu. Likewise I am Love
Which generates. I am Vâsuki 'mongst snakes.
Ananta, too I am the Nâgs among.
I am Varuṇ 'mongst aquatic beings. I
Among the manes am the Aryamâ.
Amongst the regulators I am Yam.

---

* S'ankar says कार्यकारणसंघातेभिव्यक्का बुद्धेर्वृत्तिर्धेननाा. S'ridhar भूतानां संव-
निश्रनी चेतना ज्ञानशक्तिरहमस्मि. Madhusûdan चिदभिव्यञ्जिका बुद्धेर्वृत्ति:.

† I. e. found in the course of the labours for obtaining the Amṛit,
namely the churning of the ocean.

Pralhâd I am among the Daityas. I
Am Time among the things that count.* I am
The prince of beasts among the beasts, 'mongst birds
The son of Vinatâ.† I am the wind
'Mongst purifiers. Among those that wield
Weapons, I am Râm.‡ Among the fishes, I
Am Makar, among streams the Jâhnavî.
I am the beginning, as well as the end,
The middle, too, Oh Arjun ! of creations.§
I am the science of the soul among
The sciences, of controversialists
The argument.‖ /Among the letters I am
The letter A, and 'mongst the various sorts
Of compounds I am the Dvandva.¶ I alone
Am Time eternal, the creator I
Whose faces are in all directions.$ Death

---

* It is difficult to say what this precisely means. S'ankar says काल:
कलयनां कलनं गणनं कुर्वन्नमहम्. S'ridhar कलयता.वशीकुर्वता गणयता वा मध्ये
कालोहमस्मि. Madhusûdan कलयनां संख्यानं गणनं कुर्वन्ना मध्ये कालोहम्.
Under St. 33 S'ankar says काल: कलयनामहमित्यत्रायुर्गणनात्मक: संवत्सर-
ज्ञानायायु:स्वरूप: काल उक्त: स च तस्मिन्नायुपि क्षीणे सति क्षीयते भत्र तु प्रवाहा-
त्मकी क्षय: काल उच्यते इति विशेष:. This furnishes a passable explanation.

† Garud.

‡ The son of Das'arath.

§ St. 20 (line 1280) refers to the animate creation only. This verse
to everything—S'ankar.

‖ S'ridhar says, यादरन् वीतरागयो: शिष्याचार्ययोस्तस्यानिरूपणफल: श्रुनौसौ
श्रेष्ठत्वान्मद्विभूति:.

¶ Mr. Thomson's rendering of this is quite incorrect.

$ कर्मफलविधानूनां मध्ये विश्वतोमुखो धाना सर्वकर्मफलविधाताहमिद्यर्थ:—
S'ridhar. See Chap. XI. St. 11 (line 1399) and note there.

That seizes all I am. I am the source
Of what's to be.* I am fame, and fortune, speech,
And memory, and patience, intellect,
And perseverance among females.† So
Among Sâm-hymns the Bṛihatsâm I am.
Among the metres I am Gâyatrî.
I am the Mârgas'îrsha among the months.
The spring among the seasons. I am the game
Of dice of cheats. And of the glorious
I am the glory. I am victory,
I am industry, the goodness of the good.
I am Vâsudav among the Vrishṇis. I
Among the Pâṇḍavs am the Conqueror
Of wealth. Among the Munis I am Vyâs.
I am the discerning Us'anas of those
Who have discernment. Among teachers I am
The rod.‡ I am the polity§ of those
That wish for victory. Silence I am
Mongst secrets.‖ And the knowledge I am of those
Who knowledge have attained. Whatever's the seed
Of Arjun! of all beings, that I am.
Nothing there is, or moveable or fixed,
Which is without me. Slayer of foes! no end

---

* S'ankar says उद्भव उत्कर्षोभ्युदयस्तस्मातिहेनुश्चाहं केषां भाविकल्याणानामुत्कर्षे-
तत्रियोग्यानामित्यर्थे:. With him S'ridhar and Madhusûdan concur.

† .... एना उत्तमा: स्त्रीणामहमस्मि यासःमाभासमात्रसंबन्धेनापि लौकाः
हनार्थमात्मानं मन्यन्ते—S'ankar.

‡ अदान्तानां दमनकारणम् says S'ankar. येनासंयता भावि संयता भवन्ति स
दण्डो मद्विभूनि: S'ridhar.

§ सामाद्युपायर्छदा says S'ridhar.

‖ न हि तूर्णीं स्थितस्याभिप्रायो ज्ञायते says S'ridhar.

There's of my emanations glorious.
Here their extent is but in part declared
By me./Whatever thing there is of power,
Glorious, or splendid, know all that to be
From portions of my energy produced.
Or rather, Arjun! what hast thou to do
With this variety of knowledge? I
Do stand, supporting all this universe
By but a single portion of myself.

Chapter XI.

Arjun. Gone now is my delusion by the words
Momentous and mysterious, which thou hast
Spoken for my behoof, and which concern
The Adhyâtma.* I have heard from thee at large,
Oh lotus-eyed one! of the birth and death
Of beings, and about thy greatness, too,
Imperishable. All, Oh Highest Lord!
That thou hast stated now about thyself,
Is so. But still, Oh Best of Beings! I
Desire to see thy mighty form divine.
If thou, Oh Lord! shouldst think me capable
Of looking on it, show thyself to me
Lord of Devotion! inexhaustible.
Krishna. In hundreds and in thousands see my forms,
Oh Prithâ's son! all various and divine,
Of various colours, and of various shapes.

---

* Literally, "called the Adhyâtma," but the commentators seem to
be correct in their interpretation which is followed above—आत्मानात्मविवेक-
कविषयम् say S'ankar and S'rîdhar.

The Rudras, Vasus, and the Âdityas,
The As'vins, as well as the Maruts; see.
Off-spring of Bharat! many a wonder see
Unseen before. Now the whole universe,
Moving and fixed, observe here all in one,
Within my body, and Lord of sleep! whatever
Else too thou dost desire to see. But Oh!
Not with this eye alone of thine wilt thou
Be capable of looking at me. I
Give thee an eye divine. Do thou now see
My godly mystic power.*

Sanjaya.　　　　　　Then, Oh king!
The great Lord of Devotion, Hari, thus
Having said, showed to Prithá's son his form—
Supreme, divine, with many a mouth and eye,
Presenting many a wondrous sight, bedecked
With many a heavenly ornament, and wielding
Many a heavenly weapon, wearing flowers
And vestments heavenly, with heavenly perfumes
Anointed, full of wonders—the infinite
Deity with faces turned to every side.†
If in the Heavens all at once burst forth
The brilliance of a thousand suns, it would
Be to the brilliance of that mighty one
A parallel. Then Pându's son beheld,
There in the body of the God of gods,
All in one place, the universe complete,
Divided variously.‡ The Conqueror

---

* Compare Chap. IX. St. 5 (line 1114) and note there.

† Compare Chap. IX. St. 15 (line 1147). Here, too, S'ankar says विश्वतोमुखं सर्वभूतात्ममत्तात्.

‡ *I. e.* in its various divisions as gods, manes, men, and so forth—S'ankar.

Of wealth, then filled with great astonishment,
His hair standing on end, bowed to the God
With the head, and joining hands, thus spake:—

Arjun.   I see

Oh God! within thy body all the gods,
As well as numbers of the various beings ;
Seated upon a lotus-throne, the Lord
Brahmâ ; the sages ; and the snakes divine.
With many a stomach, mouth, and arm, and eye,
I see thee on all sides, of countless forms.
Oh Lord of all, of every form ! thy end,
Thy middle, thy beginning, I see not.
I see thee with the diadem, the mace,
The discus too—a mass of splendour bright
On every side, and hard to look upon ;
All round as brilliant as a blazing fire,
Or as the sun, immeasurable. Thou
The Indestructible, the Supreme One
That's to be known; thou the support supreme*
Of the universe; thou the inexhaustible
Protector of everlasting piety.†
The eternal person dost thou seem to me.
I see thee, of beginning, middle, end,
Devoid; of power infinite; with arms
Unnumbered; with sun and moon for thy eyes ;
With mouths like to a blazing fire ; and heating
By thy own splendour all this universe.
The interspace betwixt the earth and sky,
And all the quarters too, dost thou pervade

---

* निधान परमाश्रय इत्यर्थ: says S'ankar. प्रकृष्टाश्रय: says S'ridhar. But
see St. 38 (line 1509) and Chap. IX. St. 19 (line 1160).

† Compare Chapter IV. 7 (line 523).

Oh mighty one! looking upon this form
Of thine, miraculous and terrible,
Frightened are the three worlds. For here these bands
Of gods do enter thee;* some frightened pray
With joined hands ; companies of sages great
And Siddhas crying "Hail" praise thee with hymns
Expressive.† The Âdityas, the Sâdhyas too,
The Rudras, Vasus, Vis'vas, and the Winds,
The Ushmaps, Yakshas, and the Gandharvas,
The Asurs, and the Siddhas, all amazed
Look at thee. Looking on thy mighty form,
With many a mouth and eye, Oh large-armed one!
With many an arm, and stomach, thigh, and foot,
Fearful with many a jaw, sorely afraid
Are all the worlds as well as I.   At sight
Of thee, Oh Vishṇu! with eyes blazing, large,
With mouth wide open, and with numerous hues,
Brilliant, the Heavens touching, I retain
No courage, no tranquillity, afraid
Much in my inmost soul. Looking upon
Thy faces, dreadful with the jaws, and like
The last Fire of Destruction, pleasure none
I feel, the quarters cannot recognise.
Oh Lord of gods pervading the universe
Have mercy! All these Dhṛitarâshṭra's sons,
Together also with the crowds of kings,
Bhîshma, and Droṇ, this charioteer's son too,
Hastening together with our champions chief,

* प्रविश्रान्तो दृश्यन्ते says S'ankar. द्वारणं प्रविशन्ति says S'rîdhar, unnecessarily, I think.

† पुष्कलाभिः संपूर्णाभिः says S'ankar. पुष्कलाभिःपरिपूर्णायाँभिः says Madhusûdan.

Into thy mouth, horrific* by thy jaws,
And fearful, enter. Some appear with heads
All smashed within the spaces 'twixt the teeth
Stuck down. As flow towards the sea alone,
The volumes of the rivers' waters fierce,
So do these heroes of the human world
Enter thy blazing mouths.† As butterflies
With force increased‡ enter a blazing fire
To be destroyed, even so to be destroyed
These men with force increased enter thy mouths.
Devouring all the people from all sides,
Thou lickst them over and over with thy mouths
Blazing. Oh Vishṇu! thy fierce splendours heat
The universe, filling it with their rays.
Tell me who thou art with this awful form.
My salutations be to thee, Oh first
Of gods! have mercy! I desire to know
Thee the Primeval one, for Oh thy deeds
I understand not.

Krishna.   I am Death, I am he
Who causes the destruction of the worlds,
Developed,§ and am now engaged about
The overthrow of the worlds. Without thee even,
The warriors in the adverse hosts arrayed
Will cease to be. Therefore be up, obtain
Glory, and conquering thy enemies,

---

* विकृतानि says S'rídhar. Horrific by reason of the ruggedness and distortion.

† Compare Chap XI. 21 (line 1438).

‡ समृद्ध उद्धृत: says S'ankar. बुद्धिपूर्वकं समृद्ध: says S'rídhar.

§ प्रवृद्धो वृद्धिगन: say S'ankar and Madhusûdan. प्रवृद्ध: अत्युन्कट: says S'rídhar.

Enjoy a prosperous kingdom. I have myself
Already killed them, Savyasâchin![*] be
Merely the instrument. Droṇ. Bhîshma, and Karṇa,
Jayadrath, and all other warriors too,
Heroic, do thou kill—all killed by me.
Be not distressed; do fight; and in the field
Thou shalt defeat thy foes.

Sanjaya.   Hearing these words
Of Kes'av, with joined hands, the crownèd one
Trembling, with salutations, once more spoke
To Kṛishṇa, overwhelmed with fright, his throat choked up,
Bowing.

Arjun. Oh Lord of minds, by thy renown
Attracted and delighted is the world—
Fitly. In all directions frightened fly
The demons, and the hosts of Siddhas too
Salute thee all. Why should they not salute
Thee, Higher than Brahmâ, First Cause of him too?
Oh Infinite High-minded one! Oh Lord
Of gods, who dost pervade the Universe!
Thou the Indestructible one, that which is,
That which is not, and that which is beyond.[†]
Thou art the primal lord, the ancient Being,

---

* Arjun, so called as he could shoot arrows with his left hand, सव्येन वामेन हस्तेन साचितुं शरान्संभर्तुं शर्लिं यस्य—S'ridhar.

† S'ridhar says सद्व्यक्तमसदव्यक्तं च तायां परम्. Madhusûdan सद्विभिमुखेन प्रनीयमानमस्तीति । असन्निर्विषमुखेन प्रतीयमानं नास्तीति ॥ अथवा सद्व्यक्तमस-दव्यक्तं तमेव तथा तयरं तायां सदसद्भ्यां परं मूलकारणं यदक्षरं ब्रह्म तदपि तमे-व तद्विन्नं किमपि नास्तीत्यर्थः ॥ S'ankar's comments are not quite clear. Comp. Chap XIII. 12 (line 1185).

Thou art the last receptacle of this world,*
Thou art the subject, thou the object,† thou
The final goal, Oh polymorphous one!
'Tis thou pervadest all.   Thou art the Wind,
Thou Yam, Fire, Sea, Moon, and the sire of men,
And thou the great grandsire. A thousand times
Obeisance be to thee, and yet again
Obeisance to thee! In front, from behind,
Obeisance be to thee, from every side!
Thou all! Thou art of power infinite,
Of glory unmeasured! All dost thou pervade,
Therefore art all! Whatever was said by me
Contemptuously, taking thee to be
My friend—" Oh Krishna," " Oh Yâdav," or "Oh friend."—
Not knowing this thy greatness, or from want
Of caution,‡ or through friendship; and whatever
Dishonour I did thee in mirth, what time
We sported, sat together, ate our food,
Or took repose, sometimes in company§
Sometimes alone, Oh Undegraded one!
For that I do apologize to thee,
The unbounded one. Of all this universe,
Moving and fixed, thou art the father, thou
Its great and venerable Lord. To thee

---

* Compare St. 18 (lin 1424). S'ankar says निधीयतेऽस्मिञ्जगत्सर्वं महाप्रलयादौ. S'rídhar has जयस्थान.

† I use subject and object in something like the philosophical sense, as meaning the knower and the known.

‡ विक्षिप्तचित्ततया says S'ankar.

§ S'ankar says तत्समक्षं तच्छब्दः क्रियाविशेषणार्थः. S'rídhar says (after explaining एक: by सखाग्भिना) तत्समक्षं तेषां परिहसतां सखीनां समक्षम्; with this Madhusûdan agrees.

No equal is, matchless in power throughout
All the three worlds. Whence can there be a greater ?
Therefore I bow to thee, prostrate myself,
And would propitiate thee, Praiseworthy one !
Oh be thou pleased, Oh Lord ! to pardon me,
Even as a father does his son, a friend
His friend, or as a husband his beloved.
Seeing this form, unseen before, I feel
Delight, but also fear overpowers my heart.
Be pleased, Oh world-pervading Lord of gods !
Lord ! show me that same form. I wish to see
Thee with the mace and diadem, wheel in hand.
That same fourhanded form, Oh all-formed one !
Oh thousand-handed God ! once more assume.

Krishna. Oh Arjun ! pleased, I have now shown to thee
Through my power mystic* this my shape supreme —
Glorious, and universal, infinite,
Primal, and seen before by none but thee.
Not by the study of the Veds, nor yet
Of sacrifices,† not by alms, not acts,
Nor yet by rigid penances, can I
Be seen, Oh bravest of the Kurus ! here
Upon this world of mortals, in this form,
By any one but thee. Be not distressed,
Be not perplexed, seeing this form of mine,

---

* योग again. Compare Chap. VII. St. 25 (line 980).

† S'ankar says वेदा (Calc. Ed. यज्ञा) ध्ययनैरेव यज्ञाध्ययनस्य सिद्धत्वात्पृथ-
ग्यज्ञाध्ययनग्रहणं यज्ञविज्ञानोपळक्षणार्थम्. So too S'ridhar वेदाध्ययनव्यतिरेकेण
यज्ञाध्ययनस्याभावाच्चज्ञशब्देन यज्ञविद्या कल्पसूत्राद्या लभ्यन्ते वेदानां यज्ञविद्याना
चाध्ययनैरित्यर्थ:. A suspicion, however, occurs to one's mind. Is not
यज्ञवेदाध्ययने: meant ? And see St. 53 (line 1570).

So dreadful.   Free from fear and with pleased heart,
See once more now that same old form of mine.

Sanjaya. Having said thus to Arjun, then, the son
Of Vasudev showed once more his own form.
And the Great One once more in gentle shape
Comforted him so frightened.

Arjun.   Seeing now
This shape of thine, Janârdan! human, mild,
I have come to my right mind, and have returned
To my state normal.

Krishna.   Difficult to see*
Is this form of mine which thou hast now seen,
Even the gods do constantly desire
To see it. Not by penance, not by alms,
Not by the Veds, not by the sacrifice,
Can I be seen as thou hast seen me now.
But 'tis by worship fixed on me alone,
Oh Arjun! that I can be truly known,
Seen and amalgamated with,† Oh slayer,
Of foes! in this shape. He, Oh Pàndu's son!
Who acts performs for me, to whom I am
The highest object, who's my devotee,
Free from attachments, and from hatred free
Towards all beings, he to me does come.

Chapter XII.

Arjun. Of all the worshippers who meditate
On thee, devoted always thus, and those

------

* *I. e.* difficult to get a sight of.
† प्रवेष्टुं मोक्षं गन्तुम् S'ankar. प्रवेष्टुं तादात्म्येन S'ridhar.

Who on the Indestructible, Unseen,
Do meditate, which know devotion best?

Krishna. By me are those the most devoted deemed,
Who with the highest faith imbued, their minds
Steadying on me, worship me, constantly
Devoted. Those, upon the other hand,
Who bridling all the senses, equable
Throughout, intent upon the good of all,
Worship the Indestructible, Unseen,
Ineffable, which doth all permeate,
Unthinkable, indifferent,° and fixed,
And changeless, come to me. For those whose minds
Are to the Unseen attached, greater's the toil,
Because the goal unseen† is hard to reach
For the embodied ones. But to those men
Who worship me, upon me meditating
With a devotion towards me alone,
Who offering up to me their every act,‡
Give themselves up to me, Oh Pṛithâ's son!
And who still fix their minds upon me, I
Without delay stand the deliverer
Out of the ocean of the mortal world.
On me alone place thou thy mind, on me
Thy resolution fix, in me alone

---

*   The original is कूटस्थ on which S'ridhar says कूटे माया-
प्रपञ्चे अभिष्ठानत्वेनावस्थितम्, which follows S'ankar's interpretation.
The other meaning which is expressed by the word 'indifferent' viz.
निष्क्रिय, or passively looking on, is also stated by S'ankar.

† अक्षरात्मिका says S'ankar i. e. The Indestructible. अव्यक्तविषया ग-
तिनिष्ठा says S'ridhar i. e. firm adherence to the Unseen. Madhusûdan agrees with S'ankar and renders गति by गन्तव्यं फलभूतं ब्रह्म.

‡ Compare Chapter III. St. 30 (line 461).

Wilt thou reside hereafter,* there's no doubt.
But if thou canst not firmly fix thy mind
Upon me, then, Oh Conqueror of wealth !
By the devotion of repeated thought,†
Endeavour to attain to me. If, too,
Thou art unequal to repeated thought,
Then be intent exclusively on acts
For me ; because thou wilt perfection reach
Even acts for me performing. If again
Thou art unequal to this too, forsake
All fruit of action, being self-restrained,
To me alone devoted.‡ Knowledge is
Superior to repeated thought ; above
Knowledge is meditation valued ; more
Than meditation is the abandonment
Of fruit of acts ; from that abandonment
Results tranquillity. That devotee
Of mine is dear to me, who's friendly, kind,
Who hates no creature, to whom "mine" is not,
Who is from egoism free, and equable
In pain and pleasure, patient, self-restrained,
Always devoted, and contented, firm
In his determinations, with his mind
And faculty of fixed resolve on me
Concentrated. He through whom never the world

---

* मदात्मना वासं करिष्यसि S'ridhar and Madhusûdan.

† Compare Chap. VIII. St. 8 (line 1025). S'ankar says चित्तस्यै-
कालिमन्नालम्बने सर्वतः समाहृत्य पुन:पुन: स्थापनमभ्यासस्तत्पूर्वको योग: समाधानलक्षण:.
S'ridhar and Madhusûdan concur.

‡ मद्योगमास्थितो मयि क्रियमाणानि कर्माणि संन्यस्य यत्करणं तेषामनुष्ठानं मद्योग-
ःनमाश्रित:—Sankar. S'ridhar says मद्योगं मदेकत्वरणम्. Madhusûdan,
as usual, combines both explanations.

Is agitated, whom the world too never
Does agitate, who's free from joy wrath fear
And perturbation, he is dear to me.
That devotee of mine, who is unconcerned,
Pure, wise, impartial, free from all distress,
Who doth renounce all acts for fruit,* he's dear
To me. He who rejoices not nor hates,†
Grieves not, does not desire, abandoning
Good and ill,‡ worships me, is dear to me.
Alike with respect and with disrespect,§
Alike to friend and foe, alike in heat
And cold, in pleasure and in pain, quite free
From all attachments, taking blame and praise
As equal, talking little, satisfied
With anything, homeless, of steady mind,
The man who worships me is dear to me.
And those, too, of my worshippers who taste
This holy nectar as thus shown above,
Imbued with faith, and given up to me
As the highest object, they are most dear to me.

Chapter XIII.‖

Krishna. This frame is called the Kshetra, Oh Kunti's son!
And learned persons call him who knows this
The Kshetrajna. And, offspring of Bharat! know

---

* Compare Chap. IV St. 19 (line 558); 'for fruit' is not in the original but must be supplied.

† Compare Chap. II. St. 56 *et seq.* (line 310 *et seq*).

‡ Comp. Chap. IX. St. 28 (line 1197).

§ *I. e.* Unmoved whether he is respected or the reverse.

‖ The relation of this Chapter with what has gone before is thus stated by S'ankar. In the seventh Chapter, two forms of the Supreme Being have been stated, by means of which he acts as the

I am the Kshetrajna in all Kshetras.   I
Do think the knowledge of Kshetrajna and Kshetra
To be true knowledge.   Hear from me in brief
What this Kshetra is, what it is like, what change
It undergoes, from what it comes ; and what
Is he, what are his powers :—all which is sung
By sages variously in various hymns,
With all distinctions, and in passages,
Teaching the Brahma, settled, argued out.*
The elements, and egoism, fixed resolve,
And the unseen, the senses ten, the one,
The five sense-objects, hatred, and desire,
Pleasure, pain, body, courage, consciousness,
Thus is described the Kshetra, accompanied

---

creator, preserver, and destroyer of the universe. Now in this
Chapter, the truth about the Supreme Being is to be expounded,
and as a means to that, the two forms of Kshetra and Kshetrajna
are explained. S'ridhar observes, that Krishna has said already that
he delivers his worshippers from this mortal world. Now such
a deliverance cannot be effected without real knowledge of the soul.
Therefore to communicate that knowledge is the object of this
Chapter, in which matter and spirit are distinguished from each
other. Madhusûdan, as we have already observed on sundry occasions, combines the two explanations into one.

    * 'Sages'=Vasishtha and others, says S'ankar. S'ridhar and Ma-
dhusûdan add योगशास्त्रैः. 'Variously'=in various ways—S'ankar.
S'ridhar says, " as the object of meditation &c., in the form Vairāj
&c." 'Various hymns,'=hymns from the Veds, concerning ordinary
and extraordinary actions, actions with special desires &c.—S'ridhar.
' Passages &c.,'—सूत्र refers to those that indicate generally, and पद
to those that describe specifically, the Brahma—S'ankar and S'rī-
dhar. 'Argued out,' applies, according to S'ridhar, to passages like
कथमसन: सज्जायेत or कोह्येवान्यात्क: प्राण्यात् &c.

With changes, briefly.* Absence of vanity
Of ostentation and of hurtfulness,
Patience, straight-forwardness, devotedness
To a preceptor, firmness, purity,
And self-restraint, towards objects of sense
Indifference, absence of egoism,   .
Perception of the evil of birth and death
And age and sickness and distress,† release
From all attachments, disregard of son,
Wife, home,‡ and constant equability
Upon the approach of good or evil, of me
Worship exclusive with a firm resolve,§
Frequenting lonely places, and distaste
Of men's society, and constancy
About the knowledge of the Adhyâtma,‖ thought

---

* Compare Chapter VII. St. 4 (line 908 *et seq.*) and the Sânkhya Sûtras Chap. I. Sûtra 61. Sânkhya Sûtra II. 13. shows the meaning which the word बुद्धि has in the Sânkhya system. 'The one' is the mind. S'ridhar says एते चेच्छादयो दृइयत्वान्नात्मधर्मो अपि तु मनोधर्मो भत:- क्षेत्रान्त:पातिन एव | उपलक्षणं चैतत्संकल्पादीनाम्; with this Madhusûdan, and we may add, S'ankar agree.

† This is the first step towards वैराग्य or indifference to worldly enjoyments. S'ankar suggests another interpretation in which दु:ख and दोष (evil and distress) would be in apposition—दु:खान्येव दोषा:—which is probably better than the one adopted in the text. S'ridhar also proposes जन्मादिषु दु:खदोषयोरनुदर्शनम्.

‡ Compare Chap. XII St. 19 (line 1645).

§ Comp. Chap. XIV. St. 26 (line 1845) also XII. 6 (line 1626). अनन्ययोगेन S'ankar renders by अपृथक्समाधिना. Madhusûdan says नान्यो भगवतो वासुदेवात्परोस्त्यत: स एव नो गतिरित्येवं निश्चयेन.

‖ *I. e.* knowledge about the soul and so forth—S'ankar. Compare Chap. XV. 5 (line 1870).

About the benefits of knowledge true*—
This is called knowledge, what conflicts with this
Is ignorance. What's to be known I will say,
Which known one reaches immortality.
The Highest Brahma, which has no beginning,
Which can't be said to be or not to be.†
On all sides it has hands and feet, on all
Eyes, heads, and faces, and on all sides ears;
It stands pervading all. Possessed of all
The qualities of all the senses, still
Devoid of all the senses; unattached;
Supporting all; devoid of qualities
Yet their supporter; 'tis without, within
All creatures; moving and immoveable;
Through subtlety unknowable; it stands
Afar and near; not different, in things,
It still stands as though different. And this thing,

---

* By this thought, says S'ankar, there results the effort to acquire the knowledge.

† S'ankar says that words express meanings by indicating a class, a quality, an action, or a relation, but none of these is possible in the case of the Brahma; and therefore neither the word सत् nor the word असत् can be applied to it. S'ridhar says विधि-मुखेन प्रमाणस्य विषय: सच्छब्देनोच्यते निषेधविषयस्त्वसच्छब्देनोच्यते इदं तु तदुभयवि-लक्षणमविषयत्वादित्यर्थ:; with this Madhusûdan agrees. See Chapter IX. St. 19 (line 1164) and XI. 37 (line 1507). The difference between those passages and this is, that in this the application of the terms सत् and असत् to the Brahma is denied, while in those the Brahma is identified with both सत् and असत्. Mr. Thomson reconciles the two by saying that the Brahma cannot be called either, because it is both. The expression सच्चासच्चाभ्यामनिर्वचनीय, which in effect means the same thing as the expression under discussion, is frequently used to designate the 'Mâyâ.' See on the whole passage Notes and Illustrations.

It should be known, supports all things that are,
Devours, and does create them.   It's the light
Even of the brilliant bodies, and is said
To be beyond all darkness.   Knowledge 'tis,
The object too of knowledge, and the goal
To be attained by knowledge, placed in the heart
Of every one.   Thus have I spoken in brief
Of Kshetra, of knowledge, and of object too.
My devotee discerning this becomes
Fit to be one with me.*   Nature and spirit,
Know both to be without beginning, know
Also that Nature doth produce as well
The emanations as the qualities.†
Nature is said to be the power that makes
The body and the senses work, and spirit
Is said to be the power through which are felt
Pleasure and pain.‡   For spirit with Nature joined
Enjoys the effects that from the qualities

---

* *I. e.* to attain 'Moksha' or final emancipation.

† The emanations (विकारा:), according to S'ankar, are बुद्धयादिदे-
हेन्द्रियान्ता:, and the qualities (गुणा:) सुखदु:खमोहप्रत्ययाकारपरिणता:. In
this S'ridhar concurs. The two include, therefore, the body, as well
subtle as gross, and the various feelings and so forth.

‡ 'The body and the senses.'—I thus render कार्यकारण, following the
commentators. The ordinary sense of that expression will not do, for
what can be the कर्तृत्व (working or activity) of a कार्य (effect)? 'Is
said to be,' *scil.* by Kapil and others, says S'ridhar. The notion
that activity is all due to 'Nature' and not to the soul has occurred
before in the Gîtâ. See *inter alia* Chap. III. St. 27 (line 452). Enjoyment, however, is not the function of dead matter, but of the soul.

Of Nature* flow. And the connection 'tis
With qualities, that brings about its births
In good or evil wombs. The Being Supreme
Within this frame is called the supervisor,
The mentor, the supporter, the great lord,
The enjoyer, and the soul supreme. Whoever
Thus knows spirit, Nature, and the qualities,
Is never again born, in whatever way
He may have lived.† By meditation some
Behold the soul in themselves by themselves;
Others see by the Sânkhya-yog; and some
See by the Karmayog;‡ and others yet
Who learn not in this way, from others hearing,
Worship perform, and hearing steadily,§
They also cross beyond the reach of death,
Prince of the Bhârats! And whatever thing
Immoveable or moveable is produced,
Know thou, 'tis from the union of Kshetra
And Kshetrajna. He sees who sees the Lord
Supreme, alike in all existences,
And undestroyed himself though they be all

---

* By the qualities (गुण) are meant here their manifestations as
सुखदुःख &c. as in line 1706. Hence we have rendered the simple word
गुण in the original by ' effects of qualities.' In the next line qualities
is interpreted by S'rîdhar to mean 'senses.' This seems, however,
unnecessary, though it is the result involved in the proposition.
The qualities lead to action good and bad, and that leads to birth
in good and bad wombs.

† Comp. Chap. VI. St. 31 (line 844). 'In whatever way'=though he
may have transgressed rules, says S'rîdhar.

‡ See Notes and Illustrations.

§ With faith, from preceptors, says S'ankar.

Destroyed; because seeing the Lord alike
Present in all things, one does not oneself
Destroy one's soul,° then to the seat supreme
Proceeds. He sees who sees all acts performed
By Nature, and his soul not working. When
One looks upon all separate entities
As in one thing existing,† and on all
As emanating from that one alone,
Then one the Brahma attains.‡ This soul Supreme
Oh Kunti's son! being inexhaustible,
Without beginning, void of qualities,
Even in the body works not, is not stained.
As through its subtlety space is not stained,
Though all-pervading, even so the soul,
Though present in all bodies, is not stained.
As lights up all this world the sun alone,
So does the Kshetrajna light up this Kshetra,
Offspring of Bharat! Those who, by the eye
Of knowledge, see this difference between
Kshetra and Kshetrajna, and the release of beings
From Nature,§ they attain to the Supreme.

---

* Not to have true self-knowledge is here regarded as a sort of self-destruction, and he who sees the Supreme Being in everything escapes this self-destruction, because he has true knowledge of the soul. Comp. S'ankar on Îśâvâsyopanishad St. 2.

† S'ridhar says:—"existing in one thing"=at the time of the deluge, existing absorbed in Nature which is one of the powers of God. "Emanating"=at the time of creation.

‡ As S'ankar remarks, this is again a restatement of the same doctrine as that laid down in the preceding lines. When one sees that all is Brahma, and that every individual thing we see is but an emanation of that Brahma and nothing else, then, one attains Brahma.

§ S'ankar and the other commentators say on this:—भूतानां प्रकृति. राविद्यालक्षणाप्रक्काख्या तस्या भूतप्रकृतेर्मोक्षणमभावगमनम्. Comp. Chap. VII. St. 14 (line 940).

Chapter XIV.

Krishna. Further I will declare to thee the best—
The highest—sort of knowledge, which obtained,
All sages reach perfection, being freed
From this life.* They being by this knowledge helped,
Assume my qualities; they are not born
At the creation, do not suffer pain†
At the destruction. The great Brahma‡ is
A womb for me, in which I cast the seed.
From that, offspring of Bharat! are then born
All things that are. The bodies which, Oh son
Of Kuntî! are produced from all the wombs,
Have for their womb this great Brahma, and I am
Their father—giver of the seed. Produced
From Nature, large-armed one! the qualities—
Goodness, Indifference, and Badness too—
Within the body do bind down the soul,§
Embodied, inexhaustible. Of these,
Goodness being pure, enlightening, free from pain,
The soul, Oh sinless one! with knowledge binds

---

* For 'being freed from this life' the original has 'hence' which S'ankar explains by 'after the [end of the] confinement to this body.'

† The pain, namely, of repetition of births.

‡ Brahma here means the प्रकृति 'Nature,' which has been spoken of before.

§ I. e., according to S'ridhar "brings the soul into contact with pleasure and pain and illusion and so forth, which are the effects of the qualities."

And happiness.* Indifference, know thou,
Consists in being charmed,† and that—the cause
Of craving and attachment—Kunti's son!
With action the embodied soul binds down.‡
Badness, know thou, is born of ignorance,
And the deluder of all creatures; that
Oh Bharat's child! binds down with laziness,
And heedlessness, and sleep.§ Goodness unites
With happiness; with action, Bharat's child!
Indifference; while Badness doth unite
With heedlessness, all knowledge wrapping up.
Indifference and Badness lying low,
Offspring of Bharat! Goodness then doth stand;
Indifference and Goodness being thus,
Badness; and when Goodness and Badness are
Such, then Indifference. When in this frame
At all its portals, is the light produced
Of knowledge, then should one know Goodness there
Prevailing. When Indifference prevails,
Prince of the Bhârats! then are avarice

---

* That is to say, a person in whom this first quality predominates
acquires knowledge, and gets all worldy happiness, and calmness,—for
that is the meaning of अनामय 'free from pain,' according to
S'ridhar.

† Here I follow S'ridhar and Madhusûdan. S'ankar says गौरिकादिनिष्ट-
्ासक्तम्—the appropriateness of which I cannot clearly perceive.

‡ A man in whom this quality predominates is full of desires
for all sorts of things which he has not, and is strongly attached
to those which he has. And thus he is ever given up to *exertions*
for acquiring new things, or preserving those which he has acquired.

§ प्रमाद (heedlessness) says S'ridhar means अनवधान 'inattention;'
आलस्य (laziness) means अनुद्यम (absence of work and activity); and
नेद्रा (sleep) चित्तप्रसादो लय: (drooping or cessation of intellect).

Activity, performance of acts too,
Attachment, and want of tranquillity,*
Produced. Whereas when Badness does prevail,
Oh Kuntî's son! absence of light and work,†
Delusion, and heedlessness, are produced.
If Goodness being prevalent, one dies,
One then attains the stainless worlds of those
Who know the Highest.‡ If Indifference,
One is then born 'mongst those who are attached
To acts. And one that under Badness dies,
Is born within the wombs of the ignorant.
They say the fruit of actions good is pure,
And of the quality of Goodness ; pain
The fruit is of Indifference ; the fruit
Of Badness ignorance. From Goodness flows
Knowledge ; as also from Indifference
Flows avarice ; from Badness, ignorance,
Heedlessness, and delusion. Up those go
Who stick to Goodness ; in the middle stop
Those of the quality of Indifference ;
And those go downwards whose behaviour
Is of the lowest quality. What time
The seer sees no one but the qualities

---

* 'Activity' (प्रवृत्ति) S'rîdhar explains by नित्यं कुर्वंद्रपना "always doing something or another;" 'performance of acts' (कर्मणामारम्भ:)
he exemplifies by 'rearing up large mansions &c;' 'attachment'
(स्पृहा) is desire to get everything that is seen; want of tranquillity
(अशम) he renders by perpetual agitation of mind—"this I will
do now, and then that, and then the other."

† Absence of work (अप्रवृत्ति) doing nothing at all. अत्यन्तमप्रवृत्ति:—
S'rîdhar.

‡ *I. e.* Hiranyagarbha and so forth, says S'rîdhar. The elements
such as महत् &c.—S'ankar. Madhusûdan agrees with S'rîdhar.

As agents,° and knows that which is above
The qualities, into my essence then
He comes. And when the embodied soul transcends
All these three qualities from which are born
All bodies,† then is it from birth and death
And age and pain relieved, and then attains
To immortality.

Arjun. What are the marks,
Oh Lord! of one who these three qualities
Transcends, what is his conduct, how does he
Transcend all these three qualities.‡

Krishna. He's said

To have transcended the three qualities,
Oh Pāṇḍu's son! who hates not when they come
Light, and delusion, and activity ;§
And does not wish for them when they are not ;
Who standing like one unconcerned is never
Shaken by the qualities,‖ who never moves¶

---

* Again the oft-repeated idea. Seer is simply one who sees.

† As to 'transcending the qualities' compare *inter alia* line 271. देहसमुद्भवान् is by the commentators interpreted as equivalent to देहोत्तिबीजभूतान्—S'ridhar says that देह is the परिणाम (development) of the qualities.

‡ S'ridhar says that this question and its answer are a repetition in another form of what has been said about a स्थितप्रज्ञ in Chapter II.

§ These are respectively the effects of the three qualities. They are according to S'ridhar only indications, and all the respective effects are to be understood here. Mr. Thomson erroneously takes them to stand for the qualities themselves.

‖ *I. e.* so as to lose all discrimination—S'ankar. ' Qualities' stands for the effects of the qualities, pleasure, pain &c. says S'ridhar here as before.

¶ स्वरूपावस्थ एव भवति says S'ankar, न व्याप्रियते says Madhusûdan, न चलति says S'ridhar. It seems to mean "never deviates from the determination formed by him."

But ever is steady, thinking the qualities
Exist;* who is calm; to whom pleasure and pain
And gold, stone, sod are all alike; to whom
Equal are things as well disliked as liked;
To whom Both praise and censure of himself
Are equal; who towards the side of friends
Or foes, in honour or dishonour too,
Is still alike; and who all acts forsakes;
And he who with devotion worships me—
Devotion all-exclusive† —he transcends
These qualities, and fits himself to be
One with the Brahma. I the image am‡
Of the Brahma, and of immortality
All inexhaustible, of piety
Eterne, and of unbroken happiness

Chapter XV.

Krishna. They say the As'vattha inexhaustible§
Grows with its roots above, its boughs below;
The Chhandas are its leaves; whoever it knows
Doth know the Veds. Upwards and downwards too,

---

* Comp. III. 28. (line 456) with which S'ankar likens this completely by supplying अन्यान्यविदमन्. Mr. Thomson thinks the two differ, but I do not see the distinction he draws.

† Most of the elements making up this passage are noted elsewhere. Compare Chap. II. St. 56 et seq. Chap. V. St. 20, VI. 7, 8, 9, VII. 14, XII, 13 et seq.

‡ प्रनिष्ठा (image) is thus explained by S'ridhar प्रनिष्ठा प्रतिमा घनीं. भूतं ब्रह्मगहं यथा घनीभनप्रकाश एव सूर्यमण्डलं तद्वादिस्यथे:. Madhusûdan says कलिनहृपरहितमकालिनं रूपम्; and afterwards प्रनिष्ठा पर्याप्ति:.

§ Compare for this and following verses Kathopanishad V. 15.

Extend its branches,   by the qualities
Enlarged, their sprouts being objects of sense.
Downwards extend the roots that in this world
Of mortals lead to action.   Here not thus
Is its form known; nor is its end, its source.
Nor its supports.   But with the weapon strong
Of unconcern, hewing the As'vattha down,
With its roots firmly fixed, then should that seat
Be sought for, from which those who do repair
To it return not—thinking that one rests
On that same Primal Being from whom the course
Eternal emanates.*   Those who are free
From pride, delusion, who have overcome
The evils of attachment, and dispelled
Desires, who to the Adhyâtma are gvien up,
Who are free from the pairs of opposites,
Called pain and pleasure—undeluded these
Go to that seat Imperishable.   That seat
The Sun lights not, nor Fire, nor yet the Moon.†
That is my seat Supreme, going to which
One comes not back.   A part eterne of me
It is, that in this mortal world becomes
An individual soul, and to itself
Draws out the senses with the mind as sixth

---

* The construction in the original here is not quite clear, but I
follow the commentators, according to whom, the clause beginning
with the words ' thinking that' explains the manner of the ' search'—
अन्वेषणप्रकार, as S'ridhar puts it.   Mr. Thomson's rendering involves,
I think, a rather unusual meaning for प्रवृत्ति, and is after all not perfectly clear or unexceptionable. 'The course' (प्रवृत्ति) is the course of
this worldly life—संसारप्रवृत्ति.

† Compare Kathopanishad VI. 1.

From Nature.* Whensoever the Soul Divine
Obtains or quits a body, these he takes
Always with him, as from their seats the wind
Takes off perfumes. And then presiding over
The ear, the eye, the sense of touch and taste
And smell, and also over the mind, the Soul
Objects of sense enjoys.† The ignorant
See not the soul quitting this frame or staying,
Enjoying, or joined with the qualities.
They see who have eyes of knowledge.‡ Devotees
With efforts see it placed within themselves.§
But those who have not purity attained
And who have no discernment see it not

---

* 'Senses with the mind as sixth'—means the five senses and the
mind. 'from Nature'—S'ridhar says that the senses are absorbed in
the Prakṛiti or Nature during sound sleep, as also at the time of the
dissolution of the world ; and from Nature the unemancipated soul
has to resume them.

† The perception and enjoyment of worldly objects by the soul is of
course indirect only—through the intervention of the senses and the
mind.

‡ 'Staying' means staying in the body ; 'enjoying', according to
S'ankar, means perceiving sound &c. while 'joined with the qualities'
means brought into contact with pleasure, pain, delusion &c. Sr'idhar
renders 'enjoying' by enjoying worldly objects, and the last phrase
he explains by joined with the senses इन्द्रियुक्त. Madhusûdan
agrees with S'ankar. S'ankar observes एवंभूनमर्प्येनमन्यन्तं दर्शनगोचरं
प्राप्तं विमूढा दृश्चादृश्चविषयभोगवज्ञाकूटचेनस्तयानेकभा मूढा नानुपश्यन्ति.

§ 'Within themselves' means within their bodies (S'ridhar) in
their intellects (S'ankar). Madhusûdan agrees with S'ankar, and
explains 'placed' by reflected.

Even after efforts. Know° that glory mine,
Which in the Sun lights up the Universe,
And in the Moon and Fire. Into the earth
Entering, I by my power support all things.
And I become the watery Moon, and give
Their nutriment to all herbs. I become
Fire, and entering into all creatures' frames,
Joined with the upward and the downward winds,
I cause digestion of the four-fold food.†
Within the heart‡ of every one I am placed,
From me all reasoning, knowledge, memory.
In all the Veds I am only to be known.
I am the author of the Vedânta. I
Am also he who knows the Veds. There are
In this world these two Beings—that which is
Destructible, and the Indestructible.
Of all things the Destructible consists;
The Unconcerned one is that which is called
The Indestructible. The Being Supreme
Is yet another called the Highest Soul,
Who, as the Great Lord inexhaustible,
Pervading the three worlds, supports them. I
Transcending the Destructible, and being
Even higher than the Indestructible,
Am in the Veds and in the Universe

---

* Comp. Kaṭhopanishad V. 15. He here returns to what he had left
off at line 1877. The intervening portion shows, according to S'ridhar,
how it comes that some souls do 'come back,' after having gone to
the 'supreme seat' in deep sleep—as taught by a Vedic text.

† See Notes and Illustrations.

‡ Compare Chap. XVIII. St. 61. (line 2322).

Known as the Best of Beings.* He who knows
Me, undeluded, thus, the Best of Beings,
Offspring of Bharat! he does, knowing all,
Worship me every. way.† Thus, sinless one!
Have I this most mysterious science declared.
One knowing this becomes, Oh Bharat's child!
Possessed of knowledge, and to his duty true.

Chapter XVI.

Krishna. Freedom from fear, and purity of heart,
Persistence in pursuit of knowledge too,
Almsgiving, self-restraint, and sacrifice,
Study, and penance, and straightforwardness,
Harmlessness, and renunciation, truth,
Freedom from anger, and tranquillity,
Not playing the informer, to all beings
Compassion, freedom too from avarice,‡
Mildness, absence of vain activity,
And patience, modesty, highmindedness,§
Courage, cleanness, absence of vanity

---

* See Notes and Illustrations.

† The original is सर्वभावेन which is rendered by S'ridhar as in the text—सर्वप्रकारेण. S'ridhar then adds ततश्च सर्वज्ञो भवति. I. e. 'Then he becomes all-knowing.' S'ankar does not construe the word 'all-knowing' in this way, but as it is taken in our translation. On सर्वभावेन he says सर्वःमचिन्तया 'thinking me to be the soul of all.' But see Chap. XVIII. St. 62. (line 2324).

‡ So S'ridhar. S'ankar renders it by 'the senses not being affected even after contact with their objects.'

§ The original is तेज: 'glory.' S'ankar renders it by प्रागल्भ्य, so does S'ridhar. S'ankar says expressly तेज: प्रागल्भं न त्वग्गता दीप्ति:—not the mere bodily glory.

And of malignancy,* all these belong
Offspring of Bharat! to him who is born
To heavenly endowments. Pride, conceit,
And ostentation, anger, harshness† too,
And ignorance are his, Oh Pṛithâ's son!
Who is to demoniac endowments born.
Endowments heavenly are thought to be
Means for salvation; for captivity,‡
Demoniac. Grieve not, Oh Pâṇḍu's son!
To heavenly endowments art thou born.
Two sorts of creatures have been in this world
Created, heavenly and demoniac.
The heavenly have been spoken of at length,
Hear the demoniac from me, Pṛithâ's son!
Creatures demoniac action know not
Nor yet inaction;§ and veracity,
Behaviour as ordained, and purity,
Are not in them. "The universe", say they,
" Contains no truth; it is without a Lord,

---

* 'Absence of malignancy' (भद्रोह) means according to the commentators परजिग्यांसाराहिंल्य or अहिंसन, freedom from a desire to injure others.

† Pride (दर्प) *i. e.* of wealth and learning; and conceit (अभिमान) is the same thing as vanity, believing oneself to deserve great respect and so forth—according to the commentators. Ostentation (दाम) धर्मैध्वजित्वम् say S'ankar and S'ridhar. Madhusûdan adds धार्मकत्वयात्मनः ख्यापनम् (making a show of piety); harshness=निष्ठुरत्व says S'ridhar, परुषवचन says S'ankar.

‡ *I. e.* freedom from this world.—संसार—and being tied down to it, respectively.

§ *I. e.* That which should be done, for the attainment of real good, and that which should not be done, as productive of real mischief.

And is of all fixed principle devoid,
Without connections mutual, and indeed
Designed for pleasure."*   Holding to this view,
These men of little knowledge, ruined souls,
Of cruel actions, the world's enemies,
Are born for its destruction. Harbouring
Insatiable desires, and full of pride,
Folly, and ostentation, they adopt
False notions through delusion, and behave
In modes impure. Indulging boundless thoughts†
Ending with death ; to enjoyments of this world
Given up, resolved that that‡ is all ;   bound down
With nets of hopes in hundreds ; given up
To anger and desire ; they wish for heaps
Of wealth, the pleasures of this world to enjoy,
Unjustly. "This have I received to-day ;
This wish I shall obtain. This wealth is mine ;
This shall be mine. I have destroyed this foe ;
And others too I will destroy. I am God,
I am enjoyer, I am perfect,§ strong,
Happy, and wealthy. I am of high birth

---

  * See Notes and Illustrations.

  † *I. e.* Always during life thinking of preserving or acquiring something चिन्तामास्मयोगक्षेमोपायालोचनात्मिकाम् says Ânandagiri.

  ‡ *I. e.* enjoyment of worldly good, referring to the expression in
the line preceding, which literally means 'enjoyment of things which
are the objects of wish,' काम्यन्त इति कामा: शब्दादय: says S'ankar ; and
see Ânandagiri's gloss पारत्रिकं तु नास्ति सुखमिति निश्चयवन्तं इत्याह एनावदिति.

  § S'ankar says सर्वप्रकारेण च सिद्धोहं सपत्न: पुत्रै: पौत्रैर्नप्तृभि:—that is to
say, blessed with children, grand children, and great grand children.
Madhusûdan says similarly, possessed of companions such as sons,
servants &c. S'ridhar's view seems to me to be better. He renders it by
कृनकृत्य: literally 'One who has done all he need do.'

Who else is like me ?   I will sacrifice*
I will make gifts, rejoice." By ignorance
Deluded thus, tossed round by numerous thoughts,
Surrounded by delusion's net, attached
To the enjoyments of this world, they fall
Down into Hell impure·   Full of the pride
And madness caused by wealth, highly esteemed
But by themselves, void of humility,†
They sacrifices but in name perform,
Merely for show, against the rules prescribed.
These enemies,‡ cruel, meanest of men,
Indulging vanity, censoriousness,
Desire, pride, wrath, brute force,§ and hating me
In their own bodies and of others too,‖
Unholy, to this world¶ I do hurl down

---

* S'ankar and Madhusûdan take this to mean यज्ञैनाप्यन्यानभिभविष्यामि.
S'ridhar renders it by दक्षिनान्तेरम्यः सकाशान्महतीं प्रतिष्ठां प्राप्स्यामि.

† स्तब्धः is rendered by अप्रणतात्मानः by S'ankar, अनम्राः by S'ridhar
and Madhusûdan.

‡ *I. e.* of God, say the commentators.

§ बल is said by S'ankar to be परामिभवनिमित्त and by Madhusûdan
परराभिभवनिमित्तशरीरसामर्थ्यविशेष.

‖ This and the two preceding lines explain, according to S'ridhar,
how the sacrifices are "against prescribed rules." He says.... आत्मदेहे
परदेहेषु च चिरंशेन स्थितं मां प्राद्विषन्तो यजन्ते दम्भयज्ञेषु श्रद्धया अभावादात्मनो
वृथैव पीडा भवति तथा पश्वादीनामप्यविभिना हिंसया चैतन्यद्रोह एतावदेशिष्यत इति
प्राद्विषन्त इत्युक्तम्। अभ्यसूयकाः सन्मार्गवर्तिनां गुणेषु दोषारोपकाः. Hence it appears that the words, "hating me in their own bodies and of others
too" refer to the trouble to oneself involved in performing sacrifices
without faith, and to the animals that are killed for these useless
sacrifices.

¶ The original संसारेषु, S'ankar and Madhusûdan explain by नरक-
संसरणमार्गेषु, and S'ridhar by जन्ममृत्युमार्गेषु.

Perpetually into demoniac wombs.
Coming into demoniac wombs, each birth
Deluded still, never coming to me,
Oh Kunti's son! they go down into Hell.
Three are the ways to Hell, which to the soul
Are ruinous—desire, wrath, avarice.
Therefore should one this triad still renounce.
Released from these three ways to darkness, man,
Oh Kunti's son! behaves so as to achieve
His own good, then reaches the highest goal.
He* who abandoning the ordinances
Of scripture, acts as he himself desires,
Does not attain perfection,† happiness,
Nor yet the seat supreme. Therefore for thee,
Between what should be done and what should not
To make distinctions, the authority
Is scripture. Hence, knowing what is laid down
In scripture ordinance, all acts here perform.

Chapter XVII.

Arjun. What is the state‡ of those who, full of faith,

---

* S'ridhar observes that this is said with the view of showing that release from the 'triad' is not to be accomplished except by the performance of prescribed duties.

† सिद्धि, the original, has occurred before also several times. S'an-kar here explains it to mean 'fitness for the attainment of the *sum-mum bonum*' पुरुषार्थयोग्यता. S'ridhar renders it by तत्त्वज्ञान 'right knowledge.'

‡ The original is निष्ठा which also occurs at Chap. III. St. 3 (line 376), where we have rendered it by 'path'. Here S'ridhar renders it by स्थिति or आश्रय, S'ankar by अवस्थान. It is not difficult to see, however that the apparent difference is only owing to the context, and that in substance the different renderings express the same idea.

Worship perform, Oh Krishṇa! abandoning
All scripture rules—Goodness, Indifference,
Or Badness?

Krishna. Faith is of three kinds in men,
'Tis the result of dispositions.* Hear
About it; 'tis Good, Bad, Indifferent.
The faith of all, offspring of Bharat! is
Conformable to their hearts. Mortals here
Are full of faith, and whatsoever one's faith
Is, that is one oneself.† The Good the gods
Worship. The Indifferent the Rakshases,
And Yakshas. And the Bad worship the hosts
Of demons and the manes. Know that those
Who practise dreadful penance, unordained
By Holy Writ, with ostentatiousness,
And pride, full of attachment, and desire,

---

* स्वभाव is explained जन्मान्तरकृतं धर्मादिसंस्कारो मरणकालेऽभिव्यक्तः
स्वभाव उच्यते—S'ankar; so too the other commentators. And compare
the note at Chap. VII. 20 (line 967) *suprâ*. and at line 469.

† "According to their hearts," S'ankar's gloss on the original is
this विशिष्टसंस्कारोपेतान्तःकरणानुरूपा. S'ridhar सत्त्वनारतम्यानुसारिणी. Madhusûdan agrees with S'ankar, for he says प्राग्भवीयान्तःकरणवासनाहेत-
निमित्तकारणवैचित्र्येण श्रद्धावैचित्र्यमुक्त्वा तत्प्रादानकारणान्तःकरणवैचित्र्येणापि
नद्वैचित्र्यमाह.—He then goes on सत्त्वं प्रकाशशीलत्वात्सत्त्वप्रधानत्रिगुणा (*sic.*
णम्?) पश्चीकृतपञ्चमहाभूतारब्धमन्तःकरणम्.—"Full of faith." S'ridhar
says त्रिविधया श्रद्धया त्रिकियन्त इत्यर्थः. S'ankar says श्रद्धामय: and Madhusûdan प्राचुर्येणातिमङ्गश्रद्धा प्रस्तुना •• अन्नमयो यज्ञ इतिवत्. It seems to
mean, that the "faith" of each person is the dominant principle in
him, and according as that is Good, Bad, or Indifferent, the man himself is Good, Bad, or Indifferent. This last is the meaning of the
words immediately following.

And stubbornness, and folly, torturing
The various portions of their frames, and me
Within those frames,* are men whose conduct is
Demoniac.   The food that is liked by them
Is also three-fold.   So the sacrifice,
The alms-giving, and the penance. Listen, now,
To their distinctions, thus:—Those kinds of food
Which do increase life, energy, and strength,
Health, happiness, and relish,†—savoury,
And oleaginous, of substance full,‡
And pleasant, are by Good men liked.   Those kinds
Which are too hot, and bitter, acid, salt,
Sharp, rough, and burning, which occasion pain,
Grief, and disease, are by the Indifferent
Desired.   The food cold, tasteless,§ stinking, stale,
Impure, and even the leavings, by the Bad
Are liked.   Good is the sacrifice performed
According to the ordinances, by those
Who wish not for the fruit, but have resolved
Within their minds that it must be performed.
But know that sacrifice Indifferent,
Prince of the Bhârats! which is all performed

---

* Compare Chap. XVI. St. 18 (line 1989).

† प्रीति, the original, is rendered by अभिरुचि by S'ridhar and Madhusûdan. Ânandagiri says परेषामवि संतन्नानां दर्शीनात्वरमी हर्वे:.

‡ स्थिरा:, the orginal, S'ridhar renders by देहे सारांशेन निरकालावस्थायि न:. In this S'ankar and Madhusûdan concur.

§ S'ankar says यातयामं मन्दपक्रं निर्वीर्यमेत्य गतरसेनोक्तत्वान् Madhusûdan quotes this, and adds विरसतां प्राप्तं शुष्कम्. S'ridhar says यातयामं दीर्घावस्थां प्राप्तमित्यर्थः गतरसं निश्शीडितसारम्. पर्युषित, which we have rendered by stale, all the commentators explain to mean, cooked and allowed to remain in that state for one night.

For show, or with an eye towards the fruit.
That sacrifice do they call Bad, in which
There are no Mantras, and no food, nor wealth
Dealt out,* devoid of faith, not in accord
With the ordinances. The paying reverence
To Gods, and Bráhmaṇs, teachers, and the wise,†
And purity, straightforwardness,‡ and life
As celibates, and harmlessness—all this
Is called the penance bodily. That speech
Which sorrow causes not, and which is true,
Pleasant, and beneficial, and likewise
The study of the Veds§—all this is called
The penance wordly. Next, calmness of mind,
Mildness, and silence,‖ and restraint of self,
And purity of heart—all this is called
The penance mental. Practised with full faith
By men, devoted, not desiring fruit,
This penance three-fold is called Good. And that
Which is for honour, reverence, and respect,¶

---

* That is to say, a sacrifice in which no food or Dakshiṇâ is given to Bráhmans.

† I. e. Others than "teachers" who have right knowledge गुरुद्यनिरिक्ता अन्ये तत्त्वविद्:—S'ridhar.

‡ I. e. doing what is prescribed, not doing what is prohibited.

§ This includes the recitation of them, and therefore forms part of the ' penance wordly.'

‖ This is included in the ' penance mental,' as silence or the ' government of the tongue' is a consequence of mental restraint, and here according to S'ankar, the effect is put for the cause.

¶ ' Honour,' people saying " this is a very holy person" and so on ; ' reverence' people washing his feet and so forth ; ' respect,' people rising to receive him and so on—S'ankar.

And with much show performed, that is here called
Indifferent—'tis uncertain, transient too.
But that's described as Bad, which is performed
Under a foolish view,* with self-distress,
Or for another's ruin.   The gift of alms,
That's made because it ought to be, to one
Who can't repay,† and at a proper place,
And proper time, and to a proper man,
Is called Good.   That, however, which is made
For a return, or with an eye to fruit,‡
And with reluctance, that is said to be
Indifferent.   And it is described as Bad,
When given at an improper place or time,
To an improper man, without respect
Or with disdain.   *Om, tat,* and *sat* are called§
The three-fold designation of the Brahma.
By that the Brâhmans, as well as the Veds,
And sacrifices, were created.‖ Hence
All acts of penance, gift, and sacrifice,
That are ordained, with those who know the Brahma,
Always after repeating *Om* commence.
The various acts of penance, sacrifice,
And gift are done by those who do desire
Salvation, saying *tat*, without an eye
To fruit.   Existence, goodness, to express
Sat is employed.   Likewise, Oh Pṛithâ's son !

* Under a determination arrived at without proper discrimination.
† So the commentators interpret अनुपकारिणे.
‡ Heaven &c. as a reward for the act of liberality.
§ वेदान्तेषु. 'In the Vedântas or Upanishads' says S'aṅkar; शिष्टैः:—' by the learned'—S'rîdhar.
‖ As to the whole of this passage see Notes and Illustrations.

About auspicious* actions the term *sat*
Is used. Perseverance in giving alms,
Penance, and sacrifice, are also called
Sat, and so too are called all acts for this. †
Whatever penance is performed, whatever
Is offered up or given, whatever is done,‡
Without faith, that is *asat,*   Pritha's son !
And is nought either here or after death.

———

Chapter XVIII.

Arjun. Killer of Kes'i ! large-armed one ! Oh Lord
Of minds ! I do desire to know the truth
About Renunciation, and. about
Rejection also, as distinct from that.

Krishna.   The sages by Renunciation mean
The casting off of acts done with desires ;
And it is called Rejection by the wise
To disregard the fruit of every act.§
" Action should be rejected as an evil, "
Say some wise men ;‖ and others say, that acts

———

* प्रशस्ते विवाहादौ S'unkar माङ्गलिके विवाहादिकर्मणि S'ridhar, *i. e*
marriage &c.

† S'ankar says यज्ञदानतपोर्ष्यिमयथा यस्यभिधानत्रयं प्रकृनं तदर्थीयमीश्वरा-
र्थीयमिश्यैनत्. S'ridhar says यस्य चेदं नामत्रयं स एव परमात्मा भधेः फलं यत्र
अत्रत्रर्थं कर्मे ॰ ॰ तत्सिद्धये यदन्यत्कर्मे क्रियते ॰ ॰ नत्कर्मे तदर्थीयम्.

‡ Praise, salutation &c. says S'ankar.

§ In the first case, the act itself is not done. In the other it is
done, but without an eye to the fruit. S'ridhar refers back to Chap. V.
St. 13 (line 676 *et seq.*) and IV. 20 (line 559 *et seq.*) for संन्यास and त्याग.

‖ हिंसादिदोषवत्त्वेन त्यन्यकर्म says S'ridhar. दोषवत् may also mean 'like
an evil.'

Of sacrifice, of penance, or of gift,
Ought not to be rejected. Listen now
Prince of the Bhârats! to my judgment firm
Concerning this Rejection. Of three kinds,
Oh valiant one! Rejection is described
To be. Now* acts of sacrifice, and gift,
And penance too, rejected should not be,
Should be performed of course. Gift, sacrifice,
And penance—all do purify. the wise.
But even these acts should be, Oh Pṛithâ's son!
(It is my excellent and settled view)·
Performed without attachment, and without
Desire of fruit. Of necessary acts
Renunciation is not fit. 'Tis said
That their rejection through delusion's bad.
When one rejects acts merely because
They are hard, through fear of bodily distress,
By a Rejection thus Indifferent,
He surely will not get Rejection's fruit.
When necessary actions are performed,
Because, Oh Arjun! they must be performed,
Rejecting all attachments and all fruit,
Then such Rejection is thought to be Good.
The man of talent, whose doubts are destroyed,
Who is full of Goodness, and who doth reject
All fruit and all attachment,† likes not acts
Pleasant, to unpleasant‡ ones is not averse.

---

   * Here he states his judgment.

   † These words are supplied from the commentary. The original is simply त्यागी 'one who rejects.'

   ‡ कुशल, S'ridhar renders by सुखकर, and as an example he gives निदाघे मध्यान्हस्नानादि i. e. bathing at midday in summer.

For any creature, 'tis impossible
All action to reject.* But he is called
Rejecter† who rejects the fruit of acts.
Agreeable, and disagreeable,
And mixed,—the fruit of acts of three sorts thus
Falls to the non-rejecter after death,
Never to the renouncer,‡ large-armed one !
From me the five conditions§ learn, which are
Required for the completion of all acts,
And in the Sânkhya system‖ are declared—
The agent, the substratum, various kinds
Of senses, all the movements various,
The Deities¶ the fifth. Whatever act,

---

* Compare Chap. III. St. 3 (line 382).

† The original is त्यागी. I have thought it necessary to take the liberty of coining a word 'rejecter' as a synonym for this.

‡ The original is संन्यासी, but S'ridhar is, I think, right in saying that the word here means the same thing as त्यागी. He refers to Chap. VI. St. 1 (line 738-39).—Madhusûdan expressly dissents from this. S'ankar and he take the word in its ordinary sense, rendering it by परमहंसपरिव्राजक.

§ कारणानि S'ankar renders by निर्वर्तनानि (the printed copy has निर्वर्तनानि, I think wrongly). In what follows, says S'ridhar, it is intended to show how the fruit of acts does not accrue to the renouncer.

‖ S'ankar and Madhusûdan interpret this to mean the Vedânta-S'âstra. S'ridhar, too, does the same, but he gives also the alternative meaning—Sânkhya S'âstra.

¶ The agent = one who has the egoism to think himself the doer of acts; substratum = the body, the substratum for the manifestation of desire, aversion, pleasure, pain &c.; various senses=the twelve senses—the means for the perception of sound &c.; various movements i.e. of the internal winds, downwards, upwards, &c.; deities=those which preside over the several senses (आदित्यादि चक्षुरादनुग्राहकम) or the power that controls all (सर्वप्रेरकोन्तर्यामी वा says S'ridhar).

Just or its opposite, a man performs,
With body, speech, or mind, its causes are
Those five.   That being so, whoever sees
The agent in the soul immaculate,
Is not of right views, being unrefined
In mind, and he sees not.*   He who does feel
No egoism, whose intellect's not stained,
Destroying even these worlds, does not destroy,
Is not tied down.†   The prompting to all acts
Is three-fold—knowledge, and its object too,
And subject; so in brief all action is
Three-fold—the agent, and the instrument,
And the object.‡   In the list of qualities,§
Knowledge, and act, and agent, are declared
To be of three sorts, in conformity
To the division of the qualities.
These, too, learn as they are. When one perceives
In all things one thing inexhaustible,
One undivided in divided ones,‖
That knowledge, know, is Good.   But that which sees
In all things various entities distinct,
That knowledge, based upon variety,¶

---

* Compare Chap. XIII. St. 29 (line 1742) and other passages.

† Compare Chap. II. St. 38 (line 249).

‡ Knowledge *scil.* that a particular thing is a means to something desired; its object is that which is such a means; and the subject he who has the knowledge. When these co-exist, we have action. The 'instrument' *scil,* of action, is the senses, &c.; 'object' is that which the agent desires.

§ The system of Kapil—the Sânkhya Philosophy.

‖ Compare Chap. XIII. St. 16 (line 1699) one all-pervading principle under all the apparently distinct entities.

¶ This states in brief what is explained in the preceding lines. And compare मृत्योः स मृत्युमाप्नोति य इह नानेव पश्यति ।

Know thou to be Indifferent. And that
Which looks on only one created thing
As everything, given up to it, without
Reason, devoid of truth, and low, is Bad.*
The necessary action that's performed
Without attachment, without love or hate,†
By one not wishing for its fruit, is called
Good. But then that which is performed by one,
Full of desires, or even of egotism,‡
And which occasions toil, Indifferent
Is called. The action through delusion done,
Without regard to consequences, loss,
One's power, or harm to others, is called Bad.
The agent, from attachment egotism
Free, and possessed of boldness, energy,
And by success or ill-success unmoved,
Is called Good. But the agent who desires
The fruit of acts, who's of affection§ full,
Cruel, impure, and covetous, who feels
Delight and grief, is called Indifferent.

---

* एकस्मिन्कार्येदेहे बहिर्गे प्रनिमादौ सक्तमेनाबानेशान्मेश्वरो या नान: परमन्नानि
यथा नम्रक्षपणकादीना शारीरान्तर्वैनिंदेहवारिमाणो जीव ईश्वरो वा पाषाणादार-
चोदिमात्रम् (?) S'ankar.

† Love for children &c., or hatred for foes &c.

‡ The commentators reject the rendering 'egoism' here as rendered pleonastic by the other expressions. They render it by 'pride of
learning, piety &c.' Five lines further on, the word is again similarly interpreted by S'ridhar; Ânandagiri says there (interpreting
S'ankar's words) कर्तीहमिति वदनश्रीलो न भवतीत्यर्थ:.

§ *Scil.* for children &c., according to S'ridhar, as before, but
Ânandagiri says कर्मविषयो राग:.

And he is Bad who is of judgment void,
Who has no application, is headstrong,
Crafty, malicious, lazy, melancholy,
And slow.^ᵃ Now the division three-fold learn
Of intellect and firmness,† Conqueror
Of wealth! which I shall now exhaustively
And with distinctions mention. The intellect
That knows salvation, and the being tied down,
Security, and insecurity,
What should be done, and what should not be done,
And action and inaction,‡ Prithâ's son!
Is Good.   But that through which one understands
Improperly what should be done, what not,
Impiety, and piety, Oh Pârtha!
That is Indifferent. That intellect
Which sees impiety as piety,
And all things too the wrong way, covered up
By darkness, that is Bad, Oh Prithâ's son!

---

* अयुक्तोऽसमाहित: says S'ankar अनमि (न ?) हित: says S'rîdhar. The
original for 'malicious' is नैष्कृतिक: which S'ankar interprets by परवृत्तिच्छे-
दनपर:. Lazy (भलस:) means disinclined to work अनुद्यमशील:; slow.
(दीर्घसूत्री) means one who takes too long a time to do any work.

† Madhusûdau explains the two words thus बुद्धेरध्यवसायादिवृत्तिमत्या:
भूनेश्च तद्वने:. The word here rendered by 'intellect' is the same that
has been before translated by 'faculty of fixed resolve' and like
expressions. Firmness is the strength of that faculty.

‡ Compare Chap. XVI. St. 7. (line 1952). S'rîdhar's interpretation here is the same as on that passage. S'ankar, however, says
here प्रवृत्ति: प्रवर्तनं बन्धहेतु: कर्ममार्गे: निवृत्तिर्मोक्षहेतु: सन्यासमार्ग:. So
Madhusûdan, also, who adds as to कार्याकार्ये &c. कार्यं प्रवृत्तिमार्गे कर्म-
णा करणमकार्यं निवृत्तिमार्गे कर्मणामकरणम् भयं प्रवृत्तिमार्गे गर्भवासादिदु:खमभयं
निवृत्तिमार्गे तदभावम्.

That firmness is good firmness, by which one
Controls the movements of the mind and breath
And senses through devotion, and which never
Doth swerve.* But that, Oh Pritha's son! by which
One hugs desire and piety and wealth,†
Wishing through strong attachment for the fruit,‡
Oh Arjun! is Indifferent. And that
By which the senseless man abandons not
Folly, sleep, fear, despondency, and grief—
That firmness, Pritha's son! is Bad. Now hear
Chief of the Bhârats! the descriptions three
Of happiness. That in which one is pleased
After habituation,§ and arrives
At the end of pain, which is like poison first,
But in the end like nectar—that is called
Good, and it flows from knowledge of the soul

---

* योग 'Devotion' is here rendered by समाधान by S'ankar and Madhusûdan, and चिन्निकारय by S'ridhar. 'Which never swerves' (अव्यभिचारि-
ण्या) S'ankar renders by समाधानानुगतया. Madhusûdan by अविनाभूतया
which he construes with योगेन and explains further by समाधिव्याप्तया.
The meaning is that this firmness of mind always adheres to devotion, and thereby always controls sense, breath, and mind.

† These are three of the so-called पुरुषार्थ—omitting the highest
मोक्ष or 'final emancipation;' 'Hugs' (धारयते)=प्राधान्येन धारयते (S'ridhar) मनसि निस्यकर्तव्यरूपानेव धारयते meaning 'regards as essential.'

‡ 'The fruit'=the fruit of the action performed with an eye to the
three things mentioned. प्रसङ्ग 'attachment' is interpreted by Madhusûdan to mean 'the belief of oneself being the real agent in
the action.'

§ By repetition of enjoyment—not at once as in the case of the
pleasures of the senses,

Free from obscurity.* That happiness
Is known to be Indifferent, which comes
From contact of the object and the sense,
Which is like nectar first, and in the end
Like poison. That's described as Bad, which, first
As well as in its consequence, deludes
The soul, and flows from sleep and laziness
And heedlessness.† There is nought on this earth,
Nor yet among the gods in Heaven, which
Is free from these three qualities produced
From Nature. The offices, killer of foes!
Of Brâhmaṇ, Kshatriya, Vais'ya and S'ûdra are marked
According to the qualities produced
From Nature.‡ Penance, patience, purity,
Sedateness, self-control, and rectitude,
Knowledge, experience, in a future world
Belief§—these are the duties natural

---

* S'ankar who gives this meaning in common with the other
commentators also suggests the following as to आत्मबुद्धि viz.
आत्मनी बुद्धि:, which would mean 'one's own mind.' Mr. Thomson
adopts this meaning of आत्मबुद्धि and renders प्रसाद by 'serenity.'
The meaning is not inadmissible. But I prefer the other, as in
this there is not much propriety in the employment of the word
आत्म. Comp. Chap. II. St. 65 (line 340), Chap. XVII. St. 16 (line 2060).

† प्रमाद, a word which has occurred before in this work—S'ridhar
renders it by कर्तव्यावधारणरहित्य.

‡ Compare Chap. IV. St. 13 (line 536). The word for 'nature'
here is स्वभाव which is rendered by प्रकृति and compare also Chap.
V. St. 14 (line 632).

§ As to knowledge and experience see Chap. II. St. 41 (line
495). The original word answering to the next expression is
आस्तिक्य, literally 'the state of a believer that something exists,'

Of Brâhmaṇs. Courage, glory, bravery,
Skill, not to flee from battle, giving alms,
And lordliness,* the duties natural
Of Kshatriyas.   The duties natural
Of Vais'yas, too, are tending cattle,† trade,
And agriculture.   So too servitude,
The duty natural of S'ûdras.   These
Engaged in their respective duties, reach
Perfection.   Listen now how one engaged
In one's own duty does perfection reach.
By his own proper duty worshipping
Him from whom all things emanate, and who
All this pervades, perfection‡ man attains.
One's duty ill-performed is better far
Than that of others well-performed.§   No sin
Accrues to him who does the duty set
By Nature, Kunti's son! None should forsake
The duty to which he is born though evil ;
Because by evil all acts are wrapt up,
As fire by smoke.‖   He who is self-restrained,

Compare Pânini IV. 4, 60. The 'future world' is added from the commentary, and there can be no doubt that it is the ordinary and correct meaning of the word.

* ईश्वरभाव: is explained to mean a proper exercise of authority.

† गोरक्ष्य is taken to apply to cattle generally; पाशुपाल्य say the commentators.

‡ *I. e.* eligibility for the path of knowledge ज्ञाननिष्ठा योग्यताछक्षणा-सिद्धि:—S'ankar and Madhusûdan.

§ Compare Chap. III. St. 35 (line 475).

‖ Comp. Chap. XVIII. St. 7 (line 2124). The evil is not stated by the commentators but seems to be the quality of 'fettering' the soul so frequently spoken of. S'ridhar infers from this, that as the

Whose thoughts are not attached to any thing,*
Free from desires, doth the perfection reach,
Supreme, of freedom from all action,† through
Renunciation. Learn from me in brief
How one who has perfection reached attains
The Brahma, Oh son of Kuntî ! the highest state
Of knowledge.‡ With an intellect full pure
And self-restrained, with firmness casting off
Sound and all other sensuous objects, freed
From love and hate, frequenting lonely spots,
Eating but little, with speech, body, mind,
Restrained, to meditation constantly
And to devotion and to unconcern§
Given up, abandoning all egoism,
And vanity, desire, wrath, stubbornness,
And all belongings,‖ free from thoughts of "mine,"¶
And tranquil, man the fitness does obtain
To be one with the Brahma. And thus become

---

good elements in 'fire' are used to the exclusion of the smoke, so
the good portion of action should be accepted, and its 'evil' portion
abandoned in the manner stated in the next stanza.

   * *Scil.* wife, child &c. says S'ankar.

   † सग्यो मुक्त्यवस्थानरूपां सिद्धिम् say S'ankar, पारमंश्यचर्यौम् says
S'ridhar referring to Chap. V. St. 13 (lines 678-9) and distinguishing
it from Chap. V. St. 8 (line 662).

   ‡ This, according to the commentators, shows what that attainment of the Brahma is which has been spoken of just before.

   § Devotion =concentration on the soul alone. Unconcern see
line 856.

   ‖ Comp. Chap. VI. St. 10 (line 771) also line 562 referred to in the
note there.

   ¶ Comp. Chap. II. St. 71 (line 362). Madhusûdan says देहजीवनमात्रेपि
ममकाररहितः.

One with the Brahma, and with a tranquil soul,
One grieves not, wishes not, towards all beings
Alike; supreme devotion to me then
One reaches; through devotion truly knows
Who I am, and how great; then knowing me
Truly, into me enters.[○] Even all acts
Always performing, on me resting, he,
The inexhaustible eternal seat,
Favoured by me, attains. To me all acts
By the mind offering,† given up to me,
Practise devotion, with the faculty
Of steady resolution ;‡ and thy mind
Always upon me fix. Fixing thy mind
On me, thou by my favour shalt surmount
All dangers. But if thou through egotism§
Listen not, ruined shalt thou be. If thou,
Through egotism, thinkst "I shall not fight," vain

---

* 'Become one with the Brahma' at the opening of this passage
(ब्रह्मभून:) of course cannot mean absorbed into the Brahma. S'ridhar
renders it by ब्रह्मण्यवस्थितः. It would seem to mean 'one who has
comprehended fully his own identity with the Brahma.' As to the
'supreme devotion,' S'ankar refers to Chap. VII. St. 16 (line 952).

† Comp. Chap. V. St. 13 (line 679) and note there.

‡ बुद्धियोगम् S'ankar renders by समाहितबुद्धित्वम् 'having the faculty
of fixed resolve (बुद्धि) concentrated.' S'ridhar says व्यवसायात्मिन्न या
बुद्ध्या योग:; Madhusûdan says पूर्वोक्तसमस्तबुद्धिलक्षणं योगम्. I do not
think that there is any substantial difference between these interpretations.

§ पण्डितोहमिति says S'ankar—that is to say, through pride of your
own cleverness. So too S'ridhar and Madhusûdan. The latter on
the same word in the next line but one says नाहमेोहं क्रूरं कर्मे न
करिष्यामीति मिथ्याभिमानम्. According to this 'pride of piety' is the
meaning there.

Is that resolve of thine. For nature* will
Compel thee., What, Oh Kunti's son! tied down
By thy own duty born of Nature,† thou
Dost through delusion not desire to do,
That same thing 'gainst thy own will shalt thou do.
Arjun! the Lord is seated in the heart
Of every creature, causing to turn round,
Through his delusion, creatures mounted on
An engine. Seek asylum every way‡
With him, offspring of Bharat! Thou shalt reach,
Favoured by him, supreme tranquillity,
And the eternal seat. Thus I have declared
To thee this knowledge more mysterious
Than any mystery. Thinking of this
Fully, act as thou wishest. Hear once more
My words, the most mysterious of all—
Strongly I like thee, therefore do I speak,
For thy behoof. Upon me fix thy mind,
Become my worshipper, my devotee,
To me bow down, to me alone shalt thou
Attain. I tell thee true, thou art dear to me.
Forsaking all thy duties, come to me
As thy sole refuge. From all sins I will

---

* Nature = क्षत्रस्वभाव: (the nature of Kshatriyas) says S'ankar.
रजोगुणद्वरेण परिणता सती says S'ridhar. Madhusûdan combines the two
thus क्षत्रजस्वारम्भको रजोगुणस्वभाव:.

† Comp. St. 43 (line 2244 *et seq.*) *suprâ.*

‡ Comp. Chap. XV. St. 19 (line 1922). The commentators
here render the expression by सर्वात्मना. Madhusûdan adds मनसा
वाचा कर्मणा. And Ânandagiri says the same thing. This may be
taken as the explanation of सर्वप्रकारेण by which S'ridhar renders the
expression at Chap. XV. St. 19.

Release thee. Grieve not. *This* thou shalt not speak
To one who does no penance practise,† never
To one void of devotion, nor to one
Who wishes not to hear, nor yet to one
Who carps at me. He who this mystery
Supreme unto my devotees will speak,
Fully devoted to me,‡ shall attain
To me undoubtedly. Amongst all men,
To me there is none dearer, nor shall be
Another dearer on the earth, than he.
And this our sacred dialogue whoever
Shall study, he shall have performed for me
The sacrifice of knowledge,§ I do think.
Also the man who will even hear with faith,
And without carping, he too shall be freed,

---

* इदं शास्त्रम् says S'ankar. It means all that has been taught in the Gitâ.

† अनपरक = धर्मानुष्ठानहीन says S'ridhar. 'Devotion,' *scil.* towards God and the Preceptor, say the commentators. Compare the last stanza of the Chhândogyopanishad यस्य देवे परा भक्तिर्यथा देवे तथा गुरौ || नस्यैते कथिता ह्यर्थाः प्रकाशन्ते महात्मनः. On 'who wishes not to hear,' परिचर्यामकुर्वते say the commentators, that is to say, who does not serve some preceptor in order to hear it. Comp. Chap. IV. St. 34 (line 610). S'ankar adds that all the elements mentioned must co-exist to make one eligible for learning this doctrine.

‡ With the belief that in spreading knowledge of it, he is serving and devoting himself to me. S'ankar and Madhusûdan. S'ridhar says स मयि भक्तिं करोति ततो निःसंशयः सन्मामेव प्राप्नोति, which involves a bad construction as to the first part, but as to असंशयः a more grammatical one than S'ankar's which is adopted in the text.

§ That is the best sacrifice, Comp. Chap. IV. St. 3? (lines 606-7).

And shall attain to the bright worlds of those
Who do good deeds.* Hast thou, Oh Pṛithâ's son!
Listened to this with an attentive mind?
Is thy delusion caused by ignorance
Destroyed, Oh Conqueror of wealth!

Arjun.   Destroyed

Is my delusion; by thy favour too
Oh undegraded one! I recollect
Myself.† And free from all doubt‡ now I stand.
I will do as thou bidst.

Sanjaya.   Thus did I hear

This dialogue of the high-minded son
Of Pṛithâ and the son of Vasudev—
Wonderful, causing the hair to stand on end!
By Vyâs's favour, this devotion§— this
Mystery supreme—I heard from Kṛishṇa's self,
Lord of Devotion, who propounded it
In person. And Oh king! once and again
Thinking about this wondrous dialogue
And holy, 'twixt Kes'av and Arjun, I
Often rejoice! Oh king! once and again
Thinking about that form most wonderful

---

* Comp. Chap. VI. St. 41. (line 874) where we have rendered it
world of Holy Beings.

† S'ankar says स्मृतिश्चात्मनस्तविषया लब्धा यस्या लाभात्सर्वग्रन्थीनां विप्रमोक्षः, षट्त्वानुसंधानरूपा स्मृति; says S'ridhar.

‡ गतो धर्मविषयः संदेहो यस्य, S'ridhar—i. e. doubts as to whether fighting with relatives was right.

§ I. e. favour in giving him a superhuman power of seeing and hearing. 'Devotion'—S'ankar says that the composition is called 'devotion' because it relates to 'devotion.' योगार्थस्याङ्क्त्योति योग;.

Of Hari, great is my astonishment,
And often I rejoice ! Wherever Kṛishṇa
Lord of Devotion, where the archer, son
Of Pṛithâ, there, I think, prosperity,
And fortune,° victory, justice eterne !

---

* श्री and भूति are thus distinguished by S'aṅkar श्रियो विशेष-
विस्तारो भूति:, and thus by S'ridhar श्री राड्यलक्ष्मी:–भूनिद्वरोनराभिवृद्धि:.
Madhusûdan agrees with S'ridhar only substituting राड्यलक्ष्या वि-
वृद्धि for the vaguer अभिवृद्धि of S'ridhar.

NOTES AND ILLUSTRATIONS.

Lines 25-27—पर्याप्त and अपर्याप्त. There is a great difference of opinion as to the true meanings of these words in St.
10. Two opposite meanings have been proposed. The one is
'limited and unlimited' which we have adopted. The other is
'sufficient and insufficient.' For the sense adopted by us,
which is consistent with the traditional strength of the two
armies, compare Mâgh. I. 27. And see Wilson's Essays on
Sanskrit Literature Vol. III. 116.

Lines 32-33—Compare Wilson's Essays on Sanskrit Literature Vol. III. p. 116; and see p. 117 as to the names of the
several conchs in lines 37-43.

Line 53—The Ape was Hanumân.

Lines 59-61—More literally these lines should have
run thus :—

.... I see those who are here
Assembled, anxious for the fight, and longing
To do good to the evil-minded son
Of Dhritarâshtra.

Line 75—The Gândîv is the bow of Arjun.

Line 165—There is great difference of opinion among
the commentators as to the real meaning of the words "talkst
the words of wisdom." Probably, S'rîdhar's is the simplest
explanation. You *talk*, says Krishna to Arjun, like a wise
man; but your *conduct* in lamenting for your relatives is not
so wise.

Line 174—I find that a commentator of the Dvait

School of Philosophy, namely Râghavendra Yati, interprets मात्रा to mean ज्ञानविषयः.

Line 256 *et seq.*—Of this passage, again, S'rídhar's explanation is the easiest, and to my mind most acceptable. Krishṇa, having closed what he calls the Sânkhya doctrine, now states the Yog doctrine; and says, that those who follow and act upon this Yog doctrine, never lose the fruit of anything they begin; nor do they find obstacles in their way, like those who perform all they do out of a desire for particular benefits. Those who act with desires, now wish for one thing, now for another. But those who follow the Yog doctrine desire nothing, they have one settled course of action, one fixed resolution—all they do they offer unto the Supreme Being. As to Samâdhi, which we have rendered by contemplation, Madhusûdan says as follows:—समाधीयते अस्मि-न्सर्वमिति व्युत्पत्त्या समानिरन्तःकरणं वा परमात्मा वेति नाप्रसिद्धार्थकल्पनम् ॥ अहं ब्रह्मेत्यवस्थानं समाधिस्तन्निमित्तं व्यवसायात्मिका बुद्धिर्नियत इति व्याख्याने तु एतिरेवाशृता ॥ The ultimate sense of the passage seems to be the same on all these interpretations. And that sense is, that the class of persons described here are not in that settled state of mind which is necessary for the performance of every act as offered to the Supreme Being. Contemplation is of course contemplation of the Brahma to whom every act is to be offered up. Our translation of जन्मकर्मफलप्रदा is not quite accurate according to the interpretations of the commentators, though in substance it appears to be not incorrect. S'ankar takes the compound to mean 'promising a new birth as the fruit of action'—and this interpretation seems to be preferable to the others suggested. In accordance with this the lines should run thus:

And which doth promise as the fruit of acts

New births—the flowery talk, Oh Prithâ's son!

"The effects of the three qualities" are the affairs of this world. Compare Mâlavikâgnimitra (वैगुण्यं द्रव्यमत्र लोकचरितं नाना- रसं दृश्यते). "Free from them," as stated in the footnote, is explained by the commentators to mean free from desire, which is the ultimate meaning of "free from the effects of the three qualities," as the whole of what is called the business of this earth is performed with some desire or another. "Resting in courage" means preserving courage and patience under the sufferings flowing from the pairs of opposites mentioned just before. The last words, it need scarcely be said, mean that one should not be over-anxious to obtain what one has not or to preserve what one has. One ought to be indifferent to such things. As to the three qualities see note on Chapter XIV.

Lines 275-7—This is a rather difficult Stanza, and I cannot make up my mind to accept the construction of it proposed by the commentators. Nor does Mr. Thomson's construction appear to me to be suitable to the context. I would, with some diffidence, suggest the following. Having said that the Veds are concerned with actions done out of a desire for particular benefits, Krishna gives here a simile by which to illustrate that assertion. As you can resort to a large reservoir of water for various objects, such as drinking, bathing &c., so if you look to the Veds, you will find there the means of accomplishing various purposes. You can perform the S'yen-sacrifice, if you want to destroy an enemy. You can perform the Jyotishtom, if you want to attain to Heaven, and so on. In one word, a man can find in the Veds the means of accomplishing various desires of one class, as he can find in a large reservoir the means of accomplishing various desires of another class. But then, Krishna goes on to say, perform the actions prescribed, but do not entertain the desires,

Line 286—The argument as to the meaning of बुद्धियोग contained in the note on this line seems to me to derive further support from Stanza 50 (lines 289-291). There बुद्धि and योग must be taken to mean the same thing, as they do on S'ankar's interpretation. Otherwise we have to resort, as S'rídhar resorts, to the introduction of an idea which is not in the original. S'rídhar says तस्मात्तदर्थीय योगाय युह्यस्व.

Lines 297-99—काञ्ज which we have rendered by 'taint' may also mean 'snare.' श्रोतव्य and श्रुत in line 299 are taken by Madhusûdan to mean the fruit of actions about which you have heard or are to hear. This seems to be confirmed by S'ankar's interpretation of 'what thou hast heard' in the next line. Râghavendra Yati, the dualistic commentator already once mentioned, takes it to mean all actions whatever—सर्वकर्मेति लक्षणमेतत्.

Line 308—Pleased in and by oneself. S'ankar says that this means enjoying happiness, independently of any external gains, in one's own self as प्रत्यगात्मा; S'rídhar says as परमानन्दस्वरूप which is substantially the same thing. Râghavendra Yati says आत्मन्येव परमात्मन्येव स्थित: सन् तदेकचित्त: सन्नीति यावत् । आत्मना परमात्मना तन्प्रसादेनेत्यर्थं: । तुष्ट: संतोषयुक्त: ॥

Line 386—The active senses are speech, hands, feet, &c. See Thomson's Gítá p. 22n.

Line 396—Spiritual is a word which I have adopted here, simply in order to avoid a long periphrasis, not because it is an accurate rendering of the original यज्ञार्थ. The sacrifice here appears to mean the daily offerings to and worship of the Deities which would fall within the नियतं कर्म or 'action prescribed' spoken of in line 392.

Line 409—Compare Manu. III. 118.

Line 415—As to समुद्भव, it should be also remembered,

that in कर्मसमुद्भव Mr. Thomson does not understand that word in the same sense as in ब्रह्मसमुद्भव.

Line 429—Compare Îs'opanishad Stanza 2.

Line 485—In support of the commentator's interpretation of the word 'this' here, we may refer to Gîtâ VI. 33-4 and XI. 45, 46, where the construction is somewhat similar. There is first a general expression, as to which we do not know exactly the specific thing to which it is to be applied, and then in the next Stanza we are introduced to that specific thing.

Line 488—On further consideration I am not satisfied with the rendering of the word कामरूप in the text. The lines should run thus :—

Knowledge is enveloped by this constant foe—
This foe, Desire—of men of knowledge, who
Oh Kuntî's son ! is like a fire, and who
Is never filled.

कामरूपवैरी means 'this enemy in the shape of desire.' This is the interpretation countenanced by the commentators, and it appears to me more appropriate than the one adopted in the text from Meghadût St. IV. The last lines with a similar correction might run thus :

And do thou by thyself restrain thyself,
And, Large-armed one ! destroy this enemy—
The enemy, Desire—who is hard to tame.

Line 504—Manu is the first man of the Solar dynasty of Indian kings. Ikshvâku was one of his descendants and one of the ancestors of the hero of the Râmâyan.

Lines 531-2—The meaning of these lines, as the commentators say, is that God confers favours having regard to what is asked of him. To those who ask for worldly fruit, he gives that ; to those who want final emancipation he gives that. The favours conferred are in conformity with the prayers with which men "come to me." For the latter part of the passage, compare Gítá VII. 22 and IX. 23 (lines 973 ; 1180). The meaning is that, to whomsoever the prayers may be addressed in name, they really go to Vishṇu in the end.

Lines 535-6—This is contrasted with the fruit of knowledge. The fruit of action is worldly good, which is got much sooner than the fruit of knowledge, namely, final emancipation.

Lines 552-555—The meaning of this is that the actions which ordinary people suppose to be a man's actions are really not his, that is to say, not of the soul. Comp. Chap. IV. lines 661 *et seq.* When there are no external marks of action, when ordinary people think a man to be utterly inactive, then is the real time of the activity of the soul. Compare also Chap. II. 353 for another aspect of much the same fact.

Line 567—मत्सर. I have rendered it by envy, following Madhusûdan. It may also mean simply enmity to others, as the other commentators render it.

Line 570—Wholly free = free from the bonds of virtuous and other actions (S'ankar) ; from attachment to worldly things &c. (S'rídhar); from a false notion of oneself being the doer in all one's worldly actions (Madhusûdan, and compare lines 457 *et seq.*); from the false notion identifying oneself with the body &c. or from the false notion of one's own independence (Râghavendra).

Line 573—There are some differences between the several interpretations proposed of this passage, but it is unnecessary to set them out here. The last line means that the act of offering is also Brahma—ब्रह्मैव कर्म तस्मिन् &c. (S'ankar).

Line 579—Râghavendra takes the meaning of this line to be that they offer up all their actions to Vishṇu, knowing every thing to rest on him, and abandoning the notion of their own freedom. According to S'ankar, the ultimate meaning is that they are always meditating on the unity of Brahma and Âtmâ, of the Supreme and the individual Soul. S'rídhar's meaning is that they 'destroy' their 'yajna', or sacrifice and all other actions, by means of the 'yajna' described in lines 573 *et seq.*

Line 583—'Sound and others' means, शब्द, स्पर्श, रूप रस, गन्ध—the five qualities of things which are perceived by the five senses of hearing, touch, sight, taste, and smell. The expression, of course, stands for all worldly objects.

Line 587—In speaking of penance &c. as the ' offering', there is of course a figure involved. Penance and the rest stand in the position of the offering in the ' yajna' or sacrifice which the persons referred to perform, the yajna meaning the act or acts performed as worship of the Supreme Being. Doing penance, studying the Veds &c., are thus among the modes of worshipping the Supreme Being adopted by different persons. Knowledge here is interpreted by S'ankar to mean knowledge of the meaning of the S'âstras S'rídhar takes स्वाध्यायज्ञान to be one idea—namely knowledge of the meaning of the Veds acquired by a study of them. See Manu III. 134.

Line 595—The winds are the winds said to exist within the body. Râghavendra says the first word ' winds' means the operations of the senses, the second the senses themselves. He takes the passage to mean that they contract the workings of the senses, and adds, ' the meaning being that the senses are reduced in their strength by limited food.' He proposes an alternative rendering :—प्राणान्वायीन्द्रियदेवान्मनःप्रभृयु. चमरैवाभीनानःप्रयन्तीत्यर्थैः अभिमन्यक्षे भगवन्नूज्ञान्वेन नियनःहारः पृथग्यक्षौ ज्ञानय्यः

Line 600—Compare Manu. III. 285.

Line 606—The superiority is owing to the fact, says S'ankar, that the sacrifice of knowledge leads to no fruit—*i. e.* such fruit as will bind one down to regeneration &c., but only to final emancipation.

Lines 671-2—The word केवल (mere) must be connected, according to S'ankar, with 'body, mind, and resolution' as well as with 'senses' though grammatically connected with 'senses' only. It signifies the absence of identification of oneself with any of these. The actions are done mechanically, but without the belief that they are one's own.

Lines 679-84—The Lord (प्रभु) means आत्मा or देही according to S'ankar. But this only in line 679, and the footnote on line 683 should therefore not be there. Râghavendra adopts this meaning in both places, saying जडमवेक्ष्य प्रभु: समर्थो जीव:. S'ridhar takes it to refer to the Deity. Action or agency— The Deity is not himself the author of human actions nor is he the cause impelling men to act. In the next line is stated the fact that the Deity has nothing to do with the acceptance of the good or evil acts of his worshippers. The popular notion that God is pleased with the good acts of his worshippers and condones their evil ones is unfounded These notions are the result of ignorance—'thence do all beings err.' We may add, that this idea of Deity is, *in some respects*, similar to that which is beginning to commend itself to some of the foremost scientific intellects of our own day.

Line 692—A Châṇḍâl is the meanest class in Hindu society. See too Mâdhav S'ankar Vijaya VI. 29 *et. seq.*

Lines 714-5—Mr. Thomson omits भन्त:सुख and भन्त- रारम: from his translation. The distinction seems to be that between happiness and amusement. The commentators render आराम by क्रीडा—sport or divertation.

Lines 724-5—Excludes the objects of the senses.

The exclusion is of course ceasing to think of them, expelling them from one's thoughts. For objects of the senses, the word here is स्पर्श, objects of touch, but it signifies the objects of the other senses as well.

Line 747—To him who has reached devotion, tranquillity is a means, says our text. But for what? ज्ञानादिप्राप्तये say S'rîdhar and Madhusûdan; मुक्तिगतमुखातिशयस्य says Râghavendra. These substantially agree, as meaning—for the acquisition of the next state, that of perfected knowledge or final emancipation. S'ankar, however, says योगारूढत्वस्य साधनमुच्यत इत्यर्थः, which I do not quite understand.

Line 754—आत्मा in this line is rendered by S'rîdhar to mean the soul which is free from connexion with mind &c. Râghavendra has the following येन आत्मना येन जीवेनेति समानाधिकरणं वा येन जीवेन कर्त्रा (तौ in Ms.). आत्मना बुद्ध्या करणेनेति व्यधिकरणं वा आत्मा मनःजितं वशीकृतं तस्यात्मनो जीवस्य आत्मा मनः बन्धुरेवेत्यादिकायैव भगवद्ज्ञानोपयोगीति यावत् ॥

Line 760—परमात्मा सम्यगाहितः हृदि संनिहितो भवति ध्यानविषयो भूत्वा परीक्षाविषयो भवतीत्यर्थः—Râghavendra.

Line 772 et seq.—Compare S'vetâs'vataropanishad II., 10 The Kus'-grass is well known as being regarded as sacred by our people.

Line 818—निर्विण्णचेतसा (instead of अनिर्विण्णचेतसा as we have taken it) is intelligible, though I think it should not be construed as Mr. Thomson seems to construe it. The meaning with that word would be—that devotion should be resolutely practiced by one with a mind indifferent (to worldly objects).

Line 843—Exists in me—compare line 1202. S'ankar says it means, that there is no obstacle to his final emancipation. 'However living,' Râghavendra says this means whether righteously or unrighteously—the man of knowledge being sure of final emancipation though he behave unrighteously.

Line 851-2—दृढ (obstinate) S'ankar renders by तन्तुनागव-दच्छेद्यम्, S'ridhar by विषयवासनानुबन्ध (? द्र) तया दुर्भेद्यम्. Râghavendra by विषयवासनानुविद्धतया दुर्भेदं साधुविषये नेतुमशक्यम्. Madhusûdan by विषयवासनासहस्रसूनतया भेनुमशक्यम्.

Line 908 *et seq.*—As to this see the note further on about the three Qualities.

Line 921—'Om' is the well known mystic particle so variously explained; see too line 1045. Sound, according to Hindu philosophers, is a function of space (शब्दगुणमाकाशम्).

Line 931—The use of the strength, says S'ankar, is merely the support of the body &c. S'ridhar says it is the strength (characterized by the quality of Sattva or Goodness) for performing one's duty.

Line 938—In the note पदार्थे: ought to be preceded by भावे:. Râghavendra agrees with S'ankar. Greater than they means greater than the qualities—superior to and untouched by them; compare line 1833. As to line 941-2, 'the result of the qualities' see the note on the Qualities on Chap. XIV.

Line 1007—स्वभाव. The rendering of this word by 'change' is exceptionable, as suggesting a difference between the Brahma and the Adhyâtma which does not seem to be intended. Brahma in its relations to the body &c. is called Adhyâtma. Râghavendra explains स्वभाव thus स्वधास्तो भावध संदेकरूपेण वर्तमानधेनि स्वभाव:. The offering is, according to Râghavendra, an act of the Deity. As to development S'ridhar cites आदित्याब्ज्ञायने वृ‍टि: &c. क्षरोभाग; might, possibly, as stated in the note, correspond to स्वभाव: (स्वो भाव:) and mean 'perishable form.' This would to a certain extent agree with Mr. Thomson's view. But the clause does not come immediately after स्वभावोध्यात्ममुच्यते—and this makes it difficult to take that clause in to assist the construction of क्षरो भाव:, when an unexceptionable meaning can be derived in another way.

Line 1017—Form = particular form of the Supreme Being. देवताविशेष says S'ankar, and S'ridhar and Madhusûdan follow him. Râghavendra says यं यमारि भावं पदार्थम्. S'ridhar and Madhusûdan agree with this also, by adding भन्यमाविंग and भन्यरारि यत्किचित् after देवताविशेष.

Line 1025—Devotion of repeated thought, is the concentration of mind on one object uninterrupted by thoughts of any other object. Râghavendra agrees with S'ridhar as to the meaning of योग here.

Line 1037 *et seq.*—Compare Kathopanishad. II. 15.

Line 1045—Compare Manu II. 83.

Line 1061 *et seq.*—Compare Manu I. 73. 'All perceptible things' signifies every thing in the world. 'The unperceived' is the Prakriti. Comp. Gîtâ IX. 8 (line 1120).

Line 1071—"Which is perceived." This rendering is based on भन्यो व्यक्तिव्यक्तात् being not equivalent to भन्य: भव्यक्त: भव्यक्तात्, but to भन्य: अभ्यक्त: व्यक्तात्. S'ankar, and S'ridhar, and Madhusûdan also, however adopt the former construction and take भव्यक्तात् to refer to "the unperceived," (अभ्यक्त) spoken of just before. I find, however, that Râghavendra has adopted the other view.

Line 1076—As to धाम Râghavendra agrees with S'ridhar, and though S'ankar renders it by पद, still S'ridhar's is probably the most suitable meaning here.

Line 1106—Not opposed to law = *i. e.* not unrighteous like the S'yen-sacrifice, says S'ankar; that sacrifice being one performed for the purpose of destroying one's foe. Directly knowable *i. e.* like happiness, says S'ankar. Not hard to practise = not hard to acquire, or learn.

Line 1122—A Kalpa is a vast period of time which measures the duration of the Universe. The beginning of a Kalpa is when the world is created. When the Kalpa ends, the world is destroyed and there is a fresh creation again.

Lne 1134—Asurs and Râkshases are demons.

Line 1144—Working= मन्त्रादौ यत्नं कुर्वत: Râghavendra.

Line 1148—क्रतव: दीक्षाद्रव्यभूर्यात्मकर्मकलापरूपबयौतिष्ठोमादय: ॥ यत्रस्तु दैक्षनौद्देशेन द्रव्यत्यागएव प्रधानं कर्म ॥ क्रुद्यपण्डववस्सामान्यविशेषभावेन भेदौ ज्ञेय: Râghavendra.

Line 1156—Rik, Sâm, and Yajus, are the three Veds.

Line 1166—The som-juice is a rather intoxicating drink taken at certain sacrifices.

Line 1187—The Bhûts are a separate class of super-human beings; विनायककमानृगणादय: say the commentators.

Line 1222—For प्रियमाण. Compare Kaṭhopanishad I. 16.

Line 1234—भाव: बमे: says Râghavendra, which would mean qualities.

Line 1236—The seven sages are well known. They are identified with the constellation Ursa Major. Sanak and the rest are four holy personages generally mentioned together, of whom Sanatkumâr appears in the Chhândogyopanishad as teacher of Nârad. Each of the fourteen Manus presides over a period of the world's life called Manvantar.

Line 1251—आत्मभावस्थ: is rendered by आत्माकारान्त:करणवृत्तौ विषयस्वेन स्थित: in Madhusûdan's commentary, and by तदीयचित्तवृ. चित्स्थ: in Râghavendra's.

Line 1259—As to Asit and Deval, see Müller's Sanskrit Literature p. 463; and Kern's Brihatsamhitâ, Pref. 41.

Line 1276—इन्त. Compare Kaṭhopanishad V. 6.

Line 1284—Marîchi is the name of one of the Maruts—the Winds, or Storm Gods as Max Müller calls them. The Nakshatras are what are called the Lunar Mansions. Vâsav is

Indra the king of the Gods. The Lord of Wealth is Kuber. There are eight Vasus. Meru is the Golden mountain. Briha-spati is the priest of the Gods. Skanda is the War-God Bhṛigu is one of the seven Ṛishis. The A'svattha is the Peepul Tree. Gandharvas are the heavenly choristers.

Line 1304—The perfect ones, S'ankar says, are those who even from birth are possessed of the highest piety, know-ledge, indifference to worldly good, and superhuman power (धर्मज्ञानवैराग्यैश्वर्यातिशय). It would be better, to retain the original word 'Siddhas' here, as in lines 1440 and 1444, reading 'Among the Siddhas, I—Am &c.'

Line 1306—Uchchaiss'ravas is the horse of Indra. Airâvat is his elephant. The thunderbolt is his weapon, the Vajra. Kâmdhenu is the cow of plenty. Vâsuki and Ananta are the chiefs of the snakes and Nâgs. The Nâgs, accord-ing to S'rîdhar, are the serpents without poison. Varuṇ is Neptune, the God of the ocean. Yam is King Death. Pralhâd s the Abdiel of Hindu mythology, the virtuous demon to save whom Vishṇu became incarnate as the Man-lion.

Line 1317—Râghavendra has the following on this somewhat obscure line कलयतामाकलयतां बंभनादि कुर्वतां यत् काल: तल ज्ञान इति धातो: सर्वमाकलयतीनि काल:—In the last line of the foot-note °कों क्षय: must be of course °कोक्षय:. The meaning of S'rî-dhar's gloss is that in line 1330, Time absolutely is spoken f; in this line, Time divided into years, months, and so forth.

Line 1320—यवताम् is also rendered by वेगवताम् in Râgha-vendra's commentary.

Line 1322—Jâhnavî is the Ganges.

Lines 1328-9—As to the letter A, see Introductory Essay ., LV. The Dvandva is selected because, as S'rîdhar points out, all the parts of it are co-ordinate with each other उभयपदार्थप्रधान:). 'I alone am Time Eternal' does not ac-

curately convey the meaning of the original. The meaning is
" Eternal Time also is nothing but myself."

Line 1334—कील्यौद्या देवनारूपाः स्त्रियः says S'rîdhar. It need
scarcely be said that Fame &c. are personified here.

Line 1337—The Gâyatrî is the metre in which that
mystic stanza is composed—तत्सवितुर्वरेण्यम् &c. As to the Mârgas'îrsha month—November–December—see the Introductory
Essay P. CXI. The commentators do not explain why
Krishṇa identifies himself with the " game of dice," among
all the practices of "cheats." We can only infer, that
it is regarded as the best mode of gaming for one who
wants to cheat his opponent. The Vrishṇis are the family
in which Krishṇa was born. Us'anas is the preceptor of the
Demons, S'ukra, one of whose names is Kavi, one who
has discernment. The श्रीज्ञानस्यदण्डनीति is well-known.

Line 1348—Polity i. e. the due employment of the
several modes of dealing with foes, such as trying to make
up things amicably, trying to introduce dissensions into the
enemy's camp, and so forth. As to silence, Madhusûdan after
repeating S'rîdhar's explanation गोप्यानां गोपनहेतुः adds गुह्यानां गो-
प्यानां मध्ये ससन्धाहश्रवणमननपूर्वकमात्मनो निर्दिध्यासलक्षणं मौनं चाहमस्मि ॥
The latter interpretation is not quite clear. And to suit the
former "'mongst secrets" ought perhaps, to be " for secrets."

Line 1357—विभूतिमत् S'rîdhar renders by ऐश्वर्ययुक्तम्, श्रीमत्
by संपत्तियुक्तम्, and ऊर्जितम् by केनापि प्रभावबलादिना गुणनातिशयिनम्.
Râghavendra has respectively सजातिनः श्रेष्ठचरितम्, संयुक्तम् and
अभिवृद्धगुरुतम्.

Line 1381—The As'vins are the physicians of the Gods.

Line 1441—The Sâdhyas are mentioned in Manu I. 22.
The Vis'vas are the so-called Vis'vedevs, the Ushmaps are the
manes. In line 1461, the charioteer's son is Karṇa.

Line 1507—Compare Manu. I. 11.

Line 1522—Yâdav, is descendant of Yadu, one of the sons of Yayâti, a famous king of the Lunar dynasty.

Line 1592-93—Râghavendra says कूटस्थं कूटे अव्याकृताकारे षाभिमानितया स्थितं कदारि खरदादभव्ट्वादचलं ध्रवं निर्विकारम्.

Line 1635—Free from distress. S'ankar renders the original of this, by गतभयः, free from fear; and S'ridhar by आविश्चन्यः, free from mental pain; Madhusûdan says परे-स्तताउग्रमानस्यापि गता नोत्तन्ना पीडा यस्य सः, one who does not feel pain even when beaten by others; Râghavendra says परकृतात्रकारे-र्यात्तमनःक्रेशः, one who feels no mental pain at injuries done.

Line 1639—शुभाशुभ (good and ill) is rendered by S'ridhar to mean पुण्यपाप, merit and sin. See line 316.

Line 1651—I have thought it better to retain the word Kshetra here than to render it by any inadequate equivalent. S'ankar says:—इतत्राणात्क्ष (?) यान्धिरणात्क्षित्रवद्धास्मिन्कर्मफलानिर्वृ्ते: क्षेत्रम्. S'ridhar इदं भोगायतनं शरीरं क्षेत्रमित्यभिभीयते संसारस्य परांभूमित्वात्. Madhusûdan, सरयस्येवासिमत्रसकृत्कर्मणः फलस्य निर्वृैतेः. Râghavendra इदं शरीरमव्यक्तमहंकारादिकं भगवदावासस्थानत्वाल्क्षीयते स्थीयतेत्र भगवतेति व्युत्तरस्था क्षेत्रमित्यभिभीयते.

—It may be interesting to transcribe here the opening of Râghavendra's comment on this Chapter. He says पूर्वैद्वयोक्तार्थसंग्रहपरोय-मध्याय: ॥ तथाहि यत्प्रथमषट्के त्रैगुण्यविषय: वेद इत्यादिना प्राचुर्येण साधनमावष्टसमा-तेह्क्त यच्च तत्र द्वितीयेध्याये न तेषामित्यादिना अनादिनित्यस्तादिना जीवस्वरूपमुक्त पच्च (?त्र in Ms.) द्वितीयपट्के भगवत्स्वरूपमुक्त यदरि सप्तमे भूमिराप इत्यादिना क्षेत्रशब्दितं भगवतावासस्थानमुक्त नत्रिप्रकर्णे (कृठ?) तयोक्त सर्वे बुद्धग्रारांहार्थे संक्षिप्यारिम-तध्याये प्रश्रपूर्व पदर्शयेनं प्रकृतिमित्यादिना. These last words refer to the following stanza, with which this Chapter begins in the copy of Râghavendra, though it is not in our copies.

प्रकृतिं पुरुषं चैव क्षेत्रं क्षेत्रज्ञमेत्र च ।
एतद्वेदितुमिच्छामि ज्ञानं ज्ञेयं च केशव ॥

It may be mentioned that Mr. Thomson refers to this stanza.

Line 1660—छन्देांभित्तित्रिवै: is rendered to mean in each of the Veds by Râghavendra. ब्रह्मसूत्रपद is not explained.

Line 1663—The ten senses are the five senses of action referred to before, and the five senses of perception, hearing &c. For body, the original is संघात which S'rîdhar renders by शरीर, S'ankar by देहेन्द्रियाणां संहति., and Râghavendra by देह For courage, the original is धृति, thus rendered by S'ankar:— यया प्रसादं प्राप्तानि देहेन्द्रियाणि प्रियन्ते, that by which the body and senses are supported when drooping. Hatred, &c. are mentioned here to show that they do not reside in the soul, the Kshetrajna, but in the mind.

Line 1669—Ostentation *i. e.* of one's own piety and so forth ; firmness is strict adherence to the path of final emancipation alone. S'ankar says as to 'perception of the evil &c.', that the evil to be observed in birth is the living in the womb and coming out of it ; of old age, the loss of one's intellectual and physical powers. On the alternative interpetation mentioned in the footnote, the meaning would be 'perception of the evil, namely the unhappiness, of birth, death, &c.' S'rîdhar's suggestion is also adopted by Râghavendra. Absence of vanity &c. are included under knowledge as being useful and necessary for its acquisition.

Line 1687—That which is, (सत्) according to Râghavendra, is the collection of effects (व्यक्तशब्दितकार्यजातम्) that is to say the collection of worldly objects—in fact the created universe. That which is not (असत्) is the great cause of the universe called the Unseen (अव्यक्तशब्दितकारणजातम्). This would mean that the Brahma is neither Prakriti nor any of its developments. Râghavendra also cites the following Smriti मूर्तामूर्ते द्वे एव ब्रह्मणो रूपे सत्त्वासत्त्वदुच्यते As to 'possessed of all the qualities' &c. compare the Vedic text. 'He sees without eyes, he hears without ears' (पश्यत्यचक्षुः स शृणोत्यकर्णः). Râghavendra proposes another rendering. He says सर्वगोन्द्रियाणि गुणान् शास्त्रीयविषयाश्चाभासयति प्रत्याययति प्रत्येति वा. 'Unattached', सर्वसंश्रयवर्जन.

नम् says S'rídhar. 'Their supporter'—this is the rendering of S'rídhar who paraphrases भोक्तृ by पालक. S'ankar says it means उपलब्धृ 'that which perceives'. 'Not different &c.' S'ankar says "It is one in all bodies like space, but it appears as if it were different in different creatures." S'rídhar says कारणात्मनाभिन्नं कार्यात्मना विभक्तं भिन्नमिव स्थितं च समुद्राज्जलं फेनादि समुद्रादन्यत्र भवति—which means that the various manifestations by themselves are different, but considered with reference to their material cause they are all one. Foam is different from ordinary sea water as a different form of water ; but substantially they are one. So different creatures are different when seen as individuals, but they are one when we see that they are all Brahma in their essence.

Line 1703—Knowledge—calling Brahma itself knowledge is rather singular. Râghavendra says ज्ञानं प्रकाशस्वरूपम्. S'ankar says ज्ञानममानित्वादि and Ânandagiri explains that by adding कर-णभ्युत्पत्यादि शेष:, so that ज्ञान means not knowledge itself but the absence of vanity &c. by which it is acquired.

Line 1726—S'ankar says 'Meditation means the absorption of all the senses, such as that of hearing &c., into the mind, aftertheir withdrawal from their objects, and the fixing of the mind exclusively on the soul. In themselves means in the बुद्धि, the faculty of fixed resolution; by themselves=by the internal organ polished and refined by meditation. Sânkhyayog is the belief that the three Qualities are different from the soul, which is the passive supervisor of their operations, of a different nature from them, and changeless. Karma-yog is performance of action in the belief that it is all offered unto the Supreme Being.'

Line 1745—S'ankar understands this to mean that the man sees everything as आत्मा, the supreme soul. Râghavendra takes 'existing in' as equivalent to 'being supported by',

Madhusúdan agrees with S'ankar, explaining स्थिरं by कठिन.

Line 1752—Though all-pervading. The commentators instance the case of mud by which space is never stained. 'All bodies,' S'rídhar explains to mean good, middling, and bad bodies. Rághavendra says नीचोच्चादिदेहे.

Line 1759—Release of beings &c. Rághavendra says this refers to the abovementioned means of final emancipation by which the soul is released from the elements and from Prakriti or Nature; or to the means of final emancipation by which souls are released from the inanimate Prakriti.

Line 1760—I had originally intended to treat the subject of the three qualities at some length. But under the circumstances I prefer to make only the following few observations upon it, It is clear enough that the three qualities indicate three different classes of living creatures, the differences being stated at length in this Chapter XIV. What is not so clear is how the combination of these three qualities into a whole in which they are in equilibrium comes to be identified with Prakriti (सत्त्वरजस्तमसां साम्यावस्था प्रकृ. तिः). According to the view of Prof. Wilson and other writers on the Sánkhya Philosophy, Prakriti is matter—matter in an undeveloped state. Now in what sense dead matter is identical with Goodness, Badness, and Indifference combined, it is rather difficult to see. On the other hand, if we take matter to be living matter, as containing, to borrow the language of Prof. Tyndall, "the promise and potency of life," the doctrine becomes somewhat more intelligible though still difficult to realize. Professor Bhándárkar, however, suggests a very different view of Prakriti, as he holds that the Sánkhya Philosophy is in its essence what, in the terminology of modern English philosophy, would be called Idealism. And according to him, therefore, Prakriti is the hypothetical cause of the soul's feeling itself limited and conditioned. I must refer to Prof. Bhâṇḍârkar's Essay itself for a clear and full exposition of this theory. It does, to a considerable extent, explain the difficulties which arise upon the other hypothesis. And it will be found, I think, that none of the passages in which Prakriti is mentioned in the Gîtâ will present any difficulty of explanation on this theory.

As to the renderings of the three names of the qualities, I need scarcely say, that I do not consider them at all satisfactory. But Goodness and Badness are the usual names for सत्त्व and तमस्; and रजस्, as the middle stage between the two, may, perhaps, be allowably rendered by Indifference. I have borrowed the words from Mr. Thomson with an alteration. Prof. Bhâṇḍârkar renders रजस् by Passion which is a more suggestive rendering. There is also a difference of opinion as to whether गुण here means quality or fetter.

Line 1764—Assume my qualities=Come into my essence ममस्वरूपतामागना: says Sankar. Suffer pain = do not fall down says Sankar; जननीवर्तन्ते says S'rîdhar, and on this our footnote is based. The contrast, however, between being born at the creation, and this expression, might, perhaps be held to indicate a different sort of pain than that of further birth, e. g. the pain accompanying a destruction of the world.

Line 1780—Charmed,=being enamoured of anything.

Line 1790—The meaning of this sentence is that each of the qualities produces the effects abovementioned, when the other two are repressed by it and it predominates.

Line 1806—We have given in the footnotes the two senses proposed for the word 'highest.' Râghavendra takes it to mean Vishṇu, or the Supreme Being.

Line 1809—स्ठर्षानिरु, says S'ankar, means among beasts

&c. Râghavendra says it means among demons &c. कर्मसङ्गिषु he says, means among men. In the next line, 'they say' is interpreted by S'ridhar to refer to Kapil and others.

Line 1821—The seer, is द्रष्टा. Râghavendra renders it by जीव:, S'ankar by विज्ञान्, and S'ridhar by विवेकी. 'That which is above the qualities' is the soul.

Line 1825—देहसमुद्भवान्=तत्तद्गुणपरिणामदेहेषु प्रकटीभूतान् (Râghaven-dra). For the other rendering see lines 1718 *et seq.*

Line 1845—After this a line has been omitted which should run thus :—He's said to be beyond the qualities.

Line 1859—'I' here must mean the man Kṛishṇa.

Line 1852—S'ankar thinks that this passage describes संसार or the course of worldly life. With him agree S'ridhar and Madhusûdan. Râghavendra says it describes the जगत्स्वरूप. A full explanation of the passage must be seen in the various commentaries. We only summarize them :—

As'vattha, Sankar and the other commentators explain to mean ' what will not remain even to-morrow in the same state' (न श्वोपि स्थास्यते). Its roots are above, that is to say the Supreme Being is its root; its boughs are the lesser beings Hiraṇyagarbha &c., (according to some) Mahat, Ahankâr and the other great elements (according to others.) The Chhandas or Veds are its leaves—to preserve the world as the leaves preserve the tree, says S'ankar. They are the causes of the fruit (salvation, and worldly good) says Râghavendra, for in this world we find leaves first and fruits afterwards. S'ridhar says that the fruits of acts are the shade of the tree which everybody requires and that is afforded by the Veds. Upwards and downwards=from the highest of created things, as we may say, to the lowest (ब्रह्मादिस्थावरान्त). Here S'ankar seems to render branches by the fruits of knowledge and action. "By the qualities enlarged" is explained only by Madhusûdhan, who takes it to refer to the manifestations of the qualities in the form of body, senses, worldy objects &c. Objects of sense are sprouts as they are attached to the senses which are as it were the tips of the branches. The roots which extend downwards are the desires for different enjoyments. These are the minor roots, the main root being already described to be the Deity. Here *i. e.* by those who are living in this world. 'Thus' means as described above. प्रपद्ये which we have rendered 'thinking that one rests,' Râghavendra takes to stand for प्रपद्येत "one should resort to or take shelter with"—avowedly violating the grammatical construction.

Line 1871—Compare line 1682 as to Adhyâtma.

Line 1894—S'ankar thus supplies the ellipses in the thoughts between this line and line 1877. When Krishṇa says that one who goes to Vishṇu's seat never returns, the question arises how can this be when all going is to end in returning (सर्वो हि गतिरागत्यन्ता). The answer is that the individual soul being a part of the supreme soul, it may well go to its fountain-head and never return. Then the difficulty arises how does the soul go at all from its fountain-head. That is obviated by saying that it is the connection with the mind &c. which occasions this. To the next question—when does this occur—the answer is given in the words "whensoever the soul &c." Then having stated that this truth is known only to some persons, not to all, he comes back from the digression.

Line 1897—Entering the earth—in the form of the Goddess Earth, say Ânandagiri and Madhusûdan. Support *i. e.*, by keeping the earth from falling down or from crumbling away. One of the moon's names is ओषधीश—Lord of herbs. The fourfold food is that which is drunk, that which is licked, that which is powdered by means of the teeth, and that which is eaten without such powdering.

Line 1904—Reasoning. The original is अपोहन which the commentators unanimously interpret to mean destruction *scil.* of memory and knowledge. But I cannot think that this meaning is quite appropriate. There is nothing suitable to the context in saying that the destruction of knowledge is occasioned by the Supreme Being. On the other hand ऊहापोह is a common expression for discussion, reasoning *pro* and *con*, and I think we may adopt that meaning here.

Line 1906—The author of the Vedânta. This means, according to S'ankar, the first expositor of the meaning of the Vedântas (Upanishads, I suppose) current in tradition वेदान्तार्थसंप्रदायप्रवर्तक. S'rîdhar agrees; and so does Madhusûdan, adding वेदव्यासादिद्वारेण. Râghavendra says वेदानामन्तो निर्णयो यस्मात्स वेदान्तः ब्रह्मसूत्रसंदर्भस्तस्य व्याख्याकरण कर्त्ता.

Line 1919—The unconcerned one. S'ankar says पुरुषोऽक्षर-स्तन्न्द्विपरीतो भगवतो मायाशक्तिः क्षराख्यस्य पुरुषस्योत्पत्तिबीजमनेकसंसारिजन्तुकामकर्मा-दिसंस्कारश्रयोक्षरः पुरुष उच्यते. Unconcerned is one rendering of कूटस्थ It may also mean, according to the commentators, delusive. Madhusûdan says केचित्तु क्षरशब्देनाचेतनवर्गमुक्त्वा कूटस्थोक्षर उच्यत इत्यनेन जीवमाहुः ॥ तन्न सम्यक् । क्षेत्रज्ञस्यैवेह पुरुषोत्तमत्वेन प्रतिपाद्यत्वात् ॥ तस्माक्षराक्षरश-ब्दाभ्यां कार्यकारणोपाधी उभावपि जडावेवोच्येते इत्येव युक्तम्. The two Beings are thus the whole collection of things in the world, and the material cause of them. The Deity is a totally different principle. See S'vetâs'vataropanishad p. 294 (Bibl. Ind. Ed.)

Line 1922—सर्वभावेन. (Every way) might be taken to mean with all one's heart. That is very nearly the meaning of the corresponding Marâṭhi expression.

Line 1927—Knowledge *i. e.* of the soul by study of the S'astras; sacrifice is the Dars'apûrṇamâs &c.; study is study of the Veds. For Renunciation see the next chapter.

Line 1949—Spoken of *scil,* according to Madhusûdan, in the descriptions of the man of steady mind (Chap. II.) the otce (Chap. XII.) the man of knowledge (Chap. XIII.) the man who transcends the Qualities (Chap. XIV.) S'ankar rs to the list at the beginning of the chapter.

Line 1936—No truth = nothing that is entitled to be ieved, such as Veds, Purâns &c. say S'rîdhâr and Madhu- an. Fixed principle = धर्माधर्मव्यवस्थानिष्ठ say the commentators . no principle based on virtue and vice, according to ich the affairs of the world are governed. अन्योन्यसंभूतम् the nmentators interpret this to mean produced by the union male and female. But it is difficult to be satisfied with i is. I have followed the rendering of Mr. Thomson, though s by no means without its own difficulties. For 'without nnexions mutual', Mr. Thomson has "arisen in certain cession." नष्टात्मान:, which we have rendered by "of ruined als," S'rîdhar renders by मलीनसचित्ता:, of impure mind ; and nkar and Madhusûdan say नष्टभावा विभ्रष्टपरलोकसाधना:.

Line 1992—Hurl into demoniac wombs i. e. according to commentators, they are born as tigers, snakes &c.

Line 1997—Ruinous to the soul i. e., according to nkar, rendering the soul unfit for any of the highest ends human beings ; according to S'rîdhar, leading to birth in a rer order of living beings.

Line 2007—सिद्धि in the Gîtâ means final emancipation (मोक्ष); efinement, the being fitted for a higher stage of life.

Line 2020—Yakshas = Kuber &c.; Rakshases = Nirriti Ânandagiri.

Line 2081—Comp. line 1045 and Manu II. 83. By that . the designation, says S'ankar. S'rîdhar suggests the alter- ive 'by the Brahma' which I prefer. For this i. e. for pen- e, sacrifice &c., or for Brahma (S'ankar.) The connexion of s passage with what goes before is stated by S'rîdhar. He s, that as it would appear that all acts of penance &c. are either bad or indifferent, this passage shows how they may attain the quality of goodness. I must say, however, that I do not understand this passage clearly.

Line 2049—Conditions—the original is कारणानि, causes. On agent (कर्ता) S'rîdhar has चिद्रचिद्ग्रन्थिरहंकारः:—egoism or self-consciousness formed of the union of *chit* and *achit.* Line 2053 refers to those who, not understanding that the soul is not among the five things necessary for action, think it to be the doer of all the acts of a human being (Compare line 445.) The stain on the intellect is the feeling 'I have done this, I shall enjoy the fruit of it' (Line 2037) and so forth.

Line 2215—Desire here means desire for carnal pleasures.

Line 2240—Nature here may be either the great principle प्रकृति or माया, which is made up of the three qualities in equilibrium, or it may mean the respective natures of Brâhmaṇs &c. In the latter case, the qualities are the causes of the natures. (S'ankar.)

Line 2304—See Kaṭhopanishad II. 6, 17 and S'vetâs'vatar III., 13.